D0024632

Logistics, Supply Chain and Operations Management
Case Study Collection

Logistics, Supply Chain and Operations Management
Case Study Collection

Editor David B Grant

HD
38.5
.L64
2016

KoganPage

LONDON   PHILADELPHIA   NEW DELHI

Publisher's note

Every possible effort has been made to ensure that the information contained in this book is accurate at the time of going to press, and the publishers and authors cannot accept responsibility for any errors or omissions, however caused. No responsibility for loss or damage occasioned to any person acting, or refraining from action, as a result of the material in this publication can be accepted by the editor, the publisher or any of the authors.

First published in Great Britain and the United States in 2016 by Kogan Page Limited

Apart from any fair dealing for the purposes of research or private study, or criticism or review, as permitted under the Copyright, Designs and Patents Act 1988, this publication may only be reproduced, stored or transmitted, in any form or by any means, with the prior permission in writing of the publishers, or in the case of reprographic reproduction in accordance with the terms and licences issued by the CLA. Enquiries concerning reproduction outside these terms should be sent to the publishers at the undermentioned addresses:

2nd Floor, 45 Gee Street	1518 Walnut Street, Suite 900	4737/23 Ansari Road
London	Philadelphia PA 19102	Daryaganj
EC1V 3RS	USA	New Delhi 110002
United Kingdom		India

© The Individual Contributors, 2016

The right of the individual contributors to be identified as the authors of this work has been asserted by them in accordance with the Copyright, Designs and Patents Act 1988.

ISBN   978 0 7494 7595 6
E-ISBN   978 0 7494 7749 3

British Library Cataloguing in Publication Data

A CIP record for this book is available from the British Library.

Library of Congress Cataloging-in-Publication Data

Library of Congress Control Number: 2016933903

Typeset by Graphicraft Limited, Hong Kong
Printed and bound in by CPI Group (UK) Ltd, Croydon, CR0 4YY

CONTENTS

FOREWORD

Case studies have long been an important part of the learning process in many disciplines – particularly in the study of business and management. In the classroom, a good case study can provide a powerful vehicle for exploring the complexity and intricacy of real-world phenomena. Nowhere is this more true than when seeking to understand the challenges facing logistics and supply chain managers today.

In the past, logistics and supply chain issues were not high on the corporate agenda and, as a result, there was little documented evidence of good and bad practice across industry sectors. Today the situation is quite different. Organizations, big and small, have come to recognize the impact that logistics and supply chain decisions can have on their overall performance. Costs, revenues and, hence, profits are directly and indirectly driven by the way in which logistics and supply chain operations are structured and managed.

We are now entering an era where competitive advantage is achieved not so much through the products or services that the business offers but rather through the way in which we design and execute the processes that create and deliver value in the marketplace. Hence the need for organizations to develop the requisite skills and capabilities necessary to achieve excellence in logistics and supply chain operations.

The collection of case studies presented in this book illustrates the diversity of challenges that businesses face as they seek to manage and hopefully improve performance in these vital areas. These cases provide a welcome addition to the expanding knowledge base that is helping to change the way in which organizations think about these critical business processes.

Martin Christopher
Emeritus Professor of Marketing & Logistics,
Cranfield School of Management, UK

EDITOR'S INTRODUCTION

Logistics, operations and supply chain management (SCM) are very much applied disciplines that enhance people's lives by producing and distributing the goods and services demanded by them, whether it is automobiles or electronic goods, food and drink, or services such as haircuts or coffee shops (Christopher, 2010). The outputs of these disciplines comprise superb customer service through product availability and service excellence; for example orders delivered on-time and in-full with no errors or retail shops that have adequate on-shelf product availability (Grant, 2012).

However, these disciplines face a number of ongoing challenges. These challenges include increasing costs, time compression to produce and deliver goods, product complexity, demand for quality of performance and service, shortages of personnel and talent, as well as the continuing globalization of supply and markets, shrinking product life cycles, risk, disruption and security, and the impact of logistics, operations and SCM on the natural environment (Grant, 2014). Knowledge created by academic study and research of these challenges allow these disciplines, which are only 150 years or so old and thus fairly recent in terms of academic thought, to progress as they mature.

Sharing that knowledge through publication, teaching and other forms of dissemination is also important to enable such progression. One form of dissemination is a teaching case study that considers an important issue, either in isolation or together with related issues, discusses possible alternatives to address the issue(s), and provides a feasible recommendation. A teaching case study is different to case studies conducted for research purposes, but is also important in the disciplines of operations management (Voss et al, 2002) and logistics and SCM (Aastrup and Halldórsson, 2008).

The International Records Management Trust noted that the origins of teaching case studies were in 'the study of law in the nineteenth century' but by 'the mid-twentieth century were increasingly used in other' disciplines including inter alia 'business and management studies' and 'engineering'. Academics and educators recognized it was insufficient to disseminate generic principles and practices of a discipline; it was also important to equip students to consider a variety of scenarios so they might easily adapt to a wide range of situations found in their post-education employment (IRMT, 1999, p1).

Regarding logistics and SCM, Van Hoek noted that 'case teaching not only provides a practical setting, it also allows for an interactive educational experience where professional skills (presenting, analysis, no clear universal solutions) can be trained' (2001, p513). He also noted that while it is important for educators to keep up to date with cases on the hot topics of today, there was a dearth of good, current and relevant logistics, operations and SCM cases at the turn of the millennium. That is still the situation some 15 years on.

This *Logistics, Supply Chain and Operations Management Case Study Collection* addresses that need, and the three related requirements, by providing a rich and varied compilation of case studies and extended exercises from across logistics, operations and SCM. The cases in the Collection contain real-life scenarios from leading companies including Volvo, Vortex, Green Cargo and the Swedish Transport Administration. The collection is also comprehensive in scope and detail. The breadth of cases includes actual events experienced by businesses of every size, from small- and medium-sized enterprises (SMEs) to multinational corporations (MNCs) in manufacturing, transportation, hospitality and other industries.

Anyone involved in logistics, operations and SCM will find the Collection extremely helpful. Directors and managers in practice will find interesting and immediate application of strategies and tactics for their own situations and challenges, and learn to identify potential pitfalls before they become chronic issues. Academics and professional trainers will have a valuable tool for academic curricula, independent learning modules, and professional training programmes either as in-class or assessed cases. The cases will allow testing of management proficiency in crisis mitigation and resolution and the expanded question and answer sections designed to measure knowledge transfer and lessons learned are particularly useful. Finally, students will learn from engaging and topical situations that are highly relevant to the logistics, operations and SCM disciplines, and both students and prospective managers will learn crucial skills to meet current challenges, qualify for professional advancement, and achieve success.

This Collection has been laid-out in two separate sections: operations management and logistics and SCM. Each section will contain a brief introduction to set the scene for the cases in it and highlight some of the unique ideas presented. On behalf of Emeritus Professor Martin Christopher, who wrote the foreword for this Collection, Kogan Page and myself, we hope you enjoy and the cases and find many productive and engaging uses for them.

Professor David B Grant

References

Aastrup, J and Halldórsson, Á (2008) Epistemological role of case studies in logistics, *International Journal of Physical Distribution & Logistics Management*, Vol 38 (10), pp 746–63

Christopher, M (2010), *Logistics and Supply Chain Management*, 4th ed, FT Prentice Hall, Harlow UK

Grant, D B (2012) *Logistics Management*, Pearson Education, Harlow UK

Grant, D B (2014) Trends in logistics and supply chain management: a focus on risk, *Journal of Supply Chain Management: Research & Practice*, Vol 8 (2), pp 1–12

IRMT (1999) Michael Roper (ed.) Writing Case Studies: *A manual*, *International Records Management Trust*, London, www.irmt. org/documents/educ_training/.../IRMT_ed_rec_writing_cs.doc.

Van Hoek, R I (2001) Logistics education, *International Journal of Physical Distribution & Logistics Management,* Vol 31 (7/8), pp 505–19

Voss, C, Tsikriktsis, N and Frohlich, M (2002) Case research in operations management, *International Journal of Operations & Production Management*, Vol 22 (2), pp 196–219

Part one
Operations management

The operations management section of this Collection contains 14 cases and extended exercises. There are four overarching themes presented in this section:

- Information technology and its relationship to risk (cases 1.1 and 1.2) and service operations (case 1.5);

- Manufacturing and production issues such as business process reengineering (case 1.3), production layout and process flows (cases 1.7 and 1.9) and quality (case 1.13);

- Production planning for aggregate demand and forecasting (cases 1.6, 1.8 and 1.14), financial analysis and planning of operations (cases 1.10, 1.11 and 1.12); and

- Sustainability as it pertains to services and public sector operations (cases 1.4 and 1.6).

These themes and topics address the challenges noted in the introduction of increasing costs, time compression to produce and deliver goods, product complexity, demand for quality of performance and service, risk, disruption and security, and the impact of operations management on the natural environment.

Professor David B Grant

The nuclear effect of computer malware
Impact of politics on computer-controlled operational processes

Lucian Tipi

AUTHOR BIOGRAPHY

LUCIAN TIPI is a Principal Lecturer in Business Systems at Sheffield Business School, Sheffield Hallam University.

Introduction

It is widely perceived that cyber-crime and cyber-attacks are perpetrated by loners, technically gifted but socially inadequate individuals who hide in their dark bedrooms for months at a time and code away relentlessly. While this may be the case at times, a number of recent cases of cyber-attacks seem to suggest that these kinds of activities are being professionalized to a high degree, with evidence emerging of likely state sponsoring having taken place. State sponsoring of cyber-attacks raises the stakes of such attacks to a new level, where politics and national interests are the main driver, rather than the more traditional motivations such as money, curiosity, technical prowess, etc.

The case study presented here is focused on malware that is specifically designed to target industrial computer-controlled systems. While in the mainstream IT/IS arena, computer security is well understood, managed and implemented, this is not necessarily the case when it comes to a wide variety of computer-controlled industrial equipment. The root causes of this is that the lifetime of industrial plant equipment is usually far longer than the lifetime of the office-based equipment, and therefore it tends to lag behind in terms of security. Also, most legacy industrial control systems have not been built with security in mind, but rather the drivers have been resilience and cost effectiveness. As the number of cyber-attacks and their diversity is on the increase, this needs to change. One of the most contentious areas of industrial production is that of the nuclear industry, with a small number of states trying to protect and control the proliferation of this industry around the world by giving international security as a main reason for this. The following case will illustrate the extent to which such control can be taken.

Useful definitions

- *BSOD:* Blue screen of death – a situation where there is an error screen displayed after a fatal system error on a Windows computer system. The system becomes completely unusable and needs to be restarted, sometimes in a 'safe' mode, to try and identify the hardware or software problem that caused the fatal error. Data is typically lost during such events if data-containing files were open at the time when the fatal error occurs.

- *Computer operating system:* Essential software that manages computer hardware and all other software resources and provides common services for computer software applications. Application software require an operating system to function (unless in an embedded system).

- *Computer worm:* Malware that replicates itself in order to spread to other computing systems. Unlike a computer virus, it does not need to attach itself to an existing computer file in order to self-replicate. The effect of the worms does not typically consist in damage to computer files, but rather damage to the computer systems affected by them; these can range from consuming network bandwidth, to clogging up systems, to altering the behaviour of computer systems, etc.

- *Industrial control system:* A control system used in industrial production. Such systems include supervisory control and data acquisition (SCADA) systems, distributed control systems (DCS) and other smaller control systems, e.g. programmable logic controllers (PLC). The systems are found in industrial plants and critical infrastructure.

- *Malware:* A piece of software that has been designed with a malicious purpose in mind. The effects of malware can be the disruption of computer operation, the gathering of sensitive information, gaining access to computer systems, etc.

- *Production computer network:* An industrial computer network whose purpose is to connect the various computer-controlled industrial equipment found on a production plant.

- *Zero-day vulnerability:* A previously unknown vulnerability in a computer application or operating system, one that developers have not had time to address and patch. The name 'zero-day' is due to the fact that the developers have had zero days to fix the problem – no fix is available. Once a software patch is available, it is no longer a zero-day vulnerability. Zero-day vulnerabilities are exploited by individuals and companies who sell them to government agencies/other stakeholders for use in cyber-attacks.

THE NUCLEAR PELLET FACTORY:
how to calibrate your centrifuges properly

This case study is based on a real attack on an enriched uranium pellet (manufactured to fuel nuclear power plants) production facility that caused significant costs and delays (estimated at years) to the facility.

Siavash is an industrial systems control engineer who started working at the Nuclear Pellet Factory two years ago. Recently he has been given the task of setting up centrifuge production line 3. He is very excited to have started working here, as the production facility is being newly built, using cutting-edge TFS SCADA equipment, giving him the opportunity to fully utilize his skills and knowledge, something that he has taken to quite enthusiastically. His main area of responsibility is the installation of the facility's high-speed centrifuges that will deliver the enriched uranium necessary for the production of the fuel pellets to be delivered to a range of customers around the world.

It's a Monday morning and Siavash goes to work as normal, looking forward to this week as it was when line 3 of high-speed centrifuges was due to go live. There were only a few calibration issues to sort out, in order to make sure that the centrifuges rotate at the correct speed. This is quite important as each of the centrifuges costs over £150K and the production line contains 10 centrifuges. Should the centrifuges not be calibrated correctly, there is a risk of significant damage to them through the burning out of the high-speed electrical motors that provide their power. Siavash remembers that centrifuges number 3 and number 8 were giving him some problems last week – so he decides to make checking these out his first job of the day. He starts the computer-controlling centrifuge number 3 up and runs the diagnostic software. Once the diagnostic software finishes its run, Siavash has a look at the output data and notices that the centrifuge is actually spinning about 25 per cent slower that its nominal speed. He re-checks the calibration data, and everything seems to be normal. He decides to check his results with one of his more senior colleagues, Azim, who works nearby on line 2 of high-speed centrifuges. He calls Azim over and they both look at the output of the diagnostic software. Azim says:

Azim: Well, you know what – this is nothing that unusual, it happened to me last week on centrifuge 6 on line 2.

Siavash: Okay, so what's the problem?

Azim: I have noticed that this TFS SCADA equipment we're getting is not that well calibrated, so sometimes you just have to override the automatic calibration and input the speed values that you want out of it manually.

Siavash: Really? How do you work these out?

Azim: Well, I see from your data that centrifuge number 3 on your line is spinning 25 per cent slower than required – just increase the motor power to compensate for this and that's that problem fixed!

Siavash: Thanks Azim, this is really easy. I have a couple of centrifuges that have these issues. I'll work on them today and get them going. Then hopefully I can get the whole line 3 started tomorrow.

Siavash starts working on his problem centrifuges 3 and 8 and by the afternoon everything seems to be going according to plan. He increases the motor power for the two centrifuges to compensate for the lack of calibration and runs the diagnostic software on both. The results from the diagnostic software confirm that both centrifuges now work fine, and the required nominal speed is achieved every time during several testing cycles. Towards the end of the day, Siavash goes to his supervisor and declares with a satisfied look on his face that line 3 is ready to go into production on Tuesday (the very next day, three full days ahead of schedule).

On returning to work the next day, everything seems to be working fine, though he does need to restart the computer-controlling centrifuge 8 twice as about five minutes after starting it up in the morning the computer crashes, giving him the BSOD.

Uranium is loaded into the centrifuges and the first production run of line 3 is starting. The line is working very well and Siavash is a lot more relaxed now. He is actually contemplating a much desired pay rise that was promised to him if he manages to start production on line 3 before the end of the week.

The alarm on the production line 3 starts at just after midday that day – there is a small fire on centrifuge 3. The fire is extinguished very quickly; however, the damage that occurred during the incident means that a small quantity of radioactive material has leaked from the centrifuge. What this means is that centrifuge 3 will have to be scrapped entirely, and new equipment fitted to replace it, at a cost of approximately £200K.

Siavash and Azim attend an operations meeting later on in the week, along with a number of other industrial systems control engineers, where it transpires that most of them have been having ongoing problems with the TFS SCADA equipment and the computers that controlled these, and that BSOD occurrences have been quite frequent. A number of centrifuges have been suffering from problems as a result; several of these had motor burnouts or other mechanical damage related to their high-speed nature. At the meeting, the decision to call in one of their software developers is taken, to investigate further the nature of these problems.

Further details

The software developer specialists come into the Nuclear Pellet Factory and after extensive investigations they discover that many of the computers that control the TFS SCADA equipment used to drive the uranium enrichment centrifuges have been infected with a very sophisticated computer worm. The computer worm has used a number of zero-day vulnerabilities and its complexity strongly suggests that it was a state-sponsored malware. It is estimated by security analysts that it would have taken a team of approximately 5–10 people about 80,000 hours to develop the worm. The total cost of producing the worm is estimated to be around £5 million. The worm has affected only very specific systems – Windows machines connected to a specific range of TFS SCADA kit designed for a very specific range of industrial applications. The Nuclear Pellet Factory did not have direct access to TFS support for their equipment due to international sanctions imposed on their country. The TFS kit was purchased through third parties. The Nuclear Pellet Factory with the help of their contractors has now updated the software on their systems and no longer suffers from the computer worm that plagued them in the past.

Questions

1 Explore and discuss Siavash and Azim's thought and decision-making processes.

2 Explore the problems around dealing with malware that takes advantage of zero-day vulnerabilities.

3 Why did the engineers at the Nuclear Pellet Factory not seek support from TFS, but rather preferred to work out the problem on their own?

4 Discuss the use of 'consumer'-grade computer operating systems and networks in industrial production facilities.

5 Assuming that over a period of six months prior to the incident described in the case study, six centrifuges have been a total write-off due to malfunctions and that a further 10 centrifuges have suffered damage of, on average, £25K each, calculate the total cost to the Nuclear Pellet Factory of these breakdowns. Discuss.

6 Assuming that it takes 30 days to fully replace a damaged centrifuge and 10 days on average to fix the other types of defects, how much delay has the Nuclear Pellet Factory suffered in total? (Assume that the breakdowns occur in a sequential fashion, ie there is no overlap between the breakdowns.) Discuss.

Answers

1 Explore and discuss Siavash and Azim's thought and decision-making processes.

It is fairly clear that Siavash had two issues to deal with – his own inexperience in terms of the areas that he was working in and the supposed obvious fix that was provide to him by Azim, a more senior colleague. While it seems logical that the diagnostic software reports a state of affairs, e.g. a slower speed than expected compared with the normal calibration parameters, this thought process obviously does not consider the possibility of a malware infection – in this case a targeted computer worm. Also a weakness of their thinking is the fact that they are in effect taking a DIY approach to industrial equipment – this approach is driven by the fact that they do not have access to official TFS support due to international restrictions placed on their country. There does not seem to be a big-picture view of what's happening at the production facility – someone should have briefed Siavash about ongoing problems with the centrifuges on the various production lines but nobody seems to have spotted the pattern of failures that was occurring at the Nuclear Pellet Factory.

2 Explore the problems around dealing with malware that takes advantage of zero-day vulnerabilities.

The biggest issue when it comes to dealing with malware that exploits a zero-day vulnerability is the fact that it is a largely unknown vulnerability that is being exploited – this means that the vulnerability is not yet understood, let alone being fixed. Zero-day vulnerabilities are fairly rare; however, they can be employed to a great effect as illustrated in this case study. Using antivirus software will likely not produce any results as both the malware and the vulnerability being exploited are unknown to the security software manufacturers. In the case explored here, documenting the kinds of faults that have occurred and having the higher-level view of the situation could be used to detect unusual faults patterns. Another difficulty here is that industrial engineers, while specialists in their own right, are not really computer experts and as such may not be able to put together the pieces of the information jigsaw that they have to deal with. After all, only a very small number of computer specialists would be able to discern between just random computer failures and a possible pattern of events that may lead to computer and computer-controlled equipment problems – in other words very few people fully understand what the causes of unusual computer behaviour may be when faced with such behaviours.

3 Why did the engineers at the Nuclear Pellet Factory not seek support from TFS, but rather preferred to work out the problem on their own?

In this case the answer is self-evident; they did not have access to the official equipment support, due to sanctions that were imposed on their country by the international community, leading to the Nuclear Pellet Factory having to employ third-party suppliers and contractors to provide their equipment and software. This meant that in effect the Nuclear Pellet Factory engineers were working with 'black boxes', without fully understanding the operating parameters of the equipment that they were supposed to employ at the factory.

4 Discuss the use of 'consumer'-grade computer operating systems and
  networks in industrial production facilities.

The main problem here is that commonly used operating systems are
not really designed with 'mission critical' attributes in mind. What
this means in practice is that the usual compromise between security
features and ease of use tends to be biased towards the ease of use.
This helps with the popularity and the flexibility of these operating
systems – for example they can be used for multimedia, gaming, web
browsing, office productivity software and any other software application that can be programmed for them. While this means a high
sales volume for the operating systems, this popularity constitutes
one of their main weaknesses – they are easy to get hold of and they
are worth exploring for security vulnerabilities as finding one security vulnerability means that a cyber-attack constructed on that vulnerability is likely to have a huge impact in terms of the systems that
will be affected by the attack. Such operating systems become com-
moditized and as such they become employed in all sorts of applications – industrial, infrastructure, military, etc – increasing the risk
that attacks based on their security vulnerabilities will result in damage to essential systems and services.

5 Assuming that over a period of six months prior to the incident
  described in the case study, six centrifuges have been a total write-off
  due to malfunctions and that a further 10 centrifuges have suffered
  damage of, on average, £25K each, calculate the total cost to the
  Nuclear Pellet Factory of these breakdowns. Discuss.

Cost of 1 centrifuge total write-off = £200K
Cost of 1 centrifuge partial damage = £25K

Total cost of breakdowns   = 6 × £200K + 10 × £25K
                                = £1200K + £250K
                                = £1450K.

The total cost incurred by the Nuclear Pellet Factory is nearly £1.5
million, a huge sum of money. This is a pure loss suffered by the company; it is highly unlikely that this cost can be recouped. In this case,
given that the total cost of the malware was around £5 million, it
does not seem to make sense to produce a malware that costs more
than the damage inflicted. However, one thing to remember is that

this is likely to have been a politically motivated attack, so money would not have been a main driver.

6 Assuming that it takes 30 days to fully replace a damaged centrifuge and 10 days on average to fix the other types of defects, how much delay has the Nuclear Pellet Factory suffered in total? (Assume that the breakdowns occur in a sequential fashion, ie there is no overlap between the breakdowns.) Discuss.

Time to fully replace 1 centrifuge = 30 days

Time to repair 1 centrifuge   = 10 days

Total time needed for repairs   = 6 × 30 days + 10 × 10 days
                                   = 180 days + 100 days
                                   = 280 days.

In practice, it is unlikely that all of these breakdowns have occurred in a strictly sequential fashion; some will have occurred while other centrifuges have been repaired, etc. However, what is important to illustrate here is that the total amount of work days lost by the Nuclear Pellet Factory is indeed 280 days of work – this will have had a huge impact on their production schedules.

Real world effects of cyber-attacks

Security issues in computer-controlled production

Lucian Tipi

AUTHOR BIOGRAPHY

LUCIAN TIPI is a Principal Lecturer in Business Systems at Sheffield Business School, Sheffield Hallam University.

Introduction

It is widely perceived that cyber-crime and cyber-attacks happen in cyberspace and that their effects remain in cyberspace. However, recent attacks on industrial production facilities are proof that this is no longer the case.

While in the mainstream IT/IS arena, computer security is well understood, managed and implemented, this is not necessarily the case when it comes to a wide variety of computer-controlled industrial equipment. Issues such as lack of security and various legacy systems that are connected to unsecured networks seem to be the norm in manufacturing. The root cause of this is that the lifetime of industrial plant equipment is usually far longer than the lifetime of the office-based equipment, and therefore it tends to lag behind in terms of security. Also, most legacy industrial control systems have not been built with security in mind, but rather the drivers have been resilience and cost effectiveness. As the number of cyber-attacks and their diversity is on the increase, this needs to change. The developed countries' economies depend hugely on their infrastructure and industries, which are in turn dependent on industrial control systems for their operation, and therefore it is crucial that the security features of these control systems catches up with the security features of the mainstream computing systems.

Useful definitions

- *Airgap computer networks:* Physically isolate computer networks. This could be applicable in a production environment where the production computer network is not connected to the corporate network (which is typically connected to the internet), in order to increase security.

- *Industrial control system:* A control system used in industrial production. Such systems include supervisory control and data acquisition (SCADA) systems, distributed control systems (DCS) and other smaller control systems, e.g. programmable logic controllers (PLC). The systems are found in industrial plants and critical infrastructure.

- *Malware:* A piece of software that has been designed with a malicious purpose in mind. The effects of malware can be the disruption of computer operation, the gathering of sensitive information, gaining access to computer systems, etc.

- *Phishing:* A popular method used by cyber-criminals that attempts to acquire information such as usernames, passwords and other personal details by impersonating a trustworthy entity in an electronic communication.

- *Production computer network:* An industrial computer network whose purpose is to connect the various computer-controlled industrial equipment found on a production plant.

- *Spearphishing:* – Directed phishing attempts at specific individuals or companies. Attackers will likely gather personal information about their intended target to increase their probability of success.

QUALITY STEELS:
Mr Smith's day at the office

This case study is based on a real attack on a steel plant that caused significant damage to the company that became a victim of a spear-phishing attack.

Quality Steels is a company that specializes in the production of cast steel products. They operate a number of high-capacity blast furnaces that have standard industry computer-controlled systems, which are connected to the company's production computer network. The production network is connected to the wider corporate network which, as it is ubiquitously the case today, is connected to the internet to ensure the data and information flows necessary for the running of the day-to-day activities of the company.

Mr Smith is one of Quality Steel's employees that work in the Human Resources department and every day, when he comes into the office, he makes his usual cup of tea and turns on his computer in order to deal with his email queue. As he goes through his emails he notices an email from his bank which asks him to login into his on-line bank account and to check his current account balance as there has been an unauthorized transfer of money from this recently. Mr Smith clicks on the link provided and tries to log into his bank account. The first attempt fails, he tries unsuccessfully one more time and is about to ring his bank when, at 9.30, he gets a phone call from his manager asking him for an emergency meeting as they need to discuss an upcoming grievance case. He closes his emails thinking that he'll talk to his bank later on in the day, after the meeting with his manager.

Mr Smith's office is located in the office building of his local site, in fairly close proximity to one of the blast furnaces that produces high-grade alloy steels for one of their customers.

At 10.45, the site alarm starts ringing – this is signalling that there is a general emergency on the site and that all employees must evacuate to their designated emergency assembly areas. Mr Smith and his manager go to their designated emergency assembly site where they meet with one of their friends, Mr Jones. Mr Jones works in the blast furnace that is closest to Mr Smith's building and tells them that there is a major emergency going on at the blast furnace – the furnace could not be shut down after the normal steel production cycle. As they all wait to see what happens, the health and safety staff tell them that the emergency is likely to continue for some time and that they need to evacuate the company's site all together. In the event they have to go home for the day, as no more productive work could be done.

When Mr Smith comes back to work the next day, he finds in his inbox an all-staff email that explains what happened during the previous day – a piece of computer malware affected a number of industrial control systems (that were operating the blast furnace); these were compromised and a major control system failure became apparent leading to loss of blast furnace control. This failure led to an unscheduled shutdown of the said blast furnace, causing extensive damage and loss of production. It is expected that the affected furnace will be out of action for at least two weeks, as repair works to the heavy industrial equipment will be carried out.

Mr Smith calls his bank later on that day to follow up on the previous day's email, but they tell him that they do not send such emails to customers. Mr Smith deletes the email that asked him to check his bank account and soon forgets about the whole thing; after all he has now got to catch up on the work that he could not do on the previous day.

Mr Smith keeps an eye on the news (the Quality Steels incident makes the national news) in the coming days to see whether any similar industrial facilities have been affected, but nothing appears in the headlines for the next few weeks.

Questions

1 Explain and discuss the cyber-attack mechanism that led to the unexpected shutdown of the blast furnace at Quality Steels.

2 Following a digital forensic investigation, it was confirmed that Mr Smith's computer was the source of a piece of malware that propagated through the Quality Steels' network.
What actions should the company take in relation to the Mr Smith situation?

3 Identify and discuss the steps that Quality Steels will need to take in order to secure their systems and minimize the likelihood of such attacks occurring in the future.

4 Following the cyber-attack Quality Steels need to deal with one of their customers who will not now get their cast steel products on time. How would you advise the company to deal with this situation?

Answers

1 Explain and discuss the cyber-attack mechanism that led to the unexpected shutdown of the blast furnace at Quality Steels.

What happened here is the result of a phishing or spearphishing attack. Mr Smith received the email that was supposed be from his bank. Upon clicking on the link given in that email, an unknown, stealthy piece of malware was downloaded onto his computer. The malware was designed to propagate itself across computer networks and as such it started to do just that on the company's corporate network, then on the company's production network. One of the payloads of the malware was obviously targeting industrial control systems, as the blast furnace control system was infected and malfunctioned, leading to catastrophic consequences. Two notable aspects of this attack are the speed with which the malware was able to propagate through the company's systems and its ability to infect industrial control systems. The latter feature is not commonly found in malware and it is a recent development. It is unclear what the purpose of the attackers was here – speculating, it could be assumed that they have targeted Quality Steels in particular, as no other similar attacks were reported around the same time. The cost to the company of this attack would be substantial and it would have several distinct components – loss of production, cost of repairs, costs related to the investigation of what happened, possible costs associated with serious injuries or death following the blast furnace incident, etc.

2 Following a digital forensic investigation, it was confirmed that Mr Smith's computer was the source of a piece of malware that propagated through the Quality Steels' network. What actions should the company take in relation to the Mr Smith situation?

The actions of Mr Smith are indicative of a lack of training and awareness in relation to best practice in the area of computer security. The first steps to take would be to make sure that Mr Smith is aware of the company's computer security policy (hopefully this exists!) and that he is provided with up-to-date computer security training. It is likely that many other employees will have done the same thing as Mr Smith – Quality Steels should make sure that appropriate communications are put in place that will reach all of their employees. Training for other employees is advisable; as the company seems to have been targeted specifically, it may be that they will be under attack again in the near future.

Mr Smith's computer and emails will need analysis in order to try and ascertain the extent of the malware infection. It may be possible to trace the source of the malware via the analysis of his emails. However, this is likely to be an expensive and time-consuming exercise, and Quality Steels may not be willing to pursue this avenue. Given the nature and the magnitude of this attack, the police should be contacted and asked for assistance.

3 Identify and discuss the steps that Quality Steels will need to take in order to secure their systems and minimize the likelihood of such attacks occurring in the future.

The first thing that the company should look at is the physical separation between their corporate and production computer networks – so-called 'airgap' – while making sure that the production computer network is not connected to the internet.

Is it possible/feasible/economical to update their industrial control systems? This is not a trivial exercise; it is likely to take time and cost significant amounts of money. It is best done by building it into the schedule of production-line updates/upgrades of equipment, though this is likely to result in quite long times spent in replacing the systems.

A revision of the company's computer security policy and procedures is needed, with an emphasis on the security gaps that exist around the company's industrial production systems. The implementation and monitoring of the new procedures is essential.

In the short term, the company needs to be particularly vigilant as they have been the victim of a targeted attack, which may be repeated. The result of the attack is likely to be the same in the short term, as it will not be possible to replace/update/change the company's systems quickly.

4 Following the cyber-attack Quality Steels need to deal with one of their customers who will not now get their cast steel products on time. How would you advise the company to deal with this situation?

As the Quality Steels incident made the national news, it is likely that their customer would have heard about the incident. The company should contact their customer straight away and explore solutions with them – it may be possible that they will accept different grades of products that exist in stock, or will be happy to re-schedule. Depending on the contractual arrangements, they may be entitled to compensation; it is best for both parties to discuss this at the earliest opportunity. All of Quality Steels' customers will be anxious as a result of this incident so Quality Steels will have to go on a PR offensive to ensure that their business relationships will continue unaffected. It is important that the company explains to their customers the steps that they are taking in order to ensure that this situation will not happen again. It could be useful for Quality Steels to explore with their customers a process of building in resilience to such incidents, though this could be a double-edged sword, as it could be perceived as a weakness of the production processes that they employ.

Jewellery design and manufacture operations
Delivery delays and solutions

Brian Lawrence

AUTHOR BIOGRAPHY

BRIAN LAWRENCE is Lecturer in the School of Management at the Assumption University in Bangkok, Thailand.

Introduction

This case study explores why delays in deliveries of new jewellery items from a jewellery company, GLITZ, to shops had dramatically increased. This affected sales, and incurred penalty charges. The process for creating new designs was examined as a prelude to solving the delivery problem. It was found that the delays originated in the process of making a model sample of each new design, a necessary stage before going to full production. Each sample underwent many revisions in response to feedback. A new design-creation process reduced the sample design process from 12 weeks to 7 weeks. On-time delivery was subsequently restored.

Background

A Singaporean private equity fund bought GLITZ, a jewellery production company founded in Burma in 2007. GLITZ fits Burmese gemstones into gold or silver, fashioned into five types of female jewellery: rings, earrings, necklaces, bracelets and brooches. Its customers are retail chains in East Asia. It uses an annual display and publicity for the year's new collection of traditional and creative designs.

There are 150 new designs and 50 restyled old designs produced annually, by mid-April, ready for the shops to sell on 1 June, which has been found to be the optimum launch month for sales. The annual collection must reach the shops at least two weeks before the launch date, to enable the shops to examine and assess the new jewellery and decide what would most appeal to their clientele and how to dress the shop windows and display cabinets. It takes up to three weeks to complete this distribution from the distribution centres. This means that the new offering must reach the four distribution centres in Bangkok, Bombay, Kuala Lumpur and Singapore at least one week before that, which could take up to a week, even by air, because of security and customs procedures. The final date for completing the jewellery production is therefore seven weeks before the launch date. In other words, GLITZ has a precise lead time for its production process, finishing in early April to enable the shop launch on 1 June.

Feminine fashion changes each year and has a penchant for newness and difference. This makes lead times crucial in the fierce race with competitors in an international market. The irony is that the more consumers demand creative innovation, and as production becomes better and quicker to cope with that, the more demandingly selective will customers become. It is a never-ending, ever speedier, cycle in which producers, customers, suppliers and retailers are trapped.

The process problem

When the equity fund, EQUITAS, gained full access to all the GLITZ statistics, it discovered that although the firm was profitable (which is why EQUITAS bought it), there were some puzzling facts. Deliveries from Burma of the annual collection suffered from substantial delays and too many items missed the launch date. An official investigation was commissioned and its main findings were fed back to EQUITAS. It quickly uncovered, however, that the main issue is that too much time is wasted in the finalization of new jewellery designs. More specific findings are also explored below.

One issue is that the budget for needed materials is agreed when the first design sample is made, even though frequent changes in the design mean that the raw materials change, in type and quantity. In addition to customer complaints about delays and lost sales, there is also a re-ordering and accounting problem. Every time there is a revised design, the GLITZ buying team ignores the computer system by manually recalculating the revised list of materials and sends new purchase orders to suppliers. The frequency of this inevitably creates confusion, resulting in many discrepancies between supplies ordered and materials needed or used. Some supplies are cancelled before delivery, some are kept as inventory for possible use next year and some even arrive at GLITZ after the production has finished. The consequence is excessive cost and waste. Furthermore, as the computer system is not used for the revised order, the accounts department struggles to keep track of purchase orders, supplies received and money due to suppliers.

Another aspect that influences the production chain is that lead times also depend on supplier capacity. Only when all the materials are received can the actual production begin. The finished jewellery is sent to the four distribution centres which then deliver the new collection to retailers in response to their purchase orders based on photographs of a sample of each new style. End-customers can then see the new display in shop windows.

Starting the actual production in November to finish in April, the design and sample making must start 12 weeks before in order to make the launch date. The design team, advised by the sales team, develops entirely new designs and revisits and amends existing successful ones. Within two weeks, the production department makes a sample model of each jewellery item as per the design team's orders. This is scrutinized by the sales team to check whether it is what the designers intended. Each sample is either approved or returned for changes, in which case a revised sample is made, and sent to sales for a second check. Although the time allocated to this is ten weeks, in practice this make-and-check process can have many cycles until a final sample is agreed on, taking as many as 15 weeks, thus missing the production start date of in November, with consequent delays. Meanwhile, the accounting and costing team has made a list of the range and quantity of materials needed, but this is based on the original design sample. The GLITZ buyers use this list to order materials from suppliers. Frequent revised orders are placed, after each change in the sample design, but the accounting system is not updated. Some orders are cancelled, for which suppliers charge a penalty fee.

After receiving all the materials, based on the final agreed samples, production begins. Production takes five months (22 weeks). The new jewellery items are then sent to the four distribution centres, from which deliveries are made to shops according to their orders based on photographs and descriptions. This delivery process should take seven weeks, making a grand total lead time of 29 weeks from first designs to jewels in the shops.

In recent years, the proportion of jewellery items delayed was 25 per cent. Some of these when eventually delivered remained unsold as competitors had placed their products first. All departments were unhappy with this, as were suppliers, distribution centres, retailers and customers, as the effects rippled down the supply chain. The new owners, EQUITAS, decided to have the whole process examined to identify needed improvements, and that the technique most appropriate for this would be business process redesign.

Business process redesign (BPR)

BPR examines the performance of an existing process, to assess and if necessary redesign it. BPR provides a range of techniques to reorganize activities. It collates knowledge, experiences and ideas from the people involved in the process, inside and outside the firm. It provides an overview of the process and its problems. It reveals tasks and roles, and interactive communication between all parties. The implementation stage of a redesigned process does need people with organization development (OD) skills to manage change.

BPR has three aspects: operational, organizational and strategic. In other words, it redesigns an operation, but within the wider organizational system, and strategically rather than merely tactically. In this sense it is a systems concept, considering the whole not just one operation.

Data collection

Data was collected from many sources: documents, statistics, observations, and also interviews with the managers of design, production, accounting and buying. The statistical data obtained was:

- Number of new jewellery designs annually   200 (150 + 50)
- Total number of jewels ordered by distribution centres   28,000
- Total value of jewels ordered $5,600,000
- Number delivered on time to distribution centres 21,000
- Total value delivered on time to distribution centres $4,200,000
- Delayed items delivered to distribution centres   7,000 (25%)
- Value of delayed deliveries to distribution centres $1,866,666 (33%)
- Value of sales lost through delay $466,700 (25%)
- Penalty charges made by suppliers $190,100

Mapping the process

BPR maps the work-flow process for each function in the firm.

Step 1

The new design process starts when the sales team reviews feedback and statistics from previous annual collections (both their own and their competitors), then considers changes in fashion and trends, to identify creative themes and styles for a new collection. Designers then fashion drawings and samples based on sales input. The sales team has to approve the design.

Step 2

The design team produces the technical drawings that are submitted to sales for approval. The production team then makes the samples based on the drawings and sales ask for changes to better fit the design they originally approved or to reflect changes in trends. Even if the original samples are made on time, sales ask for many revisions, even after the allotted time is over. The sample is accompanied by a list of the materials involved. Accounting translates this into orders for materials from suppliers.

Step 3

Buyers draft purchase orders for the materials involved. The accounting budget is entered into the data system so that buyers can send specific materials orders to suppliers. Buyers place orders manually, once a month. During sample revisions and reordering, the accounting budget is not updated. Sales are allowed to keep making changes, but costing is not updated.

Step 4

Copies of the original sample are sent to the four distribution centres to enable them to decide what and how many items to order.

Step 5

When the centres' orders are received, the buyers update the draft purchase orders and send them to suppliers.

Step 6

Suppliers confirm their delivery dates for materials to GLITZ.

Step 7

When the materials are received, production begins.

Step 8

Finished jewels are sent to the distribution centres.

Step 9

Distribution centres send the ordered jewels to shops.

Each step has a specific lead time. The bottleneck is in the making and remaking of samples which has the longest lead time, which is nearly 42 per cent of the total design-production lead time of 12 plus 22 weeks.

Root causes

The root causes for the constant changes in samples and orders for the supply of materials were found to be:

1 *People*: Members of various teams work without awareness and there is no collaboration or sharing of updated deadlines. Nor are there fixed deadlines.

2 *Materials*: The specifications sent to buyers are missing information and incomplete, meaning suppliers need explanations and revisions. Components do not match the quality specifications and materials often end up being ordered one by one during the sample redesign process.

3 *Machine*: These are unique products, with components affected by changing fashion.
   The sample design depends on feedback from the sales people. GLITZ often has to invent special tools for some designs.

4 *Measurement*: There is no precise quality testing in place, no clear drawing of tested jewellery, no timeline to approve changes, no agreed deadlines for sample approval.
   The sample is often altered after already delivered to distribution centres.

Improving the redesign process

Once the process had been mapped and all statistics assembled, the solution was obvious: tighten the sample design process by limiting the number of revisions allowed and reducing the time frame in which changes have to be made. Tightening the link between buyers, accounting and suppliers is also an area that could be improved.

In order to implement these improvements, there is a clear need for cooperation between designers, sales, buyers, suppliers, accounting and production. After the initial sample is made within a lead time of one week, there cannot be more than six revisions, and these have to be completed within a reduced lead time of six weeks, thus leaving enough time for buyers to send the final accurate orders to suppliers, and accounting being able to accurately update its data. Orders for supplies should not be updated until the final design decision by sales. The new process timetable can shorten the sample design lead time by 5 weeks, from 12 weeks to 7 weeks.

Although the changes seem simple, collaboration between the teams is essential for these changes to be achievable. Cross-function meetings have to be set up, to understand the new process, agree on a transition plan and provide feedback as the changes happens. This will be an entirely new way of working for the people involved. Decisions have to be debated and shared in a harmonious professional manner; even though some people will feel change is not needed and may feel unfairly criticized by the BPR findings and recommendations, others may be triumphant that what they knew to be wrong is now being corrected.

Questions

1 Summarize the problems and their solutions.
2 Why is the value of lost sales greater than the proportion of delayed deliveries?
3 Can you think of other solutions instead?
4 Why had GLITZ not done anything until taken over by EQUITAS?
5 Is there scope in your current or past organization for cross-functional collaboration,
  in good times and bad? Would it work?

Answers

1 Summarize the problems and their solutions.

There were delays in distribution centres and retail shops receiving their complete orders. This was because of lengthy and unlimited revisions made to the original samples. Also, the orders to suppliers for materials were haphazard because of the chaotic sample stage, resulting in late, unused or missing materials. Accounting never kept track of all this. The main solution was to limit the redesign stage and to defer final orders to suppliers until the final design was agreed, which would also help accounting. The identification of problems and solutions was made through the BPR technique, based on information and data from the managers involved.

2 Why is the value of lost sales greater than the proportion of delayed deliveries?

Most of the delayed items will tend to be the more elaborate and expensive items. Hence agreement of their final samples will take longer, and their eventual delayed production will miss the launch date.

3 Can you think of other solutions instead?

Is it necessary to have as many as 150 new designs plus 50 revised designs every year? Fewer would reduce the time needed for sample making. Many firms benefit from reducing their range. A Pareto analysis (80/20) would be very useful to decide this. Also, categorization of each item (metal, stone, design features) could provide fuller sales details of the sales patterns of each distribution centre and their customer shops. From Answer 2, what would be the effect of trimming the top of the range items? Could some of the delivery periods be shortened?

4 Why had GLITZ not done anything until taken over by EQUITAS?

Oh lack of progress, thy name is inert complacency. Some owners are content to make a modest profit so long as they retain or increase their market share. All firms have problems, great or small, and to tinker with them in an unprofessional way would make things worse. It often takes a big disturbance to shock an owner into enquiry and action – a new giant competitor in a regional market, a warning from the auditors, hostile take-over bids, loss of key people or desertion by a large retail outlet in a capital city or wealthy suburb.

5 Is there scope in your current or past organization for cross-functional collaboration, in good times and bad? Would it work?

Collaboration may often be an essential part of a solution, but it is not an easy option. Honesty is required to reveal what is done well and where there is room for improvement. Discussions can turn into destructive debate with internal politics and jealousy often souring relationships. In short, trust has to be developed and sustained, often through the skill of an organizational development (OD) expert.

Note

I am grateful to K Sakultara Teerawut for permission to use some of her research material.

Sustainability in the hotel industry

The role of operating agreements in the hotel industry

Arvind Upadhyay, Francesco Pomponi, Céline Vadam and Sushil Mohan

AUTHOR BIOGRAPHIES

DR ARVIND UPADHYAY is Senior Lecturer in Logistics and Supply Chain Management at Brighton Business School.

FRANCESCO POMPONI is a Research Associate at the University of Cambridge, Centre for Sustainable Development.

CÉLINE VADAM is an international hospitality and tourism investment consultant.

DR SUSHIL MOHAN is Head of Economics Department at the University of Brighton.

Introduction

Energy consumption represents between three and six per cent of hotel operating costs and is responsible for 60 per cent of its CO_2

emissions. It has increased from 25 to 30 per cent over the last decade and is forecasted to continue growing due to more demanding
standards and the development of electronic equipment. It may be
influenced by various factors including building characteristics, hotel
features, location and operations. However, the main hotel's energy
end-use is temperature regulation (including room heating, hot water
and air conditioning), representing 69 per cent of hotels' energy consumption. Various measures can be taken within hotels to reduce their
energy consumption; some involving important technical costs, which
is a crucial parameter when putting in place a sustainable plan,
whereas others only need human care. The efficiency of these measures depends deeply on the collaboration and implication of all stakeholders. Among stakeholders, hotel chains are in the best position to
promote and implement eco-friendly policies. Indeed, due to their
size, strength and international networks, they are highly influential
in setting up trends and best practice and dispose of a range of operational, communication, training, monitoring, certification and
awarding tools to do so. An efficient tool is operating agreements,
which constrain the hotels to respect a list of technical, architectural
and operational requirements to enter a brand.

Theory of energy consumption in hotels

Energy consumption is influenced by various technical, architectural, local and management factors. Their characterization is illustrated in Table 1. All of these factors can induce significant fluctuations in energy consumption, which makes it difficult to define and
estimate energy targets in the hospitality industry as each hotel is
different.

Table 1 Factors influencing energy consumption in hotels

	Effects	Impact
Building features		
Size	The bigger the building, the more energy needed.	Medium
Shape	A hotel where all the infrastructure is condensed in the same building will be more energy efficient than a disparate property.	Medium
Age	A new building is supposed to be better insulated than an old one.	Medium
Materials	The material used is important in terms of insulation and lighting of the building.	High
Technical equipment	The choice of electronic appliances is important, as they are to be energy efficient to reduce energy consumption.	High
Hotel features		
Category	The higher the category, the higher the energy need (from 17.30 kwh PAR* for economy to 89.35 kwh PAR for luxury).	High
Facilities/services	A hotel with only a few services and facilities will consume less energy than a hotel with a lot of services and facilities.	High
Location		
Climate	Climate will impact on the use of air conditioning and heating which are more necessary according to hot or cold areas.	High
Local policies	Local energy policies impact on the prices and CO_2 emissions, as they will determine the type of energy used: gas, electricity, nuclear, wind, solar, etc.	High

	Effects	**Impact**
Operations		
Energy management	The hotel's energy management policy is crucial in controlling energy costs, as it will involve all the parties (staff, investors, guests) and will set up targets and best practices.	High
Occupancy	Occupancy will impact on the energy consumption, as more people in the building will require more energy. However, there are still spaces where energy will be required independently of the occupancy.	Medium
Operational hours	A hotel runs 24/7. However, operational hours may impact on the price of energy in certain areas (cheaper in dedicated hours).	Low

*PAR = per available room

It has been established that temperature regulation is crucial in managing hotels' energy consumption. The key is to find a balance between acceptable temperatures for guests and appropriate energy spending. In this respect, 19°C (66°F) is an acceptable average according to various worldwide health authorities. To a lesser extent, other important energy end-users are kitchens and other unidentified – including cooling and refrigeration (11 per cent each). Surprisingly, lighting/TV/radio ranks five in this classification (four per cent), followed by laundry (four per cent).

In order to reduce their energy consumption, hotels have at their disposal a range of tools and practices that can be easily implemented (Table 2), depending on the state of the hotel. Hotel owners are frequently reluctant to adopt sustainability measures in general, especially in those economic segments that are more cost sensitive such as construction costs. They also perceive eco-friendly measures as expensive. However, even if the cost of the following actions may vary, the impact on the environment and the overall cost reduction will be significant, thus justifying the investment needed. Moreover, some of the suggested actions listed in Table 2 have no financial costs: they only need human investment and care. It is important to point out that the difficulty in implementation and costs mentioned are informative and based on an industry average. They may vary depending on whether the hotel is already opened or planned and if the building is existing or newly built. Indeed, it is easier to include environment friendly technical requirements when planning a new-build rather than modifying the technical characteristics (shape, insulation, specific construction materials, equipment) of an already constructed building.

Table 2 Actions towards energy consumption reduction in hotels

	Implementation difficulty	Cost
Room heating and hot water		
Efficient building shape	Medium	Medium
Efficient isolation	Medium	Medium
In-room thermostat	High	High
Lower heating temperature	Low	Low
Air conditioning		
Lower cooling temperature	Low	Low
Better isolation	Medium	Medium
In-room thermostat	High	High
Lower cooling when no guests	Low	Low
Lighting, TV and radio		
Windows allowing natural light to stream in	High	High
Motion sensors	High	High

Table 2 *(continued)*

Low-consumption light bulbs	Medium	Medium
Energy savings mini-bar, TV	High	High
Kitchen		
Conversion of kitchen grease into bio-dynamic fuel	Low	Medium
Energy efficient appliances	High	High
Laundry		
Towel reuse	Low	Low
Linen reuse	Low	Low
Energy efficient laundry equipment	High	High
Office		
Motion sensors	High	High
Switch off computers	Low	Low
Limited usage of electronic appliances	Low	Low
Ventilation		
Energy saving ventilation system	High	High
Use of natural ventilation	Low	Low
Other		
Staff consciousness	Low	Low
Guests consciousness	Low	Low
Energy monitoring	Low	Low
Solar panels installation	Medium	High
Use of renewable energies (wind, biofuel)	Medium	High

CASE STUDY

Implementing sustainability measures in the hospitality industry is not an easy task. The present case study is based on a survey conducted among major hotel chains through questionnaires whose answers have been collected and analysed. For the sake of this case study the focus will be on the role of operating agreement as a means to increase eco-friendly policies in the hotel industry. The specificity of the context is due to the limited synergies that there are amongst hotel chains where multiple stakeholders are involved, as opposed to, for instance, the airline industry, where airline companies are grouped together under international alliances. The abundance of stakeholders involved with divergent interests and targets, creates a difficult balance between the owner's profit goals and hotel chains' standard requirements.

It is therefore challenging to develop coordinated and global sustainability actions involving all the stakeholders. For example, a hotel owner may be reluctant to implement a new energy efficient air-conditioning system required by the brand because they will see this as expensive and unnecessary, especially if the current system is still working. This is often the case, regardless of the fact the new system will have less impact on the environment and will reduce energy bills. This is especially true in lower hotel categories, which are most cost sensitive as they have lower spending power. Moreover, each hotel is different and characterized by various factors, from category to location, size to facilities, making it difficult to find a proper benchmark and 'model' to apply to each property.

In order to achieve their mission as sustainability ambassadors, hotel chains dispose of a range of operating, marketing/communication, training, monitoring, certifying and rewarding tools that they can use in their properties. Such tools are listed in Table 3 and qualified according to the impact they have on the success of a sustainable policy. As we can see, operational and communication actions are the most effective ways hotel chains can promote sustainability.

Table 3 Tools to encourage sustainability practices

	Impact
Operations	
Include sustainability measures in operating agreements	High
Sanctions for not respecting the sustainability measures	High
Include sustainability measures in brand standards	High
Communication	
Communicate sustainability best practices and hotels/chains measures taken towards employees	High
Communicate sustainability best practices and hotels/chains measures taken towards the industry	High
Communicate sustainability best practices and hotels/chains measures taken towards owners/investors	High
Communicate sustainability best practices and hotels/chains measures taken towards guests	High
Training	
Staff training	High
Raise guests' awareness	Medium
Monitoring	
Use of a monitoring system	High
Publication of sustainability reports	Medium
Set-up of sustainability targets	High
Certification	
Apply for international certification	Medium
Encourage hotels to apply for national certifications	Medium
Awards	
In-house awards to congratulate the greener hotels	Medium
Encourage hotels to apply for external awards	Medium

Among hotel chains' tools to control environment management within their hotels, operating contracts are a strong one. Indeed, operating contracts set up the rules and requirements a hotel needs to fulfil in order to enter a chain. Three types of contracts, explained below, are currently used in the hospitality sector. They are more or less binding depending on the type of commitment.

- *Lease/ownership*: the chain owns the property or pays rent to the building's owner in order to establish its hotel within the building. The chain is responsible for the operation of the hotel and manages the revenues. In this scenario, the chain is the master of the hotel and can easily implement policy. However, hotel chains are currently trying to reduce the number of hotels they own or lease, as the risk and investment for them are high.

- *Management contract*: this type of agreement involves a shared commitment between the owner of the building and the chain. The owner is responsible for the building (even if the chain insures day-to-day maintenance) and the chain takes care of operations, for which it receives a fee from the owner, calculated as a percentage of revenues. The chain can therefore operate the hotel its way but with the owner's approval. For example, the chain cannot decide to install an in-room thermostat in each room without the owner's approval, as the owner will be the one investing in this new equipment. Rather, the chain can decide to set up a towel reuse policy without asking for the owner's authorization as no costs will be involved. It is a type of contract that is more and more common, especially in the upscale to luxury segments, as it permits the chain to maintain a level of control with reasonable risks and investment.

- *Franchise*: franchise is the less demanding and costly type of contract for hotels. The owner pays a franchise fee to the chain for its authorization to use its brand name and benefits from its marketing and communication tools. The owner remains the operator of the property, giving to the chain only a low involvement in the hotel's operations: the chain cannot decide to implement sustainability policies in the hotel, unless they are mentioned in the contract (meaning that they have been preliminary negotiated and approved by both parties). This type of contract is increasingly common, especially in lower categories, as it allows chains to develop quickly and with a low level of risk and investment. However, it is unusual in the upper category levels, as chains are even more careful that their high-end guests have services and facilities of the highest quality, which they cannot control with franchise agreements, as they do not manage the property.

In the contexts described above, operating agreements come into the equation since they are linked to brand standards, as following the evolving requirements of brand standards is an obligation stated in operating agreements. An operating agreement is an independent document describing the requirements a hotel should meet to enter a brand, whatever the type of contract. In that sense, brand standards and operating agreements work together, the first one setting up the standards of a brand and the second one making sure, through law, that these standards are respected. Such a combination highlights the central role of brand standards in setting up sustainability policies at chain/group level, which will be applied at hotel level. Indeed, the flexibility and evolving status of brand standards can allow chains to adapt and be proactive towards new sustainability norms and techniques. Chains can include changes as they appear necessary and legitimate to them thanks to the combination with operating agreements. For example, if a new energy norm is introduced within the industry, a chain cannot change every single contract it has to include it. However, it can add it to its brand standards and all its hotels will have to consider it (as it is mentioned in their operating contracts that they have to respect brand standards).

Questions

1 What are the behavioural factors that affect energy consumption in the hotel sector?

2 Why are hotel chains in the best position to promote and implement environmental/
eco-friendly policies in the hotel sector?

3 What are the pros and cons of operating agreements in the hotel sector?

4 Why should energy norms and practices be included within brand standards?

5 What are the challenges in defining benchmark models for such energy norms and practices in the hotel sector?

Answers

1 What are the behavioural factors that affect energy consumption in the hotel sector?

Due to the central role temperature regulation plays towards the final figures of hotels' energy consumption, a lot can be done by the guests themselves through their behaviour. More moderate temperature settings (both for heating and cooling set-points), avoiding the use of air conditioning whilst windows are open, making sensible use of blankets/throws provided, and so on, are all behavioural factors that would significantly affect energy consumption with no or little consequence for comfort levels.

2 Why are hotel chains in the best position to promote and implement environmental/eco-friendly policies in the hotel sector?

Hotel chains are among the strongest stakeholders involved in the hotel industry due to their global reach, and the potential to educate affiliate members, guests and employees to adopting more sustainable views. More specifically, due to their size, strength and international networks, they are highly influential in setting up trends and best practice and dispose of a range of operational, communication, training, monitoring, certification and awarding tools to do so. Among those tools, operating agreements are in a very favourable position for they constrain hotels to respect a list of technical, architectural and operational requirements to enter a brand.

3 What are the pros and cons of operating agreements in the hotel sector?

Pros:
- brand recognition;
- energy saving which leads to cost saving;
- international benchmark of standards;
- education of other stakeholders towards eco-friendly aptitudes.

Cons:
- difficult to implement;
- needs long-term commitment from top management;

- frequent change in standards;
- cost–benefit analysis.

4 Why should energy norms and practices be included within brand standards?

It has been stated that energy norms and practices should be included within brand standards, so they can be proactively included and changed when necessary. Their legitimacy is protected by operating contracts, which give them a legal boundary. However, due to the complexity and diversity of each hotel, it is difficult to define benchmark models and identify energy consumption range levels and adequate sanctions. This gives hotel chains an educational and promotional role towards hotels' guests and investors, putting them into the position of sustainability ambassadors in the hotel industry.

5 What are the challenges in defining benchmark models for such energy norms and practices in the hotel sector?

It's difficult to adapt a specific model as there are various models prevalent in the hotel industry. Specifically, climates influence the way buildings are built and the hotel building stock is extremely diverse around the world in terms of architectural styles, materials used, buildings' size and shape, locations and orientations. Even more to the point, thermal comfort has been proven to vary according to the external temperature and the cultural background of each person. Such aspects create an extremely challenging environment to develop benchmark models that would suit such a massively diverse population of both buildings and people. The challenge is how to standardize these models so that they can be adapted easily all over the world. In certain countries, government rules and regulations force local hotels to adapt according to their rules.

The closure of a bank department

The cost of interrupting information supply chains

Brian Lawrence

AUTHOR BIOGRAPHY

BRIAN LAWRENCE is Lecturer in the School of Management at the Assumption University in Bangkok, Thailand.

Introduction

This case study explains how a hasty decision to close a department that helped ordinary bank staff to deal with the head office IT experts was later reversed as it had caused so many difficulties. The closure decision had been taken in a hurry by a takeover bank to cut costs, but it was a proper cost–benefit analysis that revealed the situation.

A major bank in Eastern Europe, Altberg Bank, recently merged with another big bank in Western Europe, Zollern Bank. The acquisition took place in September 2013 and was planned by Zollern Bank as part of their portfolio acquisition strategy. Though businesses can expand through increased customers and sales, portfolio building is usually quicker and brings considerations of economies of scale. Though officially called a merger, staff internally clearly understood who the majority stakeholder was. In this case, Zollern Bank was leading the strategy for the newly formed corporation. Due to technical considerations and security threats relating to hackers, it was decided to continue operating both banks on their existing IT and security systems in parallel. In an effort to minimize waste and not duplicate resources Zollern Bank, however, embarked on a cost-reduction exercise. Its management decided in January 2014, without a full appreciation of what was involved, to close Altberg Bank's special IT department (SITD), which was responsible for providing ID and password issuing services to 2,400 bank staff in one of its East European countries. The resulting confusion, errors and delays led to an investigation by the HRM director undertaken between June and September 2014. Her cost–benefit analysis ultimately seemed to show that the closure should be reversed, and the department reinstated. The following case study follows her analysis.

CASE STUDY
SITD's original purpose and role

The multitude of financial services provided by Altberg Bank meant that having only one IT system was grossly insufficient to run its operations. This large international corporation had 65 million business customers in 12 East European countries. Because of the variety of their customers' needs (which were much more complex than most personal accounts) the bank operated on 70 different computer software systems. This meant that each employee needed to access up to 10 to 25 systems at once, depending on their job responsibilities and seniority levels.

And with some customers holding several different accounts with the bank in several countries, the complexities in customer service and systems operation was further heightened. Hacking considerations also meant that security was a serious concern, as the bank was always at risk of employee default.

Employees couldn't use the same ID and password details for more than one system for security reasons, and on top of that, they had different levels of clearance to access systems depending on their roles so each new role necessitated new ID and password details, which thereafter had to be frequently altered.

The bank originally had an ID and password issuing department (IIDD) based in its head office, which was responsible for ensuring secure and traceable access for all employees in all its countries. Its main responsibility was to processes employees' requests for new or changed access ID and password details. Shortly after the department was established, it was uncovered that employees in country G found it difficult to file requests to IIDD. The details required by IIDD were technical and difficult to understand, thus meaning they were beyond the employees' technical knowledge and scope. The seemingly simple process took time and often had to be repeated because of errors and blank or incomprehensible answers. Therefore, the SITD was formed as an intermediary and established in country G. It was quite small, with six staff, two of whom were supervisors, security checkers of the work of the other four.

Security is a vital element in the running of IT systems in any financial institution.

SITD had been formed because so many staff had problems in creating secure passwords, having to routinely change them, and subsequently having to frequently ask IT for reminders or to grant them access if they had forgotten them. The procedure was far more complex than for ordinary email accounts or they had personal passwords for ordinary citizens. The function of SITD was to guide ordinary non-technically focused staff through a complicated technical process involved in requesting the Head Office IIDD to set up or change security log in details and passwords. SITD was a helpful intermediary.

Pressures leading to cost-cutting

Banking has become a very competitive business, nationally and internationally. Bank charges, service offerings and budgets have to take this into account. Employees are expensive, with their salaries, office accommodation and other related costs. Banks do not have expensive machinery, raw materials or stock inventory, but they do have expensive employees tending to expensive IT systems and equipment. When in need of containing costs, or maximizing financial results from a merger, any top management would look closely at what could be pared down.

So it was with the SITD. At a superficial glance, which is all it received, by attempting to reduce costs in a speedy attempt to satisfy shareholders with profit dividends, Altberg Bank's top management were advised to scrap the department as it was deemed to duplicate the work of the IIDD. Job duplication is obviously a costly waste. Without a full study, SITD was abolished.

The closure of SITD

The bank's employees in country G now had to deal directly with IIDD based in Altberg Bank's Head Office. However, it was soon discovered that that the original pre-SITD problems remained. Delays in the request process wasted time and distracted employees away from time spent serving customers which led to widespread complaints. Baffled and frustrated employees continued to ask the former SITD staff for help who had been moved to different departments, as they did before the department was closed. It had become almost a secret parallel world, with a ghost SITD whose staff could not now properly do their new redeployed jobs.

There was also a money penalty. Rejections by IIDD because of wrong or incomplete requests incurred a monthly penalty charge for Altberg Bank, which adversely affected country G's performance measures (productivity and costs).

The HRM director's investigation

The resulting poor service to customers was never envisaged when the change was made. In this highly competitive market where the trust and loyalty of business customers is highly influential on bottom line results, the bank has to provide quality service with minimal delay or error. The merged bank could not be seen to offer a poorer service than before.

Altberg Bank's board therefore requested and obtained the agreement of Zollern Bank's board to authorize country G's HRM director to investigate the situation and make recommendations based on her analysis of the problem.

The HRM director was tasked with the responsibility of examining and evaluating all costs and benefits, both monetary and non-monetary, for the initial closure of SITD, the delays, complaints and penalties, and the apparent non-compliance with the closure of the SITD department by the staff. She consulted with top management, staff and customers, and reviewed company records.

Findings

Data was collected for comparable periods in 2013 and 2014. This showed that there had been 6,150 requests to the old SITD. Overwhelmingly these related to five computer systems, which were concerned with ordinary banking, loans, overdrafts, credit cards and higher approval. Out of these 6,150 requests, 307 (5 per cent) were rejected. After closure, the requests directed to IIDD were numbered at 6,675, out of which 2,363 (35 per cent) were rejected; a huge increase.

Interviews with requester staff and supervisors revealed that a request now took staff between two and three hours to complete, which was much longer than the half an hour it usually took when SITD existed. The new request process was also more complicated. IIDD staff didn't seem to understand staff needs and problems, and requesters didn't understand the technical language used by IIDD staff at Head Office (and often their imperfect other language skills). Rejections, delays and repeat requests were frequent because of incompleteness, errors or language misunderstandings. The requesters' other work was compromised as their available time to serve customers was reduced.

After the closure of SITD, the complexity of filing request forms accounted for 45 per cent of all requester complaints. Rejections by IIDD accounted for 25 per cent, contact difficulty was 20 per cent and 10 per cent for errors due to poor language and technical skills.

IIDD now seemed overwhelmed by all these request problems, and urgent requests were rejected. IIDD complained that requesters often didn't respond to rejections or clarification-seeking questions (or took too long), gave foolish answers to questions and were difficult to understand.

Before the closure of SITD, the monthly IT expense paid by Country G to IIDD was US$5,900. After the closure it rose to US$19,400. When SITD was in existence, its six staff were paid a total of US$15,300 per month in salaries. The staff members were subsequently redeployed to other vacancies within the bank.

Recommendations by the HRM director

After analysing all of the costs and benefits, the HRM director concluded that the SITD should be restored, but with a reformed structure in place. It was established that there was no need for two supervisors in the team and that only one was sufficient. Therefore, it was recommended that one supervisor and two former SITD staff should have their old jobs back, and two additional new skilled and experienced IT staff recruited. Salaries should also increase by 10 per cent, offset by the loss of one supervisor's salary. This solution saves money and solves the request problems which wasted manpower, caused delays, and ultimately caused poor customer service and complaints.

Questions

1 What supply chains are involved in this case?
2 Do you agree with the top management's decision to close the SITD?
3 Do you agree with the HRM director's recommendations?
4 What alternatives do you think there were to the closure?
5 What alternatives do you think there are to restoring SITD?
6 Would consultation with the staff have stopped the decision to close SITD in the first place?

Answers

1 What supply chains are involved in this case?

This is a communication problem. Originally, in 2009, there was an internal supply chain of communication from the staff directly to IIDD requesting log in details and passwords. There was also a reverse flow of information (passwords or errors needing further clarifications or corrections). This changed in 2011 when SITD was created as it was uncovered that staff needed help. The communication chain was now from staff to SITD requesting help, from SITD to staff correcting or completing their draft requests, and from SITD to IIDD. There was also an internal chain of decision-making from top management to various parties, and back to top management giving comments and suggestions. The slow speed in getting passwords also affected the external chain of information, in responding to customer requests for advice or action.

2 Do you agree with the top management's decision to close the SITD?

In a fast-changing fiercely competitive world, management is always under pressure to make decisions to improve financial performance. The takeover management, faced with almost a doubling of systems, staff, customers, buildings, countries, regulatory authorities, and more, probably saw this as a welcome simple way to cut costs. Ideally there should have been a consultation process and a more careful evaluation of the factors involved. To their credit, top management later agreed to re-evaluate what now seemed a wrong closure decision.

3 Do you agree with the HRM director's recommendations?

The recommendations seem sensible and are needed. But there are other considerations. Human decision-making is not always fully rational or logical: we are influenced by our feelings, personality and experience. The amounts saved are not huge. The HRM director may have leaned favourably towards her own once independent Altberg Bank country staff. Or she may have wanted to impress her new bosses from Zollern Bank by not totally reversing their decision, and also making her country staff happy. She may have thought that this is a transition takeover period, and that her own country staff would try harder to master the request forms, so that in two years' time she could do another survey and report that SITD was no longer needed.

4 What alternatives do you think there were to the closure?

A self-help manual could have been prepared for them to learn to take IT responsibility, with a one-year deadline to closure. After all, almost all requests were linked to only five systems (out of a possible 25). Maybe the rarely used systems could have been handled by one or two specialists instead of everybody.

5 What alternatives do you think there are to restoring SITD?

Similarly to the answer provided for question 4, request-form training could have been organized by HRM. That would take more time and incur more expenses during the learning period, and perhaps that would have temporarily caused an even worse situation. The risk would be more customer complaints and customers lost to competitors. What if the staff still found it too difficult? Also, the interaction skills of IIDD people needed improving. That is a recruitment and/or training problem. Another option is to restore SITD exactly as it was. Its old staff are still with the bank and need no training. But that option would not have the cost savings in the director's recommendation. Top-management pride also needs to be considered. In some countries 'saving face' is a highly important part of the culture, so the HRM director's recommendations help alleviate the possible repercussions of telling them they were wrong.

6 Would consultation with the staff have stopped the decision to close SITD in the first place?

Maybe not. The requesters would have said they wanted no change. Vested interests and self-interest are usually strong forces which prevail over rational facts. And many so-called facts are debatable. Requesters would have resented Zollern Bank's approach to cost-saving aimed at Altberg Bank's operations. The symbolic weight associated to a company overtaking another and dictating new rules is also important to consider. For an effective consultation period to happen, it would have had to be scheduled after both corporations had got to know one another and had a chance to develop trust.

Note   I am grateful to K Pongpat Nitayasuth for permission to use some of his research material.

Demand covering and service level estimation in public services planning
The case of household waste recycling centres

Andrea Genovese and Mike Simpson

AUTHOR BIOGRAPHIES

DR ANDREA GENOVESE AND DR MIKE SIMPSON
ANDREA GENOVESE is a Lecturer in Logistics and Supply Chain Management at The University of Sheffield Management School.

Introduction

Concepts from location science can be very useful in planning decisions in both public and private sector contexts. Specifically, considerations about demand allocation can provide valuable insights for decision-makers.

The elements that constitute a location problem are represented by:

- facilities offering a given service;
- users requiring the service;
- a location space, in which facilities can be located and users are situated.

The most common rule utilized in location problems for assigning users to active facilities is represented by the *closest allocation* rule, assuming that each user will patronize the nearest facility offering the required service, regardless of the distance (see Figure 1).

Figure 1 Closest allocation rule

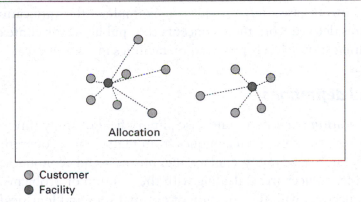

Allocation

○ Customer
● Facility

The influence of the distance on the capability of a facility to provide a service to users is captured by the *demand covering* concept. In this perspective, it is assumed that demand can be covered by a facility only if the distance between the facility and the place where the user is located is within a *covering radius* (see Figure 2). This concept is very frequently utilized in public services planning (for instance, for the design of school and healthcare facilities catchment areas).

Figure 2 Covering radius

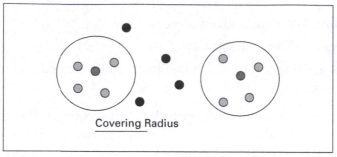

- ● Uncovered Customer
- ◯ Covered Customer
- ◉ Facility

The following case study provides an example of the applications of measures derived from these concepts to a public sector context, for estimating service levels provided by facilities in a given area.

Useful definitions

- *Location science:* A multi-disciplinary field of study (involving concepts, tools and techniques from mathematics, operational research, geography, engineering, business and economics and other subject areas) dealing with the solution of problems concerned with the selection of optimal sites and logistical configurations for locating facilities.

- *Demand allocation:* In location science, the mechanism of assigning users (or customers) who are requesting a service to a given available facility that is offering it.

- *Closest allocation rule:* In location science, a particular demand allocation rule for which users (or customers) are allocated to the closest available facility.

- *Covering radius:* In location science, a concept reproducing a sort of critical threshold. Indeed, it can be assumed that, under certain conditions, user demand can be satisfied by a facility only if the distance between the facility and the place where the user is located is within a covering radius.

Demand covering and service level estimation in public services planning: the case of household waste recycling centres

In addition to kerbside collection services and neighbourhood recycling points (located near supermarkets and retail parks), local authorities in the United Kingdom provide some special household waste recycling centres (HWRCs). These centres are provided to residents to dispose of materials that are not allowed in kerbside bins and at neighbourhood recycling points, such as: special paper, special glass, textiles and clothing, plastics, steel cans, aluminium and foil, furniture, motor oil, green waste, books, card, rubble, shoes, car batteries, scrap metal, electrical and electronic equipment, wood, household batteries, fluorescent tubes/lamps, cement bonded asbestos, plasterboard, fridges, bric-a-brac. These facilities provide a critical service to communities, as they can help in handling potentially hazardous and hard-to-treat waste and in increasing recycling rates.

Specifically, the list of currently active sites in a local authority in the North of England is provided below in Table 1. It has to be mentioned that, recently, due to budget cuts operated by the central government to local authorities, the local authority has started to implement a reduction in the working hours of the centres (originally open from 9 am to 5 pm every day). Therefore, the local authority has devised a revised schedule, shown in Table 1. Table 2 illustrates the distances (in terms of travel time, expressed in minutes) of the five centres from the 28 electoral wards in which the territory of the local authority is partitioned; furthermore, in the last column of the same table, the population of each ward is shown.

Table 1 Opening hours for HWRC facilities

Recycling centres	Opening days	Closure days
A	Wednesday to Monday	Tuesday
B	Thursday to Tuesday	Wednesday
C	Thursday to Monday	Tuesday and Wednesday
D	Friday to Tuesday	Wednesday and Thursday
E	7 days a week	None

Table 2 Travel time between wards and HWRCs and population of the wards

Travel time (in mins) Wards	HWRC sites					Ward population
	A	B	C	D	E	
W1	12	3	25	23	15	17,500
W2	20	10	29	30	20	18,600
W3	3	16	30	26	20	17,800
W4	8	8	28	24	18	18,100
W5	17	12	19	19	10	16,800
W6	13	13	19	19	5	24,000
W7	15	10	23	23	13	17,300
W8	19	14	19	21	11	16,800
W9	13	14	20	16	13	19,500
W10	22	13	30	30	21	16,400

Table 2 *(continued)*

W11	21	24	12	6	12	17,800
W12	23	16	27	27	18	19,211
W13	21	22	19	14	7	20,000
W14	22	16	24	24	14	15,400
W15	15	2	27	28	18	19,700
W16	19	10	27	28	18	17,200
W17	21	18	11	14	7	18,500
W18	11	11	24	21	14	20,100
W19	8	13	34	30	23	16,300
W20	19	12	23	24	14	18,000
W21	5	11	23	19	12	17,300
W22	20	21	19	15	9	20,200
W23	20	18	15	11	2	20,000
W24	24	22	18	20	12	16,600
W25	32	33	6	12	20	18,400
W26	19	14	16	17	9	17,900
W27	23	21	10	6	8	17,800
W28	3	13	27	22	18	17,900

Question

1 Considering the available data, the local authority is interested in understanding what the service level is that the current configuration of the HWRC sites system provides to local households, as well as estimating the effects of the changes in the opening hours on the service provision.

Answer

1 Considering the available data, the local authority is interested in understanding what the service level is that the current configuration of the HWRC sites system provides to local households, as well as estimating the effects of the changes in the opening hours on the service provision.

Several insights can be gained by applying some basic concepts from location science to this case study.

As a first attempt, due to the nature of the service, it can be assumed that users will always decide to patronize the closest facility. Namely, users coming from a given ward will always decide to bring their household waste to the closest HWRC to the ward they live in. In this way, each ward can be allocated to a facility, and the load (in terms of population) for each of the HWRCs can be evaluated. Table 3 details the allocation of wards to sites, highlighting the shortest distances between each ward and its respective closest site.

Table 3 Allocation of wards to HWRC sites

Travel time (in mins)	HWRC sites					Ward population
Wards	A	B	C	D	E	
W1	12	3	25	23	15	17,500
W2	20	10	29	30	20	18,600
W3	3	16	30	26	20	17,800
W4	8	9	28	24	18	18,100
W5	17	12	19	19	10	16,800
W6	13	13	19	19	5	24,000
W7	15	10	23	23	13	17,300
W8	19	14	19	21	11	16,800
W9	13	14	20	16	13	19,500
W10	22	13	30	30	21	16,400
W11	21	24	12	6	12	17,800
W12	23	16	27	27	18	19,211
W13	21	22	19	14	7	20,000
W14	22	16	24	24	14	15,400
W15	15	2	27	28	18	19,700
W16	19	10	27	28	18	17,200
W17	21	18	11	14	7	18,500
W18	10	11	24	21	14	20,100
W19	8	13	34	30	23	16,300
W20	19	12	23	24	14	18,000

Table 3 *(continued)*

W21		5	11	23	19	12	17,300
W22		20	21	19	15	9	20,200
W23		20	18	15	11	2	20,000
W24		24	22	18	20	12	16,600
W25		32	33	6	12	20	18,400
W26		19	14	16	17	9	17,900
W27		23	21	10	6	8	17,800
W28		3	13	27	22	18	17,900

As a result, the number of wards (and the related total population) allocated to each site can be derived, as reported in Table 4. It can be noticed that, due to the current spatial configuration of the HWRC sites, three centres (A, B and E) account for the vast majority of the demand, serving more than 90 per cent of the population. On the other hand, sites C and D serve a very limited number of wards (respectively, 1 and 2) and, therefore, a very limited quota of the total population.

Table 4 Allocation of wards to HWRC sites – summary

HWRC site	Number of wards served	Population served	% of population served
A	6	107,500	21.03
B	9	159,311	31.17
C	1	18,400	3.60
D	2	35,600	6.97
E	10	190,300	37.23

Based on the above-mentioned allocation hypothesis, it is possible to compute the average travel time for users to reach their facility. This can simply be computed as a weighted average of the travel times from each ward to the respective HWRC facility, assuming the population of the ward as the weight. Average travel times can be computed for the basic scenario in which all the centres are open (during a typical week, on Mondays, Fridays, Saturdays and Sundays); also, this measure can be calculated for the other days, in which some of the centres are closed, allowing the local authority to evaluate the impact of the closure shifts on the average travel time, assumed as an indicator of the service level provided. Table 5 shows the average travel times for all the different scenarios. It can be seen that the closure of the sole site D (on Thursdays) does not produce any major effect on the service level; Wednesdays appear to be, potentially, the most troublesome day, with just sites A and E open, and the closure of sites B (one of the major attractors, serving nine wards), C and D:

Table 5 Average travel times – scenario analysis

Scenario	Closed centres	Average travel time
Friday to Monday	None	8 min 07s
Tuesday	A and C	9 min 34s
Wednesday	B, C and D	10 min 51s
Thursday	D	8 min 24s

this is reflected in the sharp increase in the average travel time (from 8 min 07s to 10 min 51s).

Another interesting way of looking into the problem is offered by modifying the demand allocation mechanism. As an alternative, the concept of covering radius could be utilized by assuming that HWRCs are capable of attracting demand from areas within 15 minutes of travel time from their location. In this way, wards are not simply allocated to a single centre, but they could be simultaneously *covered* by more than one facility. Table 6 details the resulting analysis; highlighted cells in the table identify travel times lower than or equal to 15 minutes, signifying that the corresponding ward is covered by the centre. It can be seen that most of the wards are covered by at least one HWRC; only W12 is not covered by any facility within a 15-minute radius. Generally speaking, ten wards are covered by three HWRCs, and 11 by two HWRCs (see Table 7). This means that these wards can enjoy comparable alternatives when accessing the service; also, for these wards, impacts of site closures may be negligible, due to the presence of alternative sites. Wards W2, W3, W10, W14, W16 and W24 are just covered by a single facility; this means that impact of closure decisions must be especially carefully evaluated on these areas that are just depending on a single centre. It can also be seen that facilities C and D cover a more limited number of wards; also, for all the wards covered by these facilities (apart from W25) alternative coverage is provided by facilities A, B or E. Table 8 provides a summary, showing that, in accordance with what has been presented in Table 4, facilities B and E play a critical role in the system, covering a very large number of wards and a large proportion of the population.

Table 6 HWRCs and covered wards

Travel time (in mins)	HWRC Sites						Ward population
Wards	A	B	C	D	E	Covered by	
W1	12	3	25	23	15	3	17,500
W2	20	10	29	30	20	1	18,600
W3	3	16	30	26	20	1	17,800
W4	8	9	28	24	18	2	18,100
W5	17	12	19	19	10	2	16,800
W6	13	13	19	19	5	3	24,000
W7	15	10	23	23	13	3	17,300
W8	19	14	19	21	11	2	16,800

Table 6 (continued)

W9	13	14	20	16	13	3	19,500
W10	22	13	30	30	21	1	16,400
W11	21	24	12	6	12	3	17,800
W12	23	16	27	27	18	0	19,211
W13	21	22	19	14	7	2	20,000
W14	22	16	24	24	14	1	15,400
W15	15	2	27	28	18	2	19,700
W16	19	10	27	28	18	1	17,200
W17	21	18	11	14	7	3	18,500
W18	10	11	24	21	14	3	20,100
W19	8	13	34	30	23	2	16,300
W20	19	12	23	24	14	2	18,000
W21	5	11	23	19	12	3	17,300
W22	20	21	19	15	9	2	20,200
W23	20	18	15	11	2	3	20,000
W24	24	22	18	20	12	1	16,600
W25	32	33	6	12	20	2	18,400
W26	19	14	16	17	9	2	17,900
W27	23	21	10	6	8	3	17,800
W28	3	13	27	22	18	2	17,900

Table 7 HWRCs and covered wards – summary 1

Wards	Number
Covered by 3 HWRCs	10
Covered by 2 HWRCs	11
Covered by 1 HWRC	6
Covered by no HWRC	1

Table 8 HWRCs and covered wards – summary 2

HWRC site	Number of wards covered	Population covered	% of population covered
A	11	205,500	40.21
B	17	309,400	60.53
C	5	92,500	18.10
D	7	132,700	25.96
E	18	331,500	64.86

Table 9 provides a simple scenario analysis looking at the variation of the total amount of wards and related population covered by the HWRC system in the different days of the week. It can be highlighted that the closure of site D (happening on a typical Thursday) does not affect at all the amount of population covered; small variations can be observed on Tuesdays (when both A and C are closed), while, again, Wednesdays appear to be a critical day given the drop in coverage (82.43 per cent).

Table 9 HWRCs and covered wards – scenario analysis

Scenario	Wards covered	Closed centres	% of population covered
Friday to Monday	27	None	96.24
Tuesday	26	A and C	92.75
Wednesday	23	B, C and D	82.43
Thursday	27	D	96.24

Conclusion

The application of concepts from location science to the case afforded some useful insights. Specifically, the local authority can understand the negligible role played, in terms of demand covering and service level and number of wards served, by facilities C and D. Therefore, the reduced schedule (in terms of opening hours) for these facilities seems to be a sensible decision. The analysis highlights the pivotal role played by facilities B and D (and, to a lesser extent, of facility A), capable of providing services to a large quota of the population. Further reductions to the opening hours of the facilities could have a detrimental effect on the service level and should be carefully examined.

CASE STUDY 1.7

Job shop layout at Jones Medical Laboratories
Adjacent department method

Mike Simpson and Andrea Genovese

AUTHOR BIOGRAPHIES

DR MIKE SIMPSON AND DR ANDREA GENOVESE
ANDREA GENOVESE is a Lecturer in Logistics and Supply Chain
Management at The University of Sheffield Management School.

Introduction

Facility layout concerns both manufacturing and service operations.
Facility layout decisions consider how work areas and storage areas
are arranged to minimize the costs of movement of people, materials,
equipment and information between departments. There are several
approaches to layout problems (activity matrices, string diagrams,
flow diagrams, interrelationship diagrams, relationship charts, etc)
but all are concerned with reducing costs to a minimum. There are
several different types of layout which a factory or service provider
can use to produce a product or service and the particular layout

chosen will depend upon the volume produced and the variety of products produced. Usually organizations look at matching the appropriate process to the product characteristics and most textbooks on operations management discuss this in detail. In this case study we will look at *activity matrices* and the *adjacent department method* for organizing *job shops*.

Useful definitions

A *product layout* is characterized by high demand for the same or similar products. In this arrangement there are few variations in the product and the layout fits the dominant flow of the product through the factory (usually a line flow or continuous flow).

A *process layout* is characterized by low-volume production of any one product and the production of many different products with the same equipment (low volume; high variety). No single product has enough volume to support a dedicated set of machines. Each product has different production requirements that place different demands on the equipment. In this arrangement the layout is grouped by similar machine types because there is no dominant product flow through the facility. Thus, in an engineering company all the milling machines will be in one area, all the drilling machines in another area and all the lathes in another area. The product (or a small batch) will be sent through the factory from one area to another with a work order card which tells the operatives what work needs to be done on the item(s).

A *job shop* usually deals with low-volume and high-variety products/services. Thus, job shops have to be flexible enough to meet a variety of needs but this usually means they have a much higher unit cost than line flow or batch processes for the same product. High-quality upmarket restaurants and hospital emergency rooms are examples of job shops in that both types of organizations offer great product variety and cater to individual customer demands (low volumes). However, in a job shop environment the products do not follow the same path through the facility (it is a near random flow) and some way needs to be found of organizing a job shop to obtain the most efficient and effective layout. Fortunately, most job shops do not have a completely random flow of product but instead there are major and minor flows through the facility.

Activity matrices (sometimes called load, movement or trip frequency charts) are diagrams that show the movement of people, materials, equipment or information between departments. It is an easy way of organizing and displaying the relationships between departments to understand the movement or flow of people, materials, equipment or information so that unnecessary work can be eliminated and costs can therefore be reduced. An activity matrix looks like Table 1, initially, with all the cells in the table empty. In order to use this matrix we need to collect some data about the movement of people, materials, equipment or information between departments. For example, we can look at the number of journeys an operative, let us say a porter at a hospital, makes between the various departments in a hospital in a specified time period (day, week, month, etc). We can count the number of journeys or we can ask the porter to keep a daily log of all the journeys made, or we could look at records of job transfers if available (Table 2).

Table 1 An activity matrix (without any data added)

		To department (or workstation)					
		A	B	C	D	E	F
From department (or workstation)	A	–					
	B		–				
	C			–			
	D				–		
	E					–	
	F						–

We can then put all of the data collected into the activity matrix and produce Table 2.

Table 2 An activity matrix (with data added) for trips in a month

		To department (or workstation)					
		A	B	C	D	E	F
From department (or workstation)	A	–	10	30	20	10	10
	B	20	–	20	50	10	10
	C	50	0	–	60	25	50
	D	10	20	75	–	30	5
	E	10	0	30	20	–	20
	F	0	0	5	0	0	–

We can see that the porter travels from Department A to Department B 10 times and from Department B to Department A 20 times in a month. We can also see that the porter travels from Department D to Department C 75 times and from C to D 60 times in a month, and so on.

The objective for a job shop is to minimize the handling and transportation costs of people, materials, equipment and information within the factory/service facility between departments or workstations. This approach can be applied to both manufacturing or service job shops such as hospital departments, accident and emergency units, restaurants (especially in the kitchen area) and any service or manufacturing facility handling the flows of people or materials. It is possible to evaluate any layout by multiplying the activity level by the distance travelled and by the cost per unit distance. The objective is to minimize the cost of movement between departments. Thus, the objective function which is to be minimized is:

$$\text{Objective function} = \text{minimize} \sum_{i=1}^{n} \sum_{j=1}^{n} A_{ij} D_{ij} C_{ij} \text{ for all } i \neq j$$

Where: A_{ij} = the activity level from department i to department j; i = 1,...,n and j = 1,...,n, where n is the number of departments

D_{ij} = distance from department i to department j

C_{ij} = the cost per unit distance from department i to department j

In order to do this the following information must be collected:

1 *Activity data:* This data will need to be collected as outlined briefly earlier. Thus journeys of people or movements of items will need to be determined by either primary data collection or from logs of transfers or orders received or secondary data from records of past jobs and movements, etc.

2 *The distance between departments:* A plan or diagram of the facility can be used to estimate the distances or the actual distances can be measured if required.

3 *The cost per unit distance travelled:* Transportation/movement costs will have to be determined based on the time taken to move an item from one place to another.

A simplified approach: the adjacent department method

Very often data for the costs and the distances travelled by various components, products, etc are not available and so a simplified approach looking at the number of items travelling between departments (ie the number of return trips) can be used. This method assumes that the activities with the largest figures can be placed next to each other to minimize the objective function above. This approach minimizes the influence of cost and distance on the calculations. However, it does suffer from a number of problems, such as: what shape should the individual departments be? Is the shape of the department dependent upon the various machinery and equipment in that department? Are the departments of different sizes? How might these departments be accommodated in a new building which is a particular shape (eg square, rectangular or L-shaped) or has several floors? These are very practical questions that are specific to each individual factory or facility layout. Thus, a simplified approach is to consider the number of items travelling between each department (ie number of return trips) and place those departments with a large flow between them next to each other. This is known as the *adjacent department method*.

The adjacent department method

This method assumes that the cost per unit distance is equal for all trips. This removes the need to collect data on costs. It also assumes that the distance between departments can be categorized as adjacent (assigned 0), one department away (assigned 1), two departments away (assigned 2) and so on. These assumptions simplify the analysis and allow quick solutions to the positioning of departments (or workstations) to be generated. This simplified method is not as accurate as the objective function model in the equation above but it does give a good initial solution that can be evaluated.

Determining the optimum layout with the adjacent department method

In most management situations there is generally a requirement for a quick, good solution rather than the optimum solution. There are also numerous other constraints on the organization that may prevent the optimum solution from being implemented. Thus, a 'good' solution will often suffice.

Step 1: Determine an initial solution. A 'good' initial layout can be determined by:

1 Placing all the departments with a high number of trips between departments close together. This will give an initial solution to the layout problem.

2 Placing the departments with a few trips further away.

3 The exact shape of the building will need to be known so that distances can be determined.

Step 2: Evaluate the initial solution(s). If the solution is satisfactory, then stop. If there are solutions which may be better then continue to step 3. The evaluation method is shown in the Worked example 1.

Step 3: Change the initial solution and try to find a better
     solution. Return to step 2 and evaluate the solution.

Thus, using these three steps a suitable 'good' layout solution can be
arrived at for the departments (or for workstations) relatively quickly
and relatively easily.

The worked example shows a hospital with patient flows between
departments moving to a new building. The hospital needs to develop
a layout for the departments so as to minimize the costs of transferring patients from one department to another. Only the activity data
is available as patient trips between departments and so the adjacent
department method can be applied to solve the problem of minimiz-
ing the costs of transferring patients from one department to another.

Worked example 1: layout of hospital departments in a new building

A hospital has just built a new building with equal-sized departments
with the following shape:

Patients are normally moved from one department to another using
porters with wheelchairs and trolleys.

The hospital manager has given you the following data about the
movement of patients between departments:

An activity matrix for movement of patients between departments
(trips in a month)

		To department					
		A	B	C	D	E	F
From department	A	–	10	30	20	10	10
	B	20	–	20	50	10	10
	C	50	0	–	60	25	50
	D	10	20	75	–	30	5
	E	10	0	30	20	–	20
	F	0	0	5	0	0	–

The hospital manager wants a quick solution to this problem and
suggests that you use the adjacent department method. Your job is to
advise on the best solution to the layout problem and report back to
the hospital manager.

Solution using the adjacent department method

The original data is:

An activity matrix for movement of patients between departments (trips in a month)

		To department					
		A	B	C	D	E	F
From department	A	–	10	30	20	10	10
	B	20	–	20	50	10	10
	C	50	0	–	60	25	50
	D	10	20	75	–	30	5
	E	10	0	30	20	–	20
	F	0	0	5	0	0	–

Adjacent department method

1 *Add the return trips together:* By combining patient trips from Department A to B with patient trips from Department B to A we can simplify the activity matrix from that shown above. The assumption here is that trips from Department A to B are the same length (and cost) as trips from Department B to A and so on throughout the activity matrix. This procedure can be repeated for all pairs of departments in the activity matrix. This will simplify the calculations by cutting the number of cells in half. We can do this because the cost per unit distance has been assumed to be equal for all trips. The activity matrix now looks like the diagram below.

A simplified activity matrix for the movement of patients (trips in a month)

		To department					
		A	B	C	D	E	F
From department	A	–	30	80	30	20	10
	B		–	20	70	10	10
	C			–	135	55	55
	D				–	50	5
	E					–	20
	F						–

We can see that a patient travels from Department A to Department B ten times and from Department B to Department A 20 times in a month and by combining these figures we see that the patient trips from A to B can be summed to give 30 trips. We can also see that a patient travels from Department D to Department C 75 times and from C to D 60 times in a month and by combining these figures we see that the patient trips from C to D gives 135 trips in total. This procedure can be repeated for all pairs of departments in the activity matrix.

2 *From the matrix above the activity levels can be ranked:* This will allow departments to be positioned in the layout. The list provided below shows that Departments D and F have the least interaction and should be placed far apart, and that C and D have the highest interaction level and therefore should be placed as close as possible.

Ranked activity levels

Department pair	Activity level
C–D	135
A–C	80
B–D	70
C–E	55
C–F	55
D–E	50
A–B	30
A–D	30
A–E	20
B–C	20
E–F	20
A–F	10
B–E	10
B–F	10
D–F	5

3 *Initial layout:* We know that the building is divided up by a 2 × 3 matrix as shown below. Now it is possible to assign the departments to positions in the layout to produce an initial layout (see the layout diagram below).

D	C	A
B	E	F

   This is the initial layout based on placing those departments with the highest interaction (ie highest patient flows) next to each other. Thus, from the ranked activity levels we see that departments C and D are close together (ie adjacent and so distance is assigned 0). Also departments A and C are adjacent, departments B and D are adjacent and departments C and E are adjacent, and so on. Departments B and C; C and F; D and E; and A and E are also regarded as adjacent despite being diagonally related in the layout above.

4 *Evaluation:* The evaluation is achieved by assigning distances as 0, 1, 2, and so on. Adjacent departments are given a 0 distance. Departments separated by another department are assigned a distance of 1. Departments separated by two departments are assigned a distance of 2 and so on. Departments that are diagonally close (eg C and F) are also assumed to be adjacent. These assumptions simplify the problem of the evaluation of the layout. The smaller the number of trips between non-adjacent departments, the better the solution. This analysis gives the following:

Evaluation: number of trips between non-adjacent departments

Department pair	Activity level (A_{ij})	Distance (D_{ij})	(A) × (D)
A–D	30	1	30
A–B	30	1	30
B–F	10	1	10
D–F	5	1	5
		$\Sigma(A \times D) =$	75

This evaluation suggests we have a good solution because the value of the $\Sigma(A \times D)$ is quite low. Is it possible to change the layout of the various hospital departments to reduce this figure further?

If departments E and F are swapped around we get the following layout:

D	C	A
B	F	E

The analysis gives:

Evaluation: number of trips between non-adjacent departments

Department pair	Activity level (A_{ij})	Distance (D_{ij})	$(A) \times (D)$
A–D	30	1	30
A–B	30	1	30
B–E	10	1	10
D–E	50	1	50
		$\Sigma(A \times D) =$	120

The value of the $\Sigma(A \times D)$ is larger than the initial solution in this case and so we would reject this layout and recommend the initial solution to the hospital manager unless further analysis with another layout gave a smaller value of $\Sigma(A \times D)$.

It is possible to continue with the adjacent department method to improve the initial solution.

It is possible to consider distances and costs to evaluate a layout and the student is referred to textbooks on this matter.

> **Note** Other methods of analysis include string diagrams and inter-relationship diagrams to show the flow or number of trips from one department to another.

Jones Medical Laboratories: job shop layout

Jones Medical Laboratories is moving to a new building with equal-sized departments with the following shape:

The operations manager has given you the following data about the movement of samples requiring analysis between departments:

A simplified activity matrix for the movement of patients (trips in a month)

		To department					
		A	B	C	D	E	F
	A	–	20	30	20	10	50
	B	20	–	20	50	10	60
From department	C	10	0	–	10	25	50
	D	0	20	5	–	30	5
	E	10	0	30	20	–	20
	F	10	10	5	0	0	–

The departments are:

A   Receiving
B   Chill store
C   Staff offices

D   Analytical laboratories
E   Hazardous waste disposal
F   Chemical stores

Questions

1 The operations manager would like to achieve a good layout in the new building using the adjacent department method, but the main analytical laboratory (D) requires various services (eg gas bottles, water, fume cupboard extraction) and the receiving department (A) is fixed due to access for vehicles and so these departments must be positioned as shown in the layout below. Your job is to provide a good initial layout for the operations manager and evaluate the proposed layout.

2 A further constraint to the layout arises when the operations manager finds out that Department C must be placed next to Department A as shown below. You should develop an initial layout with this additional constraint and evaluate the proposed layout.

3 Do these constraints affect your proposed solution? If so, comment on your answer.

Answers

1 The operations manager would like to achieve a good layout in the new building using the adjacent department method, but the main analytical laboratory (D) requires various services (eg gas bottles, water, fume cupboard extraction) and the receiving department (A) is fixed due to access for vehicles and so these departments must be positioned as shown in the layout below. Your job is to provide a good initial layout for the operations manager and evaluate the proposed layout.

Add the return trips together:

		To department					
		A	B	C	D	E	F
From department	A	–	40	40	20	20	60
	B		–	20	70	10	70
	C			–	15	55	55
	D				–	50	5
	E					–	20
	F						–

From the matrix above the activity levels can be ranked.

Ranked activity levels

Department pair	Activity level
B–D	70
B–F	70
A–F	60
C–E	55
C–F	55
D–E	50
A–B	40
A–C	40
A–D	20
A–E	20
B–C	20
E–F	20
C–D	15
B–E	10
D–F	5

Develop the initial layout by placing activities with high levels of interaction together. A solution with constraints of A and D fixed is:

E	C	A
D	B	F

Evaluation: number of trips between non-adjacent departments

Department pair	Activity level (A_{ij})	Distance (D_{ij})	$(A) \times (D)$
A–E	20	1	20
A–D	20	1	20
D–F	5	1	5
E–F	20	1	20
		$\Sigma(A \times D) =$	65

The initial layout with Departments A and D fixed has a low value for the sum of the activities multiplied by the distance (using the adjacent department method); $\Sigma(A \times D) = 65$. It also takes into account the constraints. Any alternative layout is likely to have a greater value for $\Sigma(A \times D)$.

2 A further constraint to the layout arises when the operations manager finds out that Department C must be placed next to Department A as shown below. You should develop an initial layout with this additional constraint and evaluate the proposed layout.

		A
D		C

Thus, a solution with Department C in the bottom right is:

E	F	A
D	B	C

Evaluation: number of trips between non-adjacent departments

Department pair	Activity level (A_{ij})	Distance (D_{ij})	(A) × (D)
A–E	20	1	20
A–D	20	1	20
C–D	15	1	15
C–E	55	1	55
		$\Sigma(A \times D) =$	110

3 Do these constraints affect your proposed solution? If so, comment on your answer.

These constraints do not affect the layout proposed very much as Departments A and D do not interact a great deal and the initial solution, which has a $\Sigma(A \times D) = 65$, is a very good solution compared with other options. However, if other departments were to be fixed (eg C in bottom right; see evaluation above for this option) then a different solution would probably be less efficient and more costly. The solution shown has $\Sigma(A \times D) = 110$ which is low. Try some alternative layouts with the Departments A, C and D fixed and evaluate them.

Monument Engineering Ltd
Aggregate planning

Mike Simpson and Andrea Genovese

AUTHOR BIOGRAPHIES

DR MIKE SIMPSON AND DR ANDREA GENOVESE
ANDREA GENOVESE is a Lecturer in Logistics and Supply Chain Management at The University of Sheffield Management School.

Introduction

Planning how a company uses its resources can be done in several ways depending upon the type of company and the production processes involved. Very often companies selling a range of products of the same kind (eg screwdrivers) make several different sizes of the products (eg small, medium and large screwdrivers). However, the same processes and equipment are used to make screwdrivers no matter what size the items are (within reason). Thus, all the screwdrivers can be scheduled together (aggregated) when they are being planned through the production system.

Useful definitions

- *Resource management:* Deals with all the resources within the company (eg labour, materials, equipment, facilities, information, technical expertise and skills) and creates plans which are executed and controlled to produce goods and services as required by the customers. The objectives of resource management are to: (i) maximize profit; (ii) maximize customer satisfaction; (iii) minimize costs; and (iv) maximize benefits to the various stakeholders involved.

- *Aggregate planning:* Means that medium-range operations are planned in such a way that first-stage rough-cut approximations are made to create a plan of how the existing resources (eg labour and facilities) should be used to meet the projected (ie forecasted) demand.

- *Aggregation:* Refers to the combining of products into groups or families for planning purposes. Thus, in our example all the different sizes of screwdrivers are treated as simply screwdrivers. The same would apply for spanners, wrenches, handsaws, and so on.

- *Disaggregation:* Involves translating aggregate plans into detailed short-term operational plans for weekly and daily production schedules. Detailed resource requirements plans are also made at the same time.

- *Scheduling:* Is the final, detailed determination of the operational activities which must take place to make the products or services. Thus, the times employees will work, the sequence in which the items are provided and the operating times for machines are planned in detail.

- *Make to order:* the company has a policy of only making products according to customer orders. This is an important decision for aggregate planning as it limits the ability of the planner to make products in advance of anticipated (ie forecast) demand.

- *Make to stock:* The company has a policy of making products to stock (ie inventory) and then meets customer orders from stock. This is important for aggregate planning as it gives a good deal of flexibility to the planner in dealing with anticipated increases or decreases in forecast demand.

- *Assemble to order:* The company makes sub-assemblies (or buys them in) and stores them until they are required for a particular customer order when the sub-assemblies are then built up into the product for the customer. This is a more complicated method of dealing with customer orders as some manufacturing of sub-assemblies is taking place all the time but then customer orders are received and assembled as required. The company may hold substantial quantities of partially assembled sub-assemblies as intermediate stocks and these will require managing.

The role of stocks in the organization

Stocks act as a buffer between production and the customer in manufacturing organizations. Holding stocks ensures that while production may not be able to respond to rapid and large changes in demand by increasing output the customer demands can still be satisfied from the finished goods stock. Holding stock is expensive for some companies making expensive or large items (eg cars) because of warehousing costs, raw material and component costs, labour costs that are paid to make the product prior to selling the product. If the product does not sell (it may be out of date or unfashionable) the company has incurred costs that cannot be easily recovered. Aggregate planning can help to manage finished goods stock based on good forecasts and timely interventions when forecasts change or are not met.

Policy decisions need to be made by the company concerning stocks. For example, the decision to make to stock (MTS) or to make to order (MTO) is important as it depends on the type of product being manufactured and the fluctuations or seasonality of the demand for those products.

The effect that holding stocks has on the break-even point of a business

Holding stock increases the break-even point, reduces profit and increases the risks of doing business for the company. It is possible to make sufficient stock to manufacture yourself out of business – simply because you run out of money and credit.

Strategies for managing stocks and meeting customers' needs where there is seasonal demand for the products

Aggregate planning, stock-control systems, warehouse-management systems, strategic production planning, control systems and so on can all be used to manage stocks when a business suffers from a highly seasonal demand for its products.

With aggregate planning, groups of products (eg various sizes of spanners or different sizes of screwdrivers) that require the same or similar processes to manufacture the items can be lumped together (ie aggregated) to give a production plan. Strategies (chase demand, level production or a mixed capacity plan) based on a forecast demand for these products can be deployed. The forecast is important in that the first year might be planned according to forecast, but monthly (or even weekly) adjustments to that plan can, and should, be made based on actual sales or orders received.

The aggregate plan is used to minimize stocks while allowing the company to meet the needs of its customers. This is done by one of three strategies: chase demand plan, level production plan or mixed capacity plan. Diagrams illustrating these three approaches and an explanation of the effect of these on stocks and customer satisfaction (eg late delivery, long waiting periods, long or short sales order book, ability to meet customer needs immediately) are shown below.

The aggregate plan links to more detailed schedules

Clearly disaggregating the aggregate plan into a demand for specific products will depend on the forecast market demand for each individual product and the actual demand (ie orders received). From this demand and given the limitations of the processing equipment, their capacities and methods of increasing capacity such as subcontracting, over time, moving to a shift work system and so on, a schedule for each individual product to be manufactured can be produced. The forecast demand influences the aggregate planning so that stocks of items held are assessed in the light of the forecast demand. Since the role of aggregate planning is to reduce the costs and maximize profit for the business then proper consideration of the stocks held will lead to an aggregate plan that can be disaggregated into a detailed weekly or daily production plans.

Strategies for meeting demand

Various strategies can be used to meet demand if the forecast demand is regarded as a good and accurate forecast. Most strategies used are then regarded as

Reactive strategies:

- Vary the number of employees by hiring and firing staff or laying workers off.
- Use overtime or allow employees to work shorter hours.
- Change the shift system by adding a shift or eliminating a shift.
- Schedule factory shutdowns or increase employee vacations.
- Use stocks to buffer production against high or low demand.
- Consider having backlogs of orders during peak demand.
- Use flexible methods of employment (eg zero hours contracts or agency workers).

Proactive strategies

These strategies are aimed at balancing out the demand or smoothing the demand to meet the needs of the available capacity in the company:

- Produce products that are seasonal complements (eg diaries can be for a calendar year, academic year or financial year, and all have different seasonal demands which help to level the overall demand for printed diaries).
- Offer discounts and promotions to increase demand in the low season.
- Increase advertising in periods of low demand.

By these means the production facility can be maintained and seasonal variations in demand can be met or smoothed to a large extent.

Aggregate planning

Aggregate planning assumes the long-term demand has been forecast (accurately) and that planned capacity can meet this demand. The forecast demand and capacity plans are transformed into an aggregate plan that considers questions such as:

1 Should production be kept at a constant level or changed with demand?

2 Should stocks be used to meet changing demand?

3 Should stocks be produced during periods of low demand?

4 Should stocks be used during periods of high demand?

5 Should prices be changed?

6 Are shortages allowed, perhaps with late delivery?

7 Can demand be smoothed in some way?

In practice there are *three* strategies you can use to meet uneven (eg seasonal) demand with the objective of making the stock as close to zero as possible:

1 *Chase demand:* Where production more or less exactly matches demand. In theory there are no stocks but production has to be changed every period by hiring or firing full-time or part-time workers, changing production levels, changing to a shorter or longer working week, adding or dropping the night shift, using overtime, subcontracting work to another company and so on. Once the actual sales figures are known for a particular month some adjustments may be required to the spreadsheet and an entirely new plan developed and used for planning purposes. Thus, a great deal of management time and effort is put into managing the production based on the forecast demand and then modified based on the actual sales figures and closing/opening stock levels. Planning production becomes a continuous activity when using chase demand.

2 *Produce at a constant rate (level production plan):* Where production stays at a constant average demand for the planning period. Since production rate is constant and demand variable, the differences are met by building or using stocks. This means there are always inventory costs and maybe some shortage costs.

3 *Mixed policy:* This is a combination of the first two policies. Some production rate changes are made but not every period. This policy tries to compromize by having a fairly stable production, but reduces the inventory costs by allowing some changes (sometimes every quarter or as management decides). In practice this is the most commonly used plan.

There are often problems with changing production rates so they are usually changed as little as possible. There are advantages in having stable production rates:

- Planning is easier.
- Flow of products through the factory is smoother.
- There are fewer problems with changes.
- There is no need to 'hire and fire' employees.
- Employees have regular work patterns.
- Larger lot sizes reduce costs. (Compare this with Japanese approaches.)
- Stocks can be reduced as there is less variation in production rate (but not necessarily in demand).
- Throughput can be faster.
- Experience with the product reduces problems.

Thus, stocks act as a buffer between production and variable customer demands.

The aim of aggregate planning is to devise medium-term schedules for families of products that:

- Allow demand to be met with zero stock levels (ie sell everything you make).
- Keep production relatively stable.
- Keep within the constraints of the capacity plan.
- Meet any other specific objectives and constraints.

Figure 1 Chase demand

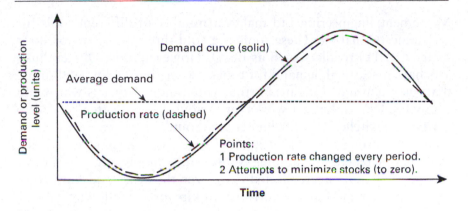

Figure 2 Produce at a constant rate

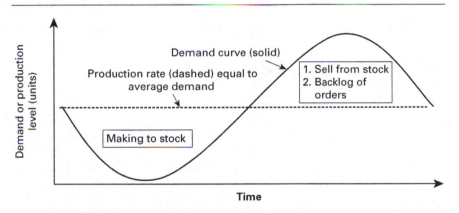

Figure 3 Mixed policy

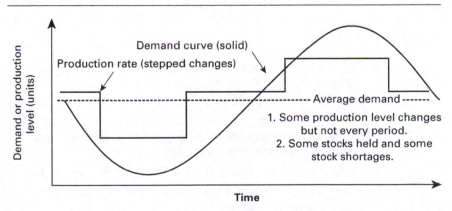

Monument Engineering Ltd

Monument Engineering Ltd makes a number of different tools for the domestic market. These tools are sold through the major do it yourself (DIY) retailers such as B&Q. However, most DIY enthusiasts have a seasonal demand for tools, especially tool kits with more than one item in, which means that when the weather is warm and sunny the DIY enthusiast works on various projects often related to gardening, kitchen refurbishment and outdoor repair jobs. Thus, there is a strong seasonal demand for tools such as screwdrivers, spanners, wrenches, plumbing tools and equipment. Monument Engineering Ltd, have collected data over the years and have forecasted the demand for screwdriver tool kits for the following year in Table 1. The maximum production of screwdriver tool kits per eight-hour day is 300 and the opening stock is 100 screwdriver tool kits in January. The company normally works seven days a week.

Table 1 Forecast demand data for screwdriver tool kits

Month	Demand (tool kits)	Month	Demand (tool kits)
January	2,800	July	8,000
February	3,000	August	7,900
March	5,000	September	6,000
April	4,000	October	4,050
May	5,600	November	2,650
June	8,000	December	5,550

Note

- The absolute maximum storage capacity of the finished goods store is 5,000 screwdriver tool kits. Opening stock in January is 100 units.
- Assume there are four weeks in a month and capacity can be changed by 300 units by not working/or working on screwdriver tool kits for a day.
- Closing stock = Opening stock + Production - Demand.
- It is useful to produce a spreadsheet for ease and speed of calculation.

Questions

1 Produce three aggregate plans for the screwdriver tool kits: (i) level production; (ii) chase demand; and (iii) mixed policy.

2 What would happen to the plans in question 1 above if the opening stock in January was 3,400 units of the screwdriver tool kits?

Answer

1 Produce three aggregate plans for the screwdriver tool kits: (i) level production; (ii) chase demand; and (iii) mixed policy.

The assumptions are that there are 28 days in a month and that the company operates for seven days a week but the production rate can be varied by changing the number of days that the factory works on the screwdriver tool kits. The current capacity is 300 units per day and the opening stock in January is 100 units.

We note that the demand is very seasonal with a low season in January to April and high season in May to September with a small pre-Christmas increase in December.

(i) Level production

Calculate the average demand and set the production level at that figure for each month.

$$\text{Average demand} = \Sigma(\text{monthly demands})/12 = 62{,}550/12 = 5{,}212.5$$
$$\text{units of screwdriver tool kits}$$

The nearest whole number of working days that can be used can be calculated:

$$= 5{,}212.5/300 = 17.375 \text{ days per month.}$$

Thus, we have to choose between 17 days and 18 days per month working on the screwdriver tool kits. If we work only 17 days per month we will not meet all the forecasted orders for the year so we choose 18 days production per month.

Then, using the following formula, we can calculate the closing stock for each month:

$$\text{Closing stock} = \text{Opening stock} + \text{Production} - \text{Demand}$$

Comments on Table 2 below are as follows:
With a finished goods store capacity of 5,000 units of the screwdriver tool kits we find that the number of units produced soon exceeds the capacity of the finished goods store. In the months February, March, April and May the finished goods store capacity of 5,000 units is exceeded. This is a time of year when the demand is fairly low and the company is largely making to stock.

Table 2 Level production plan with 18 days/month working on the screwdriver tool kits (300 units per day)

	Jan	Feb	Mar	April	May	June	July	Aug	Sept	Oct	Nov	Dec
Demand	2,800	3,000	5,000	4,000	5,600	8,000	8,000	7,900	6,000	4,050	2,650	5,550
Days worked per month	18	18	18	18	18	18	18	18	18	18	18	18
Production level (300)	5,400	5,400	5,400	5,400	5,400	5,400	5,400	5,400	5,400	5,400	5,400	5,400
Opening stock		100	2,700	5,100	5,500	6,900	6,700	4,100	1,500	–1,000	–1,600	–250	2,500
Closing stock	2,700	5,100	5,500	6,900	6,700	4,100	1,500	–1,000	–1,600		–250	2,500	2,350

There are stock-outs in August, September and October shown by the negative figures for those months in the closing stock row in the spreadsheet below. This is at the end of the high season when the stock built up earlier in the year is exhausted and when a backlog of orders is in the sales department waiting to be fulfilled. The maximum wait is approximately six days for an order to be fulfilled.

The final year-end closing stock in December is 2,350 units of the screwdriver tool kits. This stock is quite high, especially if the item is expensive to make.

Comments on Table 3 below are as follows:
If the average figure of 17 days is used the finished goods store capacity is only exceeded in April and May. However, there are stock-outs in July to December resulting in 14 days waiting in order to fulfil a customer order in September. This is poor customer service.

Table 3 Level production plan with 17 days/month working on the screwdriver tool kits (300 units per day)

	Jan	Feb	Mar	April	May	June	July	Aug	Sept	Oct	Nov	Dec
Demand	2,800	3,000	5,000	4,000	5,600	8,000	8,000	7,900	6,000	4,050	2,650	5,550
Days worked per month	17	17	17	17	17	17	17	17	17	17	17	17
Production level (300)	5,100	5,100	5,100	5,100	5,100	5,100	5,100	5,100	5,100	5,100	5,100	5,100
Opening stock	100	2,400	4,500	4,600	5,700	5,200	2,300	-600	-3,400	-4,300	-3,250	-800
Closing stock	2,400	4,500	4,600	5,700	5,200	2,300	-600	-3,400	-4,300	-3,250	-800	-1,250

(ii) Chase demand

With chase demand the number of days worked per month can be calculated and rounded down to the nearest whole number of days worked (by taking the integer) then multiplied by the 300 units produced per day to give the production level. The result of this is shown in Table 4 below.

The formula used simply takes the demand figure and divides it by the production quantity per day and rounds the number down to the nearest whole number by taking the integer. For example:

Demand = 3,100 and the production is 300 units per day therefore we get:

Number of days to be worked = Demand/units per day

= 3,100/300

= 10.333 days rounded down to 10 days.

This results in a gradual build-up of a backlog of orders because of the rounding down (see Table 4). Manually the figures can be changed when using chase demand but a more elegant automatic method can be used.

A refinement is to add the previous month's incomplete orders and subtract leftover stock to the demand figure and then divide by 300 units per day to obtain the number of days to be worked this month on the screwdriver tool kits. This is shown in Table 5 below.

Table 4 Chase demand plan with demand divided by 300 units to give days worked (with number of days rounded down)

	Jan	Feb	Mar	April	May	June	July	Aug	Sept	Oct	Nov	Dec
Demand	2,800	3,000	5,000	4,000	5,600	8,000	8,000	7,900	6,000	4,050	2,650	5,550
Days worked per month	9	10	16	13	18	26	26	26	20	13	8	18
Production level	2,700	3,000	4,800	3,900	5,400	7,800	7,800	7,800	6,000	3,900	2,400	5,400
Opening stock	100	0	0	–200	–300	–500	–700	–900	–1,000	–1,000	–1,150	–1,400
Closing stock	0	0	–200	–300	–500	–700	–900	–1,000	–1,000	–1,150	–1,400	–1,550

Table 5 Chase demand plan with refinement of subtracting the previous month's closing stock from the demand and dividing by 300

	Jan	Feb	Mar	April	May	June	July	Aug	Sept	Oct	Nov	Dec
Demand	2,800	3,000	5,000	4,000	5,600	8,000	8,000	7,900	6,000	4,050	2,650	5,550
Days worked per month	9	10	16	14	18	27	27	26	20	13	9	19
Production level	2,700	3,000	4,800	4,200	5,400	8,100	8,100	7,800	6,000	3,900	2,700	5,700
Opening stock	100	0	0	–200	0	–200	–100	0	–100	–100	–250	–200
Closing stock	0	0	–200	0	–200	–100	0	–100	–100	–250	–200	–50

The formula for this is:

Number of days to be worked = Integer [(Demand – (previous closing stock))/300)]

Thus, for example:

> If there is a backlog of orders of 300 units (–300 on the spreadsheet) as the closing stock of the previous month then we can add that to the demand forecasted for this coming month say 3,100 units. This gives:
>
> Number of days to be worked = (3,100 – (–300))/300 = 3,400/300 = 11.333 days or
> 11 days when the integer is taken. Noting that the number of days worked must be ≥ 0; it must not be negative.

This refinement allows the company to 'catch up' with the demand by taking into account the orders that were not completed and any leftover stock in the previous month. The resulting spreadsheet is now quite impressive (see Table 5) as it makes the stocks almost zero. This is because the stock outs are now limited to no more than one day of production in any month and the chase demand method is automatically controlled. This is a simple but useful refinement to the chase demand method. It would normally require some time working with the spreadsheet using trial and error to produce an optimum solution.

(iii) Mixed policy

Table 6 shows a mixed policy that has been arrived at by trial and error. This spreadsheet shows that there are some variations in the closing stock at the end of each month. These variations are larger than the chase demand method with the refinement shown in Table 5. The advantage is that there are only four changes in production level in the year and this reduces the management time and effort spent on changing production levels each period to deal with changes in the seasonal demand.

Table 6 Mixed policy

	Jan	Feb	Mar	April	May	June	July	Aug	Sept	Oct	Nov	Dec
Demand	2,800	3,000	5,000	4,000	5,600	8,000	8,000	7,900	6,000	4,050	2,650	5,550
Days worked per month	10	10	18	18	18	25	25	25	25	12	12	12
Production level	3,000	3,000	5,400	5,400	5,400	7,500	7,500	7,500	7,500	3,600	3,600	3,600
Opening stock	100	300	300	700	2,100	1,900	1,400	900	500	2,000	1,550	2,500
Closing stock	300	300	700	2,100	1,900	1,400	900	500	2,000	1,550	2,500	550

Table 7 Chase demand with opening stock of 3,400 units (with the refinement and noting that number of days worked must be ≥ 0)

	Jan	Feb	Mar	April	May	June	July	Aug	Sept	Oct	Nov	Dec
Demand	2,800	3,000	5,000	4,000	5,600	8,000	8,000	7,900	6,000	4,050	2,650	5,550
Days worked per month	0	8	16	14	18	27	27	26	20	13	9	19
Production level	0	2,400	4,800	4,200	5,400	8,100	8,100	7,800	6,000	3,900	2,700	5,700
Opening stock	3,400	600	0	−200	0	−200	−100	0	−100	−100	−250	−200
Closing stock	600	0	−200	0	−200	−100	0	−100	−100	−250	−200	−50

2 What would happen to the plans in question 1 above if the opening stock in January was 3400 units of the screwdriver tool kits?

The *level production plan* with 3400 units of opening stock has serious shortcomings if the production level is maintained at 17 days per month making the screwdriver tool kits (see Table 8 below). The finished goods store capacity is exceeded for six months from January to June and there are stock-outs in August and September. Reducing the number of days worked to 16 days or 15 days produces an equally bad aggregate plan.

For the *chase demand* situation with 3400 units of opening stock (Table 7 above) with the refinement of subtracting the previous period's stock figure (the opening stock) from the demand and setting the number of days to be worked ≥ 0 (ie greater than or equal to zero) gives a very good plan with no manufacture of the screwdriver tool kits in January (note: the spreadsheet calculation gives -2; ie minus 2 days of working which can be changed manually to zero, 0).

The *mixed policy* can simply be changed to accommodate the increased opening stock (see Table 9 below). The spreadsheet in Table 9 was arrived at by trial and error and is a reasonable attempt at stopping the worst excesses of the level production plan but it is not as good a solution as the chase demand approach. There are still only four changes in production level in the year and the finished goods store capacity is not exceeded and there are no stock-outs. Stock levels do fluctuate quite a lot and are quite high at times in the year (eg January and February).

Table 8 Level production plan with an opening stock of 3400 units in January

	Jan	Feb	Mar	April	May	June	July	Aug	Sept	Oct	Nov	Dec
Demand	2,800	3,000	5,000	4,000	5,600	8,000	8,000	7,900	6,000	4,050	2,650	5,550
Days worked per month	17	17	17	17	17	17	17	17	17	17	17	17
Production level	5,100	5,100	5,100	5,100	5,100	5,100	5,100	5,100	5,100	5,100	5,100	5,100
Opening stock	3,400	5,700	7,800	7,900	9,000	8,500	5,600	2,700	−100	−1,000	50	2,500
Closing stock	5,700	7,800	7,900	9,000	8,500	5,600	2,700	−100	−1,000	50	2,500	2,050

Table 9 Mixed policy with an opening stock of 3,400 units in January

	Jan	Feb	Mar	April	May	June	July	Aug	Sept	Oct	Nov	Dec
Demand	2,800	3,000	5,000	4,000	5,600	8,000	8,000	7,900	6,000	4,050	2,650	5,550
Days worked per month	9	9	9	18	18	25	25	25	25	12	12	12
Production level	2,700	2,700	2,700	5,400	5,400	7,500	7,500	7,500	7,500	3,600	3,600	3,600
Opening stock	3,400	3,300	3,000	700	2,100	1,900	1,400	900	500	2,000	1,550	2,500
Closing stock	3,300	3,000	700	2,100	1,900	1,400	900	500	2,000	1,550	2,500	550

Conclusion

The objective of aggregate planning is to try and keep the finished goods stock to a minimum (ie as close as possible to zero) while making sure that all customer orders are met and no stock-outs occur during the year. This will maximize profit and keep the costs of making and holding stock to a minimum. The objective of aggregate planning is to sell everything you make and have zero stocks. This depends on the forecast and regular adjustments to the aggregate plan once the true demand is known.

In practice, as the monthly sales figures are determined and compared with the forecast demand figures then the spreadsheet can be modified accordingly and a production plan and schedule for the coming month can be quickly determined. The stock levels must be checked on a regular basis to make sure the finished goods store is not nearing its capacity.

The refinement on the chase demand method leads to an automatic control of the closing stock levels in each month so that the stock holding and stock-outs at the end of each month are limited to no more than one working day production in this case. This is worth considering using if the chase demand strategy is to be used in practice.

Level production is generally inadequate with seasonal demand changes. The mixed policy is better. The chase demand method (with the refinement) is very good but requires considerably more management intervention than the other strategies.

Marketing approaches to managing demand can also be applied such as pricing changes, discounts for bulk purchases and promotions. These are generally used to shift demand away from the high season towards the low season thus attempting to level the demand to some extent and take advantage of available capacity.

The mortgage advisor
Process flow diagrams

Mike Simpson and Andrea Genovese

AUTHOR BIOGRAPHIES

DR MIKE SIMPSON AND DR ANDREA GENOVESE
ANDREA GENOVESE is a Lecturer in Logistics and Supply Chain Management at The University of Sheffield Management School.

Introduction

Process flow diagrams can be used in both manufacturing and services to show how work is carried out. Process flow diagrams provide a suitably detailed map of the way work is carried out in the organization and allow value-adding and non-value-adding activities to be identified. They also reveal, sometimes for the first time, how custom and practice have evolved in a particular work area and allow for process improvements to be identified. In services a more complex method known as service system blueprinting is used but essentially the two systems have the same logic and flows and use the same symbols. Process flow diagrams are a convenient tool for process auditing and process improvements.

Reasons for using process flow diagrams

There are many uses for process flow diagrams and some of the reasons for using process flow diagrams are:

- To understand a process and share that knowledge with colleagues.
- To develop a common understanding of the complexities of the work.
- To understand how the work flows through 'the system' and how each person contributes To that workflow.
- To make the various boundaries, components, features and properties of the work visible.
- To help in improvements, measuring and monitoring the work.
- To assist in developing alternative ways of working and organizing the workflow.
- To assess alternatives ways of working and create suitable performance measures.
- To look at customer flows and interactions with the service system.

This is not an exhaustive list and the reader is referred to specialist texts on this subject.

Useful definitions and symbols

Here are some useful definitions and explanations:

- *Flow chart:* This is a process flow diagram or process map and is a diagram representing the sequence of *activities* used to produce a unique output. Work activities can be categorized as either value creating or non-value creating. The process flow chart or process flow diagram can be used to give the most detailed view of work.
- *Activities (rectangular box):* Are the things that are done (eg actions) to add value to the work that is being processed. An activity is shown like this:

> Operation/Activity

- *Boundary (or terminator):* These define the beginning and end of the work that is being processed. That is, a boundary is the start and finish of the work or process that is being mapped. It is important to be clear where the boundaries of a particular process are so that the process flow diagram takes a clear view of what each person or department actually does before handing over to, say, another person or department. There is usually only one 'start' but there can be several 'stop' terminators. This is because the process can result in several different outcomes, particularly in services where there are naturally several different options for a customer undertaking a service interaction. A boundary or terminator looks like this:

(Start/Stop)

- *The flow (thin arrow):* The flow is the actual path through a system, mapped with the process flow diagram, which the work follows as it travels from one resource to another. Work can be seen as a flow of work through a system and this can be referred to as 'workflow'. Workflow involves the transformation of the input into an output as the work progresses (ie flows) through the system from one resource to the next. The flow is shown with an arrow like this.

⟶

- *Decisions (diamond):* This is where a decision is made about a particular item that is flowing through the system and the process flow diagram branches (or loops back) to illustrate how the decision affects the workflow through the system.

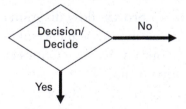

- *The move (large arrow):* This is usually used for inventory or large items that require moving from one place to another. The arrow can be vertical or horizontal.

Move ⇨

- *Delays:* These are queues or waiting and generally do not add value to the work.

- *Store:* Stock can be an input or an output of the system depending on what is going on in the organization. This is usually regarded as a non-value-adding activity.

- *Document(s) (torn paper symbol):* These are usually printed out from computer systems and can be any form of document(s) necessary for the work to be undertaken. For example, they may be invoices, receipts, contracts, information and so on. There is a symbol for a single document and a symbol for multiple documents shown.

- *Inspection (large circle):* Where an item can be inspected so that the quality of the item can be ascertained. It is often used in decision loops where only items that pass inspection can be allowed to go forward through to the next stage of the process. Usually it is regarded as a non-value-adding activity.

- *File storage (eg computer file) and database (drum shaped symbol):* Files can be stored and retrieved for use in the process flow diagram activities.

- *Same page connector (small circle with a letter):* This symbol allows activities to be connected on the same page without the use of the flow arrow symbol. This makes the diagram a little less cluttered and eliminates overlapping flows. Sometimes it can be used as a different page connector but usually another symbol is used for this on larger process flow diagrams.

In general, not all of these symbols are used in a process flow diagram and in some instances other symbols may be used depending on the charting system being used.

Symbols (which may, *inter alia*, *be used*)

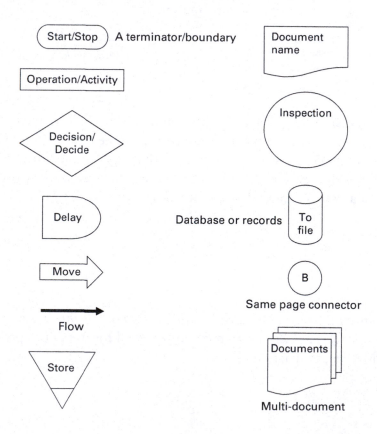

Worked example 1

You decide to go shopping for a pint of milk at a supermarket.

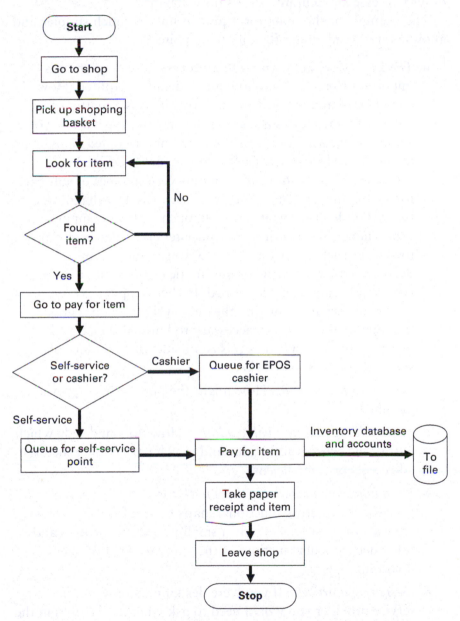

In this example it is necessary to explicitly state what you are doing to obtain your pint of milk. For more complex work a knowledge elicitation exercise might be required to establish what work is undertaken, how it is done, in which order, the decisions being made and the criteria for those decisions, inspections, delays and resources used. In fact you would need to know everything about that work in order to create an accurate process flow diagram.

The example of shopping for a pint of milk is much simpler and allows you to think about the following points:

- *The level of detail required:* In a process flow diagram it is important to understand how much detail is required. How complicated and detailed should it be? This is a matter of judgement and experience and is dependent on what it is you are analysing with a process flow diagram. Detailed analysis might be used for particularly complex processes and procedures. For example in designing certain types of software for a computer system very detailed process flow diagrams can be used to describe what should happen and the computer programmer may develop the computer code specifically aimed to achieve each activity and create the situation to make decisions either manually or automatically depending on the type of program being developed. In the shopping example it is only necessary to know that the person shopping has gone to the supermarket, it is not necessary to know if they travelled by car or bus or walked as this is outside the boundary of shopping in the supermarket.

- *Process improvements:* How might the process be improved or modified?

- *Value adding and non-value adding:* How do you decide which part of the process adds value and which part of the process adds costs or is inefficient?

- *How much involvement is there with the customer in the process?* When cross-functional maps ('swim lane' diagrams) are used the customer is only a small part of the process and other departments/functions at the supermarket become involved.

- *Designing a process:* If you were designing a process for a service provider you would need to ask what he/she does in the job and probably arrive at a narrative of what the person does. This simply 'describes' what is going on in the situation and it takes some effort to analyse this information and produce a logical process flow diagram that is an accurate representation of what work is taking place in reality. When designing a process flow diagram you would need to ask several questions about the process before the process is clearly defined. A first draft of the process flow diagram could be shown to the service provider and you could ask the service provider what he/she thought of the overall process flow diagram you have produced and ask if there is anything missing from the overall process. You would then be able to discuss potential improvements to the process.

In the case of the supermarket shopping example you need to be careful not to become too detailed in your analysis when creating the process flow diagram but there are important activities that need to be completed such as checking the 'sell by' and 'use by' dates on the milk carton or checking that the carton is not damaged and leaking or checking that it is the right sort of milk (eg full fat, skimmed, semi-skimmed, UHT, etc). These can make the process flow diagram rather complicated and perhaps this level of detail is too complicated and unnecessary to include in such a simple example. However, if it were necessary then sub-routines (ie other process flow diagrams) can be built in at appropriate places and written out on separate diagrams.

Uses for process flow diagrams

- Process flow diagrams are an essential tool in analysing the systems, procedures and processes within an organization.

- Process flow diagrams are used in benchmarking exercises to compare systems, procedures and processes between one organization and another better (or worse) performing organization (ie the benchmarking partner).

- Process flow diagrams allow you to develop very detailed explanations and descriptions of what actually happens in reality in larger complex systems and procedures. This is sometimes called 'drilling down' to show the 'ground-truth' reality of what actually happens.

- Process flow diagrams allow you to distinguish between value-creating and non-value-creating activities.

- Process flow diagrams can make types of waste in the non-value-creating activities visible such as delays, storage, batching, movement, inspection, approval and rework. Thus, in the example above the queue for the electronic point of sales (EPOS) or the cashier could be replaced by the delay symbol and that would highlight the non-value-adding work being undertaken by the shopper.

In the following exercise with the mortgage advisor we are given a narrative explanation of the process and we have to logically develop an overall process flow diagram and assess the process to see if there are opportunities for improvements. This is a common exercise to do when involved in any improvement programme.

CASE STUDY
The mortgage advisor: process flow diagrams

A customer has made an appointment to see a mortgage advisor (at a bank or building society, etc). The mortgage advisor 'meets and greets' the customer and takes the customer into a private room for discussions. The mortgage advisor confirms the meeting is about a mortgage rather than a loan. If the meeting is about a loan, the mortgage advisor suggests that a colleague of his who specialises in loans should be seen instead and makes an appointment for the customer with the loan advisor, thanks the customer and terminates the meeting. If the customer is seeking a mortgage the mortgage advisor asks about the financial situation of the customer (salary, savings, other income and outgoings) and the size of the mortgage the customer requires and the purchase price of the property. The mortgage advisor enters the information onto a database and prints out some mortgage options using the numbers entered earlier. The mortgage advisor shows the various options to the customer and the customer decides on a particular plan or may decide not to accept any plan offered at which point the meeting is terminated. The mortgage advisor prints out the relevant mortgage application form and the customer completes the mortgage application form. The mortgage advisor inspects the form and asks for any missing information not already provided by the customer. The final version of the form is agreed by the customer and mortgage advisor and the mortgage advisor photocopies the form for the back-office records department, enters the data on the computer, informs the customer that a decision will be made and the customer will be informed in five days' time, then terminates the interview.

Given this information you are asked to provide a flow chart or process flow diagram of the mortgage application procedure so that the mortgage advisor can assess if the mortgage application interview procedure and process can be made more efficient. You should comment on your answer and suggest ways to improve the process.

Symbols (which may, inter alia, be used)

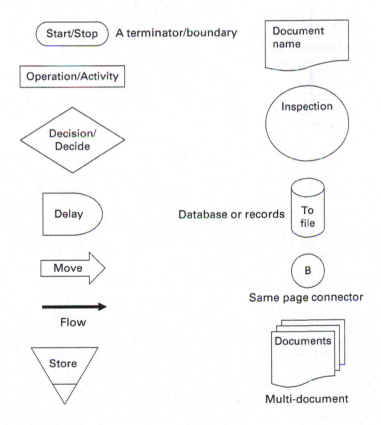

The mortgage advisor: answer

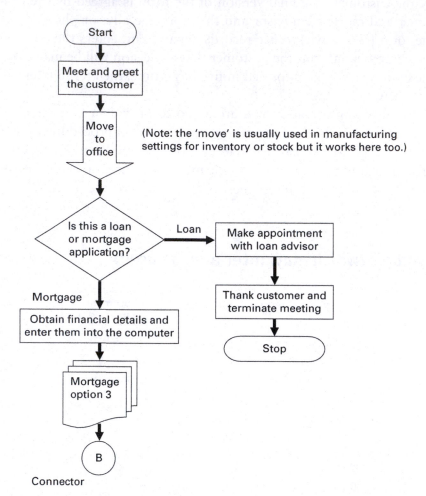

Start

Meet and greet the customer

Move to office

(Note: the 'move' is usually used in manufacturing settings for inventory or stock but it works here too.)

Is this a loan or mortgage application?

Loan → Make appointment with loan advisor

Thank customer and terminate meeting

Stop

Mortgage

Obtain financial details and enter them into the computer

Mortgage option 3

B

Connector

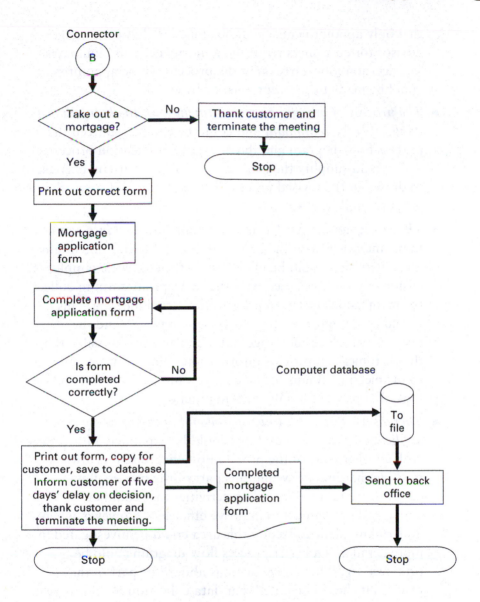

This is a very short case study with a relatively simple set of procedures for the mortgage advisor to undertake and yet there are some
problems and issues that can be easily identified from the process
flow diagram. These issues can be listed:

- *The mortgage advisor currently has to make an appointment
  for the customer to see the loan advisor.* This is a non-value-
  adding activity for the mortgage advisor. Thus, we can suggest

that only appointments should be made with the mortgage advisor for customers requiring a mortgage. This eliminates one decision loop early on in the process. These appointments could be made by a receptionist or by email.

- *The process of making an appointment with the loan advisor would then be redundant* and could be eliminated from the process flow diagram and the mortgage application process. This would simplify the process overall. It is a useful exercise to draw out the revised process flow diagram and check that it is logical and works.

- *The mortgage advisor has to collect the financial information* in the interview with the customer and this seems potentially an activity that could be made more efficient. For example, the customer could be issued with the appropriate form to collect the financial information prior to the actual meeting. This would speed up the entire process of data entry and the decision on which mortgage to take, if any. It is possible that the customer can provide information online or via email prior to the meeting. Again such a change can be drawn out and looked at to see if it will work in practice.

- *There is a lot of work towards the end of the mortgage application procedure* and this could be expanded a little more with another page of the process flow diagram. It is always possible that hidden within this part of the process flow diagram are non-value-adding activities that could be eliminated or changed to improve efficiency. However, when undertaking data collection this area could be investigated in more detail and a better process flow diagram could be produced to address any concerns about this part of the process. It should be noted that data collection for this type of study might involve several iterations of the data collection and producing process flow diagrams until both the researcher and the service provider are clear that the process has been fully mapped out.

- *There is more than one stop or boundary in this example* and this is quite common in services where more than one outcome is possible from the overall process. The customer has several decisions to make in most service operations and therefore all of these options need to be fully mapped out.

Conclusion

Process flow diagrams are used in both manufacturing and services for mapping out the flow of materials, information, people and their interactions, and so on within the process, system and organization. Process flow diagrams can be used to determine if activities and processes are value adding or non-value adding. They can also allow for improvements to processes and procedures and are routinely used in quality-improvement initiatives, process auditing and process-improvement activities. They are generally easy to use and easy to understand, but provide a very clear explanation of the processes being studied.

SABE tractors

An application of linear programming

Andrea Genovese and Mike Simpson

AUTHOR BIOGRAPHIES

DR ANDREA GENOVESE AND DR MIKE SIMPSON
ANDREA GENOVESE is a Lecturer in Logistics and Supply Chain Management at The University of Sheffield Management School.

Introduction

Linear programming represents a quintessential tool for optimal allocation of scarce resources among a number of competing activities. While originally applied in the 1940s, it still represents a powerful and general problem-solving method that encompasses several kinds of logistics and planning problems.

The term 'linear programming' derives from the fact that both the objective function (expressing the performance that the decision-maker wants to optimize) and the constraints (representing limitations to the available resources that need to be employed for achieving such an objective) can be expressed by means of linear polynomials (namely, degree-1 polynomials).

The following case study provides an application of linear programming to production planning and product mix decisions. The formulation of the mathematical model is shown, along with its solution through the application of the graphical method.

Useful definitions

- *Product mix:* Also known as product assortment, this refers to the set of product lines that a company offers to its customers. Product-mix decisions deal with planning quantities to be manufactured for each product line.

- *Feasibility domain:* In linear programming, this refers to the region of the plane containing all the feasible solutions to the problem (namely, solutions that meet all the constraints).

- *Objective function:* In linear programming, this represents a mathematical expression whose value needs to be optimized (namely, minimized or maximized), taking into account a set of specified constraints. It generally expresses a business goal in mathematical terms.

- *Optimal solution:* A solution (belonging to the feasibility domain of the problem, and usually positioned on its frontier) that optimizes the objective function (by returning its best possible value) of the linear-programming problem.

- *Degree-1 polynomial:* Also called a linear polynomial, this represents a polynomial in which the highest degree of its terms is 1.

- *Objective function isoquants:* In linear programming, straight lines representing all the possible combinations of decision variables returning the same value in terms of objective function.

SABE tractors: an application of linear programming

SABE is a tractor-manufacturing company based in a Southern European country. The logistics and production planning department has to define the product mix for the next months, taking into account the available information. The firm is manufacturing two kinds of tractors: Orchard, mainly devoted to fruit production, and Vineyard, devoted to wine production. Due to the limitations of the current plant capacity, it is not possible to manufacture more than 400 tractors per month.

An empirical formula derived by the sales department suggests that the production mix should be such that the difference between the quantity of manufactured Orchard tractors and one third of the quantity of manufactured Vineyard tractors should not be more than 150. Sales analysts also suggest that the sales of Vineyard tractors have never overtaken the sales of Orchard ones.

At the same time, the plant director is stating that, to avoid any redundancy and to keep an acceptable plant utilization rate, it is necessary to manufacture at least 200 tractors.

Taking into account that the sales price of a Vineyard tractor is €40,000, and the one of an Orchard tractor is €30,000, SABE wants to determine the monthly production mix that maximizes the turnover.

Also, the company is interested in assessing some potential future scenarios.

Questions

1 The marketing department is evaluating some changes in the pricing strategy and would like to know what would be the changes to the product mix if the price of the two tractor models were the same.

2 On the other hand, the plant director has started to think about an increase of the production capacity to 500 tractors per month and he is interested in understanding the effects of such a move.

Answers

1 The marketing department is evaluating some changes in the pricing strategy and would like to know what would be the changes to the product mix if the price of the two tractor models were the same.

2 On the other hand, the plant director has started to think about an increase of the production capacity to 500 tractors per month and he is interested in understanding the effects of such a move.

The problem can be effectively solved by using linear programming techniques.

The objective function of the problem represents the maximization of revenue. Several constraints are expressed: (i) the total maximum number of tractors that can be manufactured; (ii) an empirical formula that links the quantities to be produced for the two tractors; (iii) the fact that the sales of the Vineyard model have never overcome the sales of the Orchard one – therefore, it is reasonable to say that the manufactured quantity of Vineyard tractors should be less than or equal to the manufactured quantity of Orchard ones; iv) the total minimum number of tractors that have to be manufactured (for plant utilization purposes).

By defining as A the quantity of Orchard tractors to be manufactured, and as B the quantity of Vineyard tractors to be manufactured, the mathematical formulation of the problem can be expressed as follows:

$$Z = 30{,}000*A + 40{,}000*B \qquad Max!$$

Subject to the constraints:

$A + B \leq 400$	(1)
$A - B/3 \leq 150$	(2)
$A - B \geq 0$	(3)
$A + B \geq 200$	(4)
$A \geq 0$	(5)
$B \geq 0$	(6)

The feasibility domain is reported in Figure 1. The dotted lines report the objective function isoquants.

Figure 1 Feasibility domain of the base-case

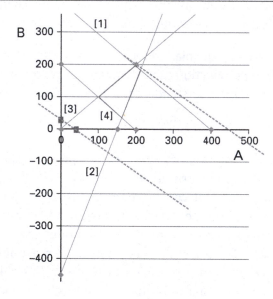

The optimal solution is attained at the intersection of constraints (1) (representing the overall capacity) and (3) (representing the impossibility of having more Vineyard tractors than Orchard ones). This means that these constraints (that are then satisfied with a strict equality sign) are the ones that are expressing the toughest limitations for SABE operations.

By solving the system of linear equations representing the constraints (1) and (3), it can be obtained: A = 200, B = 200. Therefore, 200 tractors per each model have to be produced. The total revenue can be easily derived as: Z = 30,000*200 + 40,000*200 = 1,208,000,000 euros.

Scenario analysis

If the price of the two tractors was the same, the objective function should be modified as follows:

$$Z = A + B \qquad\qquad Max!$$

Therefore, the objective function isoquants would be parallel to constraints (1) and (4). From Figure 2 below, it is possible to understand that, given the nature of the objective function and of the constraints, an infinite number of optimal solutions would be available.

If an increase of the production capacity to 500 monthly tractors was implemented, constraint (1) should have been modified as follows:

$$A + B \leq 500 \qquad\qquad (1)$$

In this case, the constraint would have been redundant; the optimal solution would have been retrieved in the intersection of constraints (2) and (3). The optimal solution can be determined by solving the system of linear equations representing the constraints (2) and (3), obtaining $A = B = 222.5$. Since tractors have to be produced as a whole, this means $A = B = 222$. Therefore, the total monthly production (due to the effect of the other constraints) just equates 448 units, leaving 52 units of capacity not utilized. Therefore, if the company still wants to operate at full capacity, an increase of the total capacity to 448 units would be recommended. Still, the increase of capacity to 500 units could be a wise move, as it could allow exploiting the plant in a better way and allowing SABE to have a capacity cushion to cope with future increases in demand and changes in the relationships between the sales of Orchard and Vineyard tractors.

Figure 2 Feasibility domain of the first scenario (both tractors have the same price)

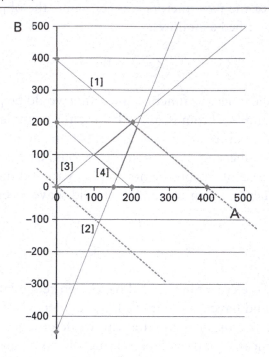

Conclusion

Linear programming has been utilized, in an effective way, to derive the optimal product mix for SABE Tractors. The scenario analysis has enabled better understanding of the role of the different constraints and the sensitivity of the optimal solution to variations in the selling prices of the different products.

Lawnmower Engines Ltd
Variable costs, break-even points and profit

Mike Simpson and Andrea Genovese

AUTHOR BIOGRAPHIES

DR MIKE SIMPSON AND DR ANDREA GENOVESE
ANDREA GENOVESE is a Lecturer in Logistics and Supply Chain Management at The University of Sheffield Management School.

Introduction

All companies aiming to make a profit must know how much it costs to make their products so that they can sell their products at a high enough price to cover their costs and make a surplus or profit on each item sold. Similarly, the company must know if the demand for their products is high enough so that they can make a profit. The income or revenue generated must cover the cost of producing each unit, but it must also recover the money that was spent on research, design, development, prototypes, market testing, packaging, marketing and launch. Thus, the company needs to know its costs in some detail. For example, the company needs to be aware that:

$$\text{Profit} = \text{Income} - \text{Total costs}$$

The total costs come from a number of sources and can be classified as:

Fixed costs (FC): Which are constant regardless of number of units made. These are items such as heating, lighting, water, rent, rates, debt repayments, salaries, and so on which do not vary with the number of units made. Research, design, development, prototypes, market testing, marketing and launch costs are fixed regardless of the number of units made.

Variable costs (VC): Which do depend upon the number of units made. These are labour costs, raw materials, components, sub-assemblies, assemblies, maintenance, consumables and any other item that varies with the number of units made. Thus the equation for variable costs can be written as:

$$\text{VC} = \text{Labour} + \text{materials} + \text{components/assemblies} + \text{maintenance} + \text{consumables}$$

Total costs: These are the sum of the fixed costs and the variable costs. Noting that n is the number of units and VCu is the unit variable cost, we have:

$$\text{Total cost} = \text{Fixed Cost} + \text{Total Variable Cost} = \text{FC} + n\text{VCu}$$
$$\text{Total cost} = \text{Fixed Cost} + \text{Number of units made} \times \text{Cost per unit}$$

Revenues/income: This rises in direct linear relationship with the number of units made and sold assuming there are no discounts for bulk purchases.

$$\text{Income} = \text{Number of units sold} \times \text{Price charged per unit}$$

Contribution: The overall contribution is the amount the total number of units sold contributes to the overall costs after the variable costs are paid for (ie the fixed costs).

$$\text{(Total) Contribution} = \text{Sales value} - \text{Total Variable Costs}$$
$$\text{Contribution per unit} = \text{Selling price of a unit} - \text{Variable costs of a unit}$$

Break-even point (B/E): This is the number of units that must be sold before an organization covers all its costs and begins to make a profit. Thus we have some formulas:

$$B/E = \frac{\text{Total Fixed Cost}}{\text{Contribution per unit}} = \text{Number of units to be sold to break-even}$$

$$B/E = \frac{\text{Total Fixed Cost} \times \text{Sales value}}{\text{Total contribution}} = \text{Sales value at break-even point}$$

Number of units at B/E × Selling price per unit = Sales value at break-even point

The number of units at B/E point can be derived:

$$n = \text{number of units sold}$$
$$FC = \text{Fixed Cost}$$
$$VCu = \text{Variable Cost per unit}$$
$$P = \text{Price charged per unit}$$

Thus:

Income = Number of units sold × Price charged per unit
Income = nP

At the break-even point, income = total costs

nP = nVCu + FC   (This is in the form of y = mx + c and can be manipulated)

Dividing throughout by the number of units, n, gives:

$$P = VCu + FC/n$$

Subtracting VCu from both sides of the equation gives:

$$P - VCu = FC/n$$

Dividing throughout by FC gives:

$$\frac{P - VCu}{FC} = 1/n$$

Therefore, after rearranging, gives the number of units at the break-even point:

$$n = \frac{FC}{P - VCu} = \text{Fixed Cost/(unit Price - unit Variable Cost)}$$

Since,

> Contribution per unit = Selling Price of a unit – Variable Costs of a unit = P – VCu

> Number of units at break-even point = $n = \dfrac{\text{Fixed Cost}}{\text{Contribution per unit}}$

Determining the variable cost for a desired profit

Using the calculations above to establish what the variable cost per unit (VCu) should be in order to make a certain desired level of profit (before interest and taxation) is useful for operations managers. Such an approach allows the operations manager to look at ways in which the variable costs can be reduced and determine what the likely profit could be (assuming all other things remain the same). As shown in the diagram in Figure 1, we know that:

> Profit = Sales value – Total Variable Costs – Fixed Costs

Rearranging this equation gives:

> Total Variable Costs = Sales value – Fixed Costs – Profit
> *Variable Cost per unit* = (Sales – Fixed Cost – Profit)/Number of units produced

Reducing the variable costs can be achieved by looking at specific parts in the bill of materials (BOM) and buying cheaper parts and raw materials that perform to the same specifications. Alternatively, buying cheaper parts and raw materials from a supplier with a lower cost base such as companies in other countries where they may have a greater comparative advantage from lower labour and material costs; or using different materials and processes to make the parts. Some of these can be achieved using value analysis and value engineering approaches and these are often used in various Kaizen cost-reduction programmes. However, at this stage we only need to know how to determine the target variable cost in order to make a certain profit and this will stimulate efforts to reduce costs.

The simple break-even point chart shown above is plotted graphically to illustrate that the fixed costs have a major effect on the

Figure 1 A simple break-even point diagram

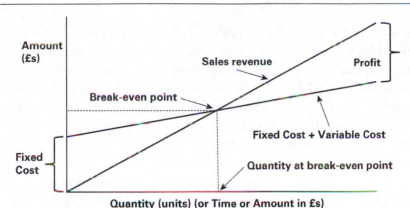

break-even point. Thus, if the fixed costs were much lower the break-even point would be lower and the profit would be increased; assuming the variable costs remain the same. Similarly, if the fixed costs were higher then the break-even point would be higher and the profit would be lower; assuming the variable costs remain the same.

The slope of the fixed cost plus the variable cost line is affected by the costs incurred from both the manufacture of the item sold and the costs incurred under fixed costs. Thus, if costs were a major problem in a company preventing the company making a profit then both fixed costs and variable costs could be targeted for reductions in order to increase the profit for the business.

The slope of the sales revenue line also has an effect on the break-even point and profit; however, operations managers are usually concerned with reducing costs and allowing the sales managers opportunities to offer discounts and lower prices while still making a reasonable profit.

All organizations grapple with these issues and making and maintaining a profitable business can be hard work in the face of strong price competition. In the following case study we see a successful business trying to establish the variable costs of making products and then attempting to see how the business might gain a greater profit from a particular deal with a customer by identifying costs that might be reduced.

We also see how apportioning maintenance and consumables to either fixed costs or variable costs affects the break-even point.

Lawnmower Engines Ltd

A company, Lawnmower Engines Ltd, has a number of departments making lawnmowers, power tools and hydraulic equipment. One department, the engine assembly department, assembles various types of two-stroke and four-stroke petrol engines. The engine assembly department makes small compact engines and manufactures to order a number of small two-stroke and four-stroke petrol engines used in lawnmowers and other applications such as quad bikes and small electrical generators. The two-stroke engines are of relatively simple construction. All the components for these engines are purchased from several suppliers and are of standard designs.

A commercial customer, Snow Mobiles Ltd, has contacted the company with a requirement for a small engine for a new snow mobile. Snow Mobiles Ltd has noted that three engines meet the requirements of the snow mobile in terms of power and physical size. However, Snow Mobiles Ltd is only prepared to pay £220 per engine but requires 2500 engines a year.

Unfortunately, Lawnmower Engines Ltd does not know which engine will be the most profitable if it were to accept the Snow Mobiles Ltd's offer but Lawnmower Engines has data for the three engines as shown below in Table 1. Lawnmower Engines knows that the fixed costs of the engine assembly department for making 2500 engines are approximately £40,000 per annum.

Table 1 Data for manufacture of the three engines

Items	Cost per unit	Engine 1	Engine 2	Engine 3
Labour	£10 per hour	4 hours	4 hours	5 hours
Test engineer	£15 per hour	1 hour	1 hour	1 hour
Pistons	£25 each	1 piston	2 pistons	2 pistons
Piston rings	£1 each	3 required per piston	3 required per piston	3 required per piston
Connecting rod	£15 each	1 required	2 required	2 required
Crank shaft	–	1 × £20	1 × £35	1 × £40
Bearings	£2 each	2 bearings	3 bearings	3 bearings
Long bolts	£1 each	4 required	6 required	6 required
Short bolts	£0.50 each	4 required	6 required	6 required
Cylinder head	–	1 × £20	1 × £19	1 × £18
Gear box	–	1 × £11	1 × £14	1 × £15
Seals	£1.00 each	2 required	3 required	3 required
Machine maintenance	£1,500 per annum	–	–	–
Gloves, oil, wipes, overalls, etc	£10,000 per annum	–	–	–

Note	The test engineer is also a labour cost and should be included in the calculations.

Questions

Your job as the operations manager is to:

1 Calculate the variable costs of manufacture for the three engines listed in Table 1. Note: the company works 250 days each year, a day is eight hours working and the company employs ten people in the engine assembly department.

2 Calculate the break-even point for each engine in terms of number of units, as a percentage of sales and in pounds sterling.

3 Which engine(s) would you recommend for the Snow Mobiles Ltd contract?

4 What is the effect of apportioning maintenance and consumables to fixed costs instead of variable costs?

5 If Lawnmower Engines Ltd wanted to make £120,000 profit on the deal with Snow Mobiles Ltd what would the unit variable cost of the chosen engine need to be? What would Lawnmower Engines Ltd need to do to achieve that profit?

6 Comment on your answer by making recommendations to Lawnmower Engines Ltd sales department concerning which engine(s) should be offered to the Snow Mobiles Ltd customer.

Note   It is a useful exercise to make a spreadsheet up to do the calculations in this case study.

Answers

1 Calculate the variable costs of manufacture for the three engines listed in Table 1. Note: the company works 250 days each year, a day is eight hours working and the company employs ten people in the engine assembly department.

The variable costs (VC) are:

$$VC = Labour + materials + components/assemblies + maintenance + consumables$$

Engine 1:
Assume that maintenance and consumables can be included as variable costs and calculated as a figure for each hour of labour.

Maintenance = £1500/(250 × 8 × 10) = £0.075 per hour of labour
Consumables = £10,000/(250 × 8 × 10) = £0.50 per hour of labour

Total per hour of labour is £0.575 per hour of maintenance and consumables

5 hours of labour gives £0.575 × 5 hrs = £2.875
6 hours of labour gives £0.575 × 6 hrs = £3.45

VC = 40 + 15 + 25 + 3 + 15 + 20 + 4 + 4 + 2 + 20 + 11 + 2 + 2.875 = **£163.875**
to make Engine 1.

Engine 2:

VC = 40 + 15 + 50 + 6 + 30 + 35 + 6 + 6 + 3 + 19 + 14 + 3 + 2.875 = **£229.875**
to make Engine 2.

Engine 3:

VC = 50 + 15 + 50 + 6 + 40 + 6 + 6 + 3 + 18 + 15 + 3 + 28 + 3.45 = **£245.45**
to make Engine 3.

Snow Mobiles Ltd is only prepared to pay £220 per engine (presumably because of the overall cost of the snow mobile to the final customer) as a result only one engine (Engine 1) is profitable for Lawnmower Engines Ltd. Engine 2 and Engine 3 will make a loss on each engine and should not be offered to Snow Mobiles Ltd.

2 Calculate the break-even point for each engine in terms of number of units and in pounds sterling.

Break-even point for Engine 1 (the other engines make a loss) can be calculated as follows:

Sales volume per annum = 2500 units × £220 = **£550,000**
Total annual variable costs = 2500 units × **£163.875** per engine = **£409,687.50**
Fixed costs are given as £40,000 for manufacturing 2500 units.

Total contribution is calculated from:

Contribution = Sales volume − Variable costs = £550,000 − **£409,687.50 = £140,312.50**
Contribution per unit = £140,312.50/2500 units = **£56.125**

$$\text{B/E point (£s)} = \frac{\text{Fixed Cost} \times \text{Sales volume}}{\text{Total contribution}} = \frac{£40,000 \times £550,000}{£140,312.50}$$

$$= £156,792.87$$

$$\text{As a percentage of sales} = \frac{£156,792.87 \times 100}{£550,000} = \textbf{28.5 per cent}$$

$$\text{B/E in Units is} = \frac{\text{Total Fixed Cost}}{\text{Contribution per unit}} = \frac{£40,000}{£56.125} = \textbf{712.7 units}$$

(of Engine 1).

Profit = Sales revenue − (Total variable costs + Fixed costs)
Profit = £550,000 − (£409,687.50 + £40,000) = **£100,312.50** for 2500 units of Engine 1 sold to Snow Mobiles Ltd

Table 2 Variable costs for the manufacture of the three engines

Items	Cost per unit	Engine 1	Engine 2	Engine 3
Labour	£10 per hour	£40.00	£40.00	£50.00
Test engineer	£15 per hour	£15.00	£15.00	£15.00
Pistons	£25 each	£25.00	£50.00	£50.00
Piston rings	£1 each	£3.00	£6.00	£6.00
Connecting rod	£15 each	£15.00	£30.00	£30.00
Crank shaft	–	£20.00	£35.00	£40.00
Bearings	£2 each	£4.00	£6.00	£6.00
Long bolts	£1 each	£4.00	£6.00	£6.00
Short bolts	£0.50 each	£2.00	£3.00	£3.00
Cylinder head	One required	£20.00	£19.00	£18.00
Gear box	One required	£11.00	£14.00	£15.00
Seals	£1.00 each	£2.00	£3.00	£3.00
Sub total for labour and materials		**£161.00**	**£227.00**	**£242.00**

Maintenance and consumables (spread over the number of man hours)

Machine maintenance	£1,500 per annum	£0.075 per hour of labour = £0.375	£0.075 per hour of labour = £0.375	£0.075 per hour of labour = £0.45
Gloves, oil, wipes, overalls, etc	£10,000 per annum	£0.50 per hour of labour = £2.50	£0.50 per hour of labour = £2.50	£0.50 per hour of labour = £3.00
Totals		**£163.875**	**£229.875**	**£245.45**

Note   The company works 250 days each year and a day is eight hours working. Note that Lawnmower Engines Limited employs ten people. Thus there are 20,000 man hours available per annum for making engines in the engine assembly department.

Note   With ten employees the maintenance and consumables costs can be spread over a man hour (including the test engineer's time too).

3 Which engine(s) would you recommend for the Snow Mobiles Ltd contract?

Only Engine 1 is profitable in that it costs £163.875 to make each engine and so only Engine 1 should be sold to Snow Mobiles Ltd.

4 What is the effect of apportioning maintenance and consumables to fixed costs instead of variable costs?

Note   Only Engine 1 is profitable and so we can do the calculations for Engine 1.

Maintenance = £1,500 pa
Consumables = £10,000 pa
Total = £1,500 + £10,000 = £11,500 pa

There are 20,000 hours available for making engines (ie 250 days × 8 hours × 10 people) but when the costs are allocated to variable costs only 12,500 hours are used for making Engine 1 for Snow Mobiles Ltd. (Note that the £40,000 fixed costs is allocated to 2500 engines.) Thus:

(12,500 hours/20,000 hours) × £11,500 = £7187.50 is the fixed costs associated with maintenance and consumables for 2500 engines.

Thus, we can modify our calculations for Engine 1, as follows:

With maintenance and consumables taken as fixed costs:

Total fixed costs = £40,000 + £7187.50 = £47,187.50

Variable cost per unit = £161.00 (without the maintenance and consumables)

Total variable cost = £161.00 × 2500 units = £402,500
Total sales = 2500 units × £220 = £550,000
Total contribution = Sales value – Total variable costs = £550,000 – £402,500 = £147,500
Contribution per unit = Selling price per unit – Variable costs per unit = £220 – 161.00 = £59.00

$$\text{B/E} = \frac{\text{Total Fixed Cost} \times \text{Sales value}}{\text{Total contribution}} = \frac{£47,187.50 \times 550,000}{£147,500} = $$

£175,953.39

Break-even point = £175,953.39 (or 31.99% or 799.78 units)
Profit = Sales – Fixed cost – Variable costs = £550,000 – £47,187.50 – £402,500 = **£100,312.50**

Thus, the break-even point increases if the maintenance and consumables are allocated as fixed costs but the profit remains the same (refer to Figure 1).

5 If Lawnmower Engines Ltd wanted to make £120,000 profit on the deal with Snow Mobiles Ltd what would the unit variable cost of the chosen engine need to be? What would Lawnmower Engines Ltd need to do to achieve that profit?

Using the calculations to establish what the variable cost per unit should be in order to make a certain desired level of profit (before interest and taxation) is useful for operations managers. We use the figures for Engine 1 as this engine will make a profit.

Profit = Sales value – Total variable costs – Fixed costs

Rearranging this equation gives:

Total variable costs = Sales value – Fixed costs – Profit
Variable cost per unit = (Sales – Fixed cost – Profit)/Number of
units produced

Thus, for the example with maintenance and consumables as variable costs and with a desired £120,000 profit required on 2500 units sold of Engine 1, we get:

VC per unit = (£550,000 – 40,000 – 120,000)/2500 units =
£156.00 per unit
**Note this is a reduction in variable costs of (£163.875 – £156.00)
= £7.875**

Thus, for the example above with maintenance and consumables as fixed costs and with a desired £120,000 profit required on 2500 units sold, we get:

VC per unit = (£550,000 – £47,187.50 – £120,000)/2500 units =
£153.125 per unit
**Note this is a reduction in variable costs per unit of (£161.00 –
£153.125) = £7.875 required to achieve a profit of £120,000.**

Thus, for a desired profit of £120,000 the variable cost per unit needs to be reduced by £7.875 regardless of the way the maintenance and consumables are allocated.

Thus, we find that the way the costs for maintenance and consumables are allocated (a) as variable costs or (b) as fixed costs; does not affect the way we might think of reducing the variable costs to achieve a certain specified profit because the value that the unit variable costs needs to be reduced is the same (£7.875) no matter which way the maintenance and consumables are allocated as costs.

6 Comment on your answer by making recommendations to Lawnmower Engines Ltd sales department concerning which engine(s) should be offered to the Snow Mobiles Ltd customer.

> Engine 1 costs £163.875 to make and will be profitable, making a contribution of £56.125 per engine. (Note: Unit contribution = Unit sales price − Unit variable costs = P − VCu.)
>
> Engine 2 costs £229.875 to make and would make a loss of £9.875 per engine.
>
> Engine 3 costs £245.45 to make and would make a loss of £25.45 on each engine.
>
> Engine 2 and Engine 3 should *not* be offered to Snow Mobiles Ltd.

Only one engine is feasible to sell to Snow Mobiles Ltd, Engine 1, which costs £163.875 to make and will sell at £220 and make £56.125 contribution on each engine. Engine 1 will become profitable for the company after 712.7 units have been made and sold to Snow Mobiles Ltd for £220 each, or £156,792.87 of sales have been made of this engine at £220 per engine with an expected **profit of £100,312.50 overall.**

Annual sales are expected to be £550,000 to Snow Mobiles Ltd, or 2500 units of Engine 1 and a contract should be drawn up for £220 per unit of Engine 1 with a specified minimum order of 2500 units per annum. This will be a profitable contract for Lawnmower Engines Ltd but if the operations manager can reduce the variable cost of making Engine 1 by £7.875 it is possible to make £120,000 profit. Therefore, alternative materials, methods of manufacture and alternative sources of cheaper components should be sought to reduce the costs of making Engine 1 and in the longer term reducing the costs of making all the engines.

While this result does not tell you which items in the bill of materials (BOM) to target to try and reduce the cost it does give an estimate of the amount the variable cost needs to be reduced.

Much more detailed analysis of the costs of each item in the product bill of materials would need to be carried out in order to identify ways of driving down the (variable) costs of making the item. It should be noted that £7.875 is approximately 4.8 per cent of the cost of making the product and could be a feasible cost reduction if the methods of manufacture were changed to a cheaper method; or if substitute materials or alternative suppliers could be found for some of the components in the product.

The engine assembly department has the capacity to make 2500 units of Engine 1 because making 2500 units of Engine 1 only uses 12,500 hours per annum (5 hours per unit × 2500 units). Note that ten people working eight hours a day for 250 days gives 20,000 man hours.

Finally

Operations managers are very interested in the details of variable costs because these provide crucial information about the amount of labour, raw materials, components, assemblies, subassemblies, consumables and maintenance that go into making a particular product. These variable cost figures may be used in setting the base price for selling the products to customers (bearing in mind the products do need to compete on price with other offerings in the market place).

These variable cost figures can also be reduced when redesigning products and various techniques such as value analysis, value engineering, cost reductions via de-specifying certain non-critical parts, using different suppliers or using alternative materials or alternative production methods can be used to drive overall variable costs down. Such cost reductions can be very useful in lowering the break-even point and making more profit for the company or even lead to price reductions when required in order to compete with other, similar products in the market. Similarly, lowering the amount of stock and work in progress in the factory can also lower the costs and lower the break-even point for the company.

However, the biggest part of the variable cost to a company is usually labour costs and if the company also has high fixed costs (ie has a lot of managers and administrators with salaries, expensive rents, high council taxes or business rates, etc) then the company can find that the break-even point is very high and the business is not very profitable (see Figure 1).

The break-even point is different if the maintenance and consumables are treated as fixed costs instead of variable costs; although the profit remains the same if everything else remains the same. If the break-even point were to be used as a key performance indicator (KPI) for the business then the maintenance and consumables should be treated in exactly the same way for each customer order. Maintenance and consumables are usually treated as variable costs because they vary directly with the number of units produced.

It is possible for companies like Lawnmower Engines Ltd to manufacture themselves out of business by making finished goods and putting them into the finished goods warehouse. If these goods do not sell then the company has spent all the money on making the products (variable costs) and managing the business (fixed costs) and the combination of costs may mean that, if the company does not have cash flow from selling other products, the company could go into debt and eventually go out of business. Thus, costs are a big issue in any business, including service businesses. Although calculating variable costs, fixed costs and break-even points might be a bit more complicated for some service businesses the same approach can be used.

Sports Co Ltd
Make or buy decisions

Mike Simpson and Andrea Genovese

AUTHOR BIOGRAPHIES

DR MIKE SIMPSON AND DR ANDREA GENOVESE
ANDREA GENOVESE is a Lecturer in Logistics and Supply Chain Management at The University of Sheffield Management School.

Introduction and useful definitions

- *Outsourcing:* Contracting with another company to do work that was once done by the organization itself. It is the process of having suppliers provide goods and services that were previously provided internally.

- *Purchasing:* The activity of acquiring services and goods for the organization. It includes all the activities necessary for fulfilling the organization's long and short-term needs.

- *Subcontracting:* Buying parts or subassemblies from outside suppliers whenever a company's capacity is insufficient to meet its needs from internal production.

Buying in a product is often called outsourcing or subcontracting and very often these terms are used interchangeably when in actual fact they are quite different as we can see from the standard definitions above. Purchasing concerns the acquisition of resources for the organization so that it can continue to make the products and services the organization provides to its customers. Essentially, the company purchases materials, a component or item from a supplier.

Usually a company that makes a part or component or item typically incurs fixed costs associated with purchasing equipment or setting up a production facility as well as fixed costs for salaries, rent, rates and so forth. Fixed costs do not vary with volume or number of units made. Fixed costs can often include costs of building or buying or leasing equipment and administrative costs. Variable costs are usually direct labour, materials, assemblies, sub-assemblies, maintenance and consumables, and anything that varies with the number of items produced. Variable costs can be eliminated to a large extent if the product or item is produced by an external supplier. Although it should be noted that the external supplier may well have a different cost base associated with producing any item or product. The economic idea of comparative advantage comes into play where a supplier in another country may have a lower cost base mainly due to lower labour costs.

Strategic approaches to purchasing include vendor rating and development and consideration of costs, quality, delivery, flexibility, technical knowledge and reliability of suppliers. However, an initial consideration is to look at the costs of purchasing an item versus the costs of making the same item within the company. This problem is called the *make or buy decision*.

Total variable costs are a function of the quantity produced and include labour, materials, and all the other costs associated with producing and distributing the product or item. By doing some algebra and calculations it is possible to determine the break-even quantity between making and buying in a particular item from a supplier (by outsourcing).

Derivation of the break-even quantity ($Q_{B/E}$)
VC = Variable cost/unit if produced within the company
P = Purchase price per unit if purchased from a supplier
FC = Fixed costs associated with producing the part or item within the company
Q = Quantity produced or required (ie the volume)

Then:

Total cost of production = (VC × Q) + FC
Total cost of buying in = (P × Q)

If the total cost of buying in is less than the total cost of making a product in the company, then buying in is the better decision; if not, then the firm should make the product or item themselves.

The break-even quantity ($Q_{B/E}$) can be identified so that the decision to make or buy in a product or item can be made. Thus, the break-even quantity can be found by the following procedure:

Set the total cost of production of the item equal to the total cost of buying in the same item, and solve for the quantity at the break-even point ($Q_{B/E}$).

(P × Q) = (VC × Q) + FC
(P × Q) − (VC × Q) = FC
(P − VC) × Q = FC

The break-even quantity ($Q_{B/E}$) is:

$$Q_{B/E} = \frac{FC}{(P - VC)}$$

Thus, if the quantity required (Q) is less than the break-even point quantity ($Q_{B/E}$), then the least-cost decision is to buy in the product or item; otherwise, it is to make the item within the organization. So when the anticipated required quantity (Q) is greater than the break-even point quantity ($Q_{B/E}$), then the least-cost decision is that the firm should make the part or item themselves. Mathematically this can be written as:

If Q is greater than the break-even quantity, $Q_{B/E}$: $Q>Q_{B/E}$; then make the item.

If Q is less than the break-even quantity, $Q_{B/E}$: $Q<Q_{B/E}$; then buy in the item.

Graphically, this can be shown as in Figure 1 below.

Figure 1

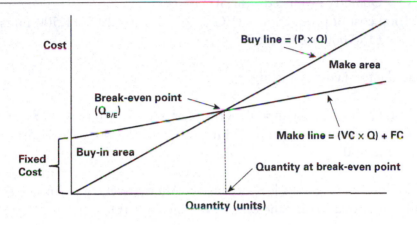

Thus, when the quantity to be made is such that making the item in the company is more expensive than buying in the item then the least-cost decision is to buy in the item (ie outsource). When the quantity to be made is such that the cost of making the item in the company is lower than buying in the item then the least-cost decision is for the company to make the item themselves. This approach is similar to an investment decision, although as noted earlier other strategic considerations are involved when selecting a supplier.

Worked example 1: make or buy decision

A manufacturing company needs to produce an item called a Dubry-Owens Adaptor used in radio-controlled models for a customer order. The manufacturing company does not have the right equipment necessary to make the Dubry-Owens Adaptor and would need to acquire the equipment at a fixed cost of £150,000. The variable cost of making the Dubry-Owens Adaptor is estimated to be £20 per unit. The manufacturing company can buy in the Dubry-Owens Adaptor at £25 per unit. The customer order is for 11,500 units. What should the manufacturing company do?

Solution:

VC = Variable cost/unit if produced by the manufacturing company
   = £20

P = Purchase Price/unit, if purchased from a supplier = £25
FC = Fixed costs associated with producing the part or item =
£150,000
Q = Quantity produced = 11,500 units
Total cost of production = (VC × Q) + FC = (£20 × 11,500 units)
+ £150,000 = £380,000

And the total cost of buying in:

Total cost of buying in = (P × Q) = (£25 × 11,500 units) = £287,500
Cost difference = (make – buy in) = £380,000 – £287,500 =
£92,500

Therefore, buying in is less expensive. Alternatively, we can use the
following equation for the break-even quantity ($Q_{B/E}$):

$$Q_{B/E} = \frac{FC}{(P - VC)} = \frac{£150,000}{(£25 - £20)} = 30,000 \text{ (units)}$$

The customer order is for 11,500 units, which is less than the break-
even point quantity ($Q_{B/E}$) of 30,000 units, therefore the least-cost
decision is to buy in the component.

Note:

There are two tests used here but either one alone is
enough to make the decision. That is:

Test 1. The first test is the cost difference which, in this example, shows that it is more expensive to make the
Dubry-Owens Adaptor than to buy in. Thus, buying in is
the least-cost decision.

Test 2. The second test is the calculation of the break-even
quantity and determining if the desired quantity (Q) is
greater or smaller than the break-even quantity ($Q_{B/E}$).
Thus, we arrive at the original guidelines:

If Q is greater than the break-even quantity $Q_{B/E}$: $Q>Q_{B/E}$;
then make the item;

If Q is less than the break-even quantity $Q_{B/E}$: $Q<Q_{B/E}$;
then buy in the item.

This point is illustrated in Figure 1 above.

It is also worth noting where the variable costs originate from when a manufacturer is making a product and this is shown in the next example. From our point of view variable costs (VC) are those costs which vary directly with the number of units made. Thus:

VC = labour + raw materials + components + assemblies and
sub-assemblies + maintenance + consumables + any other
item which varies directly with the number of units made.

Worked example 2: make or buy decision

The same manufacturing company also makes a What-u-McCall-it servo device for radio-controlled aircraft and your line manager, the purchasing manager, needs to know if the manufacturing company should make or buy this device. The device is constructed from various electronic components, a servo, a servo drive gearbox, external connectors, fastening bolts and a small die-cast metal housing. The company would need to buy some equipment to allow them to continue making this item. A local supplier can provide the What-u-McCall-it servo device ready assembled for £7.50 per unit. You are required to report to the purchasing manager given the following data:

Description	Variable costs per unit(£)
Electronic components	1.10
Servo	0.10
Servo gearbox	1.50
External connectors	0.25
Fastening bolts	0.50
Die-cast metal box	2.50
Assembly labour	0.30
Testing labour	0.50
Indirect labour	0.60
Total (£)	**7.35**
Annual fixed costs (£)	**12,000 (see note)**

Note   Assume that the equipment cost is £72,000 and has a six-year life.

Solution:

Q is the quantity to be made or purchased

Cost to buy per year = (Purchase price × Q) = (£7.50 × Q) = 7.50Q

Cost to make per year = (Variable costs per unit × Q) + annual fixed costs = (£7.35 per unit × Q) + £12,000 = 7.35Q + 12,000

By setting the costs to make equal to the cost to buy in we can find the number of units at the break-even point ($Q_{B/E}$) by solving for Q.

Cost to buy = Cost to make
$7.50Q = 7.35Q + 12,000$
$7.50Q - 7.35Q = 12,000$
$Q(7.50 - 7.35) = 12,000$

Therefore:

Q at the break-even point is $Q_{B/E} = \dfrac{12,000}{7.50 - 7.35} = 80,000$ units

$Q_{B/E}$ = 80,000 units per year at the break-even point

Thus, the value of $Q_{B/E}$ in this simple mathematical model tells you the point where the cost to buy and the cost to make are equal, that is the break-even point. For values of Q less than $Q_{B/E}$ (80,000 units), the cost of buying in is lower. For values of Q greater than 80,000 units, the cost of making the product is lower (refer to Figure 1).

Make or buy decisions at Sports Co Ltd

Questions

1 Sports Co Ltd make a variety of sporting goods products. Recently questions have been raised concerning the costs to make some of these products when compared with the opportunities to buy these products in from companies abroad. These alternative products are of equal quality and performance when in use and conform to various standards required for the various sporting bodies. Your job is to make recommendations on which products should be bought in and which products should be made by Sports Co Ltd. A number of products have been assessed and the following data has been produced in Table 1.

Table 1 Data collected

Description	Forecast volume (units)	Cost to make (£) per unit	Cost to purchase (£) per unit	Fixed costs (£) per annum
Golf clubs set	8,000	300	349	250,000
Cricket bats	5,000	23	44	135,000
Tennis racquets	9,000	70	75	80,000
Golf shoes	11,000	35	59	250,000

2 Sports Co Ltd also want to start making badminton racquets in a dedicated production facility with an estimated actual production capacity of 20,000 units per annum. The costs of making the badminton racquets are shown in Table 2 below. The production facility will cost £120,000 per annum in fixed costs. The purchase price of ready assembled badminton racquets from a trusted supplier is £42.00. Comment on the possibilities of buying in the badminton racquets.

Table 2 Data for the manufacture of badminton racquets

Description	Variable costs per unit (£)
Metal frame	15
Leather for handle	3.5
Nylon cord for head	5.5
Tensioning cord	1
Plastic insert for handle	0.5
Glue	0.5
Direct labour	6
Testing labour	3

Note   A simple spreadsheet model can be used to speed up the calculations.

Answers

1 Sports Co Ltd make a variety of sporting goods products. Recently questions have been raised concerning the costs to make some of these products when compared with the opportunities to buy these products in from companies abroad. These alternative products are of equal quality and performance when in use and conform to various standards required for the various sporting bodies. Your job is to make recommendations on which products should be bought in and which products should be made by Sports Co Ltd. A number of products have been assessed and the following data has been produced in Table 1.

Table 1 Data collected

Description	Forecast volume (units)	Cost to make (£) per unit	Cost to purchase (£) per unit	Fixed costs (£) per annum
Golf clubs set	8,000	300	349	250,000
Cricket bats	5,000	23	44	135,000
Tennis racquets	9,000	70	75	80,000
Golf shoes	11,000	35	59	250,000

Golf clubs sets calculations

VC = Variable cost/unit if produced by the manufacturing company = £300

P = Purchase Price/unit, if purchased from a supplier = £349

FC = Fixed costs associated with producing the part or item = £250,000

Q = Quantity produced = 8,000 units

Total cost of production = $(VC \times Q) + FC$ = (£300 × 8,000 units) + £250,000 = **£2,650,000**

And the total cost of buying in:

Total cost of buying in $= (P \times Q) = (£349 \times 8,000 \text{ units}) = $ **£2,792,000**

Test 1: Cost difference
Cost difference = (make − buy in) = £2,650,000 − £2,792,000 = − £142,000

Buying in is more expensive. Therefore, the least-cost decision is to make the golf clubs set.

Test 2: Number of units at the break-even point
Equation for the break-even quantity ($Q_{B/E}$) is:

$$Q_{B/E} = \frac{FC}{(P - VC)} = \frac{£250,000}{(£349 - £300)} = 5,102 \text{ (units)}$$

The company intends to sell 8,000 units, which is more than the break-even point quantity ($Q_{B/E}$) of 5,102 units, therefore the least-cost decision is to make the golf clubs sets.

Cricket bat calculations

VC = Variable cost/unit if produced by the manufacturing company = £23
P = Purchase price/unit, if purchased from a supplier = £44
FC = Fixed costs associated with producing the part or item = £135,000
Q = Quantity produced = 5,000 units
Total cost of production = (VC × Q) + FC = (£23 × 5,000 units) + £135,000 = **£250,000**

And the total cost of buying in:

Total cost of buying in = (P × Q) = (£44 × 5,000 units) = **£220,000**

Test 1: Cost difference
Cost difference = (make − buy in) = £250,000 − £220,000 = **£30,000**

Buying in is less expensive. Therefore, the least-cost decision is to buy in the cricket bats.

Test 2: Number of units at the break-even point

$$Q_{B/E} = \frac{FC}{(P - VC)} = \frac{£135,000}{(£44 - £23)} = 6,429 \text{ (units)}$$

The company intends to sell 5,000 units, which is less than the break-even point quantity ($Q_{B/E}$) of 6,429 units, therefore the least-cost decision is to buy in the cricket bats.

Tennis racquets calculations

VC = Variable cost/unit if produced by the manufacturing company = £70

P = Purchase price/unit, if purchased from a supplier = £75

FC = Fixed costs associated with producing the part or item = £80,000

Q = Quantity produced = 9,000 units

Total cost of production = (VC × Q) + FC = (£70 × 9,000 units) + £80,000 = **£710,000**

And the total cost of buying in:

Total cost of buying in = (P × Q) = (£75 × 9,000 units) = **£675,000**

Test 1: Cost difference

Cost difference = (make − buy in) = £710,000 − £675,000 = **£35,000**

Buying in is less expensive. Therefore, the least-cost decision is to buy in the tennis racquets.

Test 2: Number of units at the break-even point

Equation for the break-even quantity ($Q_{B/E}$) is:

$$Q_{B/E} = \frac{FC}{(P - VC)} = \frac{£80,000}{(£75 - £70)} = 16,000 \text{ (units)}$$

The company intends to sell 9,000 units, which is less than the break-even point quantity ($Q_{B/E}$) of 16,000 units, therefore the least-cost decision is to buy in the tennis racquets.

Golf shoes calculations

VC = Variable cost/unit if produced by the manufacturing company = £35

P = Purchase price/unit, if purchased from a supplier = £59

FC = Fixed costs associated with producing the part or item = £250,000

Q = Quantity produced = 11,000 units

Total cost of production = (VC × Q) + FC = (£35 × 11,000 units) + £250,000 = **£635,000**

And the total cost of buying in:

Total cost of buying in = (P × Q) = (£59 × 11,000 units) = **£649,000**

Test 1: Cost difference
Cost difference = (make − buy in) = £635,000 − £649,000 = **− £14,000**

Buying in is more expensive. Therefore, the least-cost decision is to make the golf shoes.

Test 2: Number of units at the break-even point
Equation for the break-even quantity ($Q_{B/E}$) is:

$$Q_{B/E} = \frac{FC}{(P - VC)} = \frac{£250,000}{(£59 - £35)} = 10,417 \text{ (units)}$$

The company intends to sell 11,000 units, which is more than the break-even point quantity ($Q_{B/E}$) of 10,417 units, therefore the least-cost decision is to make the golf shoes. However, this is a marginal case since the cost difference is −£14,000 and the difference in cost per item is £1.27. It is a management judgement if the effort to make the golf shoes is worth it.

Table 2 Summary of answer to make or buy decisions for Sports Co Ltd

Description	Forecast volume (units)	Cost difference (£)	Break-even point (QB/E) (units)	Recommendation
Golf clubs	8,000	−142000	5102	Make
Cricket bats	5000	30000	6429	Buy in
Tennis racquets	9,000	35000	16000	Buy in
Golf shoes	11,000	−14000	10417	Make

2 Sports Co Ltd also want to start making badminton racquets in a dedicated production facility with an estimated actual production capacity of 20,000 units per annum. The costs of making the badminton racquets are shown in Table 3 below. The production facility will cost £120,000 per annum in fixed costs. The purchase price of ready assembled badminton racquets from a trusted supplier is £42.00. Comment on the possibilities of buying in the badminton racquets.

Table 3 Data for the manufacture of badminton racquets

Description	Variable costs per unit (£)
Metal frame	15
Leather for handle	3.5
Nylon cord for head	5.5
Tensioning cord	1
Plastic insert for handle	0.5
Glue	0.5
Direct labour	6
Testing labour	3

Table 4 Summary of answer to make or buy for badminton racquets

Description	Variable costs per unit (£)
Metal frame	15
Leather for handle	3.5
Nylon cord for head	5.5
Tensioning cord	1
Plastic insert for handle	0.5
Glue	0.5
Direct labour	6
Testing labour	3
Total (£)	**35.00**
Annual fixed costs (£)	**120,000**

The purchase price of ready assembled badminton racquets is £42.00

Solution:

Q is the quantity to be made or purchased
Cost to buy per year = (Purchase price × Q) = (£42 × Q) = 42Q
Cost to make per year = (Variable costs per unit × Q) + annual fixed costs = (£35 per unit × Q) + £120,000 = 35Q + 120,000

By setting the costs to make equal to the cost to buy in we can find the number of units at the break-even point ($Q_{B/E}$) by solving for Q.

Cost to buy = Cost to make
42Q = 35Q + 120,000
42Q − 35Q = 120,000
Q(42 − 35) = 120,000

Therefore:

$$Q \text{ at the break-even point is } Q_{B/E} = \frac{120,000}{(42 - 35)} = 17,143 \text{ units}$$

$Q_{B/E} = 17,143$ units per year at the break-even point

Thus, the value of $Q_{B/E}$, the quantity at the break-even point, in this simple mathematical model tells you the point where the cost to buy and the cost to make are equal. For values of Q less than $Q_{B/E}$ (**17,143** units), the cost of buying in is lower. For values of Q greater than $Q_{B/E}$ (**17,143** units), the cost of making the product is lower. We know the number of units which the production line is capable of manufacturing is 20,000 units. This number is greater than the break-even point (**17,143** units) and if the production capacity can be held at 20,000 units per annum and the company can sell 20,000 units per annum then we would advise Sports Co Ltd to make the badminton racquets.

Comments

Make or buy decisions are relatively straightforward given the mathematics shown above. However, the actual decisions will depend upon a number of other factors such as quality, delivery, flexibility, technical knowledge and reliability of suppliers. Modern purchasing and supply can involve strategic approaches such as vendor rating and development that intend to drive costs down, improve quality and develop long-term relationships with suppliers that are mutually beneficial. The make or buy decision, using the mathematics shown above, is one component of assessment that can be used to help determine what to do about a particular product.

Pretty Kitchens' bag filling machine
Calculating the cost of quality

Mike Simpson and Andrea Genovese

AUTHOR BIOGRAPHIES

DR MIKE SIMPSON AND DR ANDREA GENOVESE
ANDREA GENOVESE is a Lecturer in Logistics and Supply Chain Management at The University of Sheffield Management School.

Introduction

In 1951 quality guru Dr Joseph M Juran produced his first *Quality Control Handbook* in which he analysed the costs of quality and which contained his analogy about poor quality: 'there is gold in the mine.' Juran gave a definition of quality as: 'quality is fitness for use.' This has been re-interpreted as: 'quality is fitness for purpose' by the Department of Trade and Industry (1985). Like Dr W Edwards Deming, in 1954, Joseph Juran was invited to Japan by the Union of Japanese Scientists and Engineers (JUSE). Juran's lectures to the Japanese focussed on planning, organizational issues, management's responsibility for quality and the need to set goals and targets for improvement. He emphasized that quality control should be conducted as an integral part of management control.

Juran's message is that 'quality does not happen by accident, it must be planned'. He sees 'quality planning' as part of the quality trilogy of:

- Quality Planning.

- Quality Control.

- Quality Improvement.

Juran also sees the important elements in implementing company-wide strategic quality planning as:

- Identifying customers and their needs.

- Establishing optimum quality goals.

- Creating measurements of quality.

- Planning processes capable of meeting quality goals under operating conditions.

- Producing continuous results in improved market share and premium prices.

- Reduction of error rates in the office or factory.

The theory of the cost of quality

The types of cost of quality in a manufacturing context are: waste, lower productivity, rework, warranty and guarantees, liability for defects, administration costs dealing with customer complaints, poor reputation leading to reduced ability to compete in the market and reduced market share, poor morale and motivation of employees, waste of management time dealing with quality problems and so on. These costs can be broken down into two types of cost each with two sub-categories as follows:

Control Costs – Prevention Costs and Appraisal Costs which rise with increasing quality.

Failure Costs – Internal Failure Costs and External Failure costs which fall with increasing quality.

The cost of quality can be determined from examination of the Control costs (ie Prevention and Appraisal costs) and Failure costs (ie Internal failure and External failure costs).

- *Prevention costs:* These are design of the product and production systems and these can include the choice of better materials, inclusion of features that ensure good quality (eg Poka Yoke – mistake proofing systems, Baka Yoke – fool proofing systems, Statistical Process Control SPC, design for manufacture, design of manufacturing systems, fail safes, error detection etc) and extra time to make the product. Employee training, pilot runs, testing prototypes, designing and maintaining control systems, improvement projects etc. Prevention costs often rise with increasing quality of the product.

- *Appraisal costs:* These are sampling, inspecting, testing, quality control, quality audits and administration. Appraisal costs often rise with increasing quality of the product.

- *Internal failure costs:* These are direct costs such as scrap, rework, repair, loss of materials, wasted labour, wasted machine time, extra testing, duplicated effort etc. Indirect costs are higher inventory levels, longer lead times, extra capacity needed to allow for scrap and rejects, loss of confidence etc. Internal failure costs often fall with increasing quality of the product.

- *External failure costs:* Guarantees, replacements, rework, repair, loss of reputation etc. External failure costs often fall with increasing quality of the product.

CASE STUDY
Pretty Kitchens' bag filling machine

This is a real case study based on the writer's experience of working with a client. For reasons of commercial confidentiality the names of the companies and the data and specific situations have been disguised.

The case is about the response to an inspection event at a machine that seemed to be generating a lot of problems for the company elsewhere in the business (eg telephone calls, posting out replacement bags, customer complaints). The case covers issues of inspection, analysis of the internal costs of quality (eg extra components, sending out replacement bags, handling complaints) and external costs (eg managing the complaints and making sure customers are satisfied). Some of these can be quantified from the information in the case study.

Pretty Kitchens Limited is a manufacturer of high-quality fitted kitchens. The two main product types are flat-pack DIY (Do-it-yourself) self-assembly kitchen units and contract kitchen units (pre-assembled). The company has a turnover of ~£20.4m, a profit of £1.3m before tax and employs 273 people. The company holds work-in-progress and finished goods stock of approximately £2.8m.

The company is currently having problems with creating a fittings/components pack for the flat pack self-assembly kitchen units. The automated bag-filling machine is less than perfect and there are several different types of fitting/components packs for the various types of unit. The cost and number of the individual components in each bag is given in Table 1 and Table 2 shows the data obtained from a random sample of 50 bags for a typical self-assembly kitchen unit. Pretty Kitchens produce some 4000 flat-packs a week all requiring a '10/6F B' component bag. If a customer complains of a missing component in a bag Pretty Kitchens sends out a complete component bag for that particular model of kitchen unit.

Table 1 Costs of the components for a 'perfect' (ie the correct number of components) '10/6F B' self-assembly kitchen unit bag

Item	Cost (p)	Number in a bag	Total (p)
Bolts	1.50	30	45.00
Cams	3.00	8	24.00
5mm caps (cream)	0.10	30	3.00
5mm caps (brown)	0.10	30	3.00
Sink clips	2.28	2	4.56
Shelf supports	0.92	32	29.44
F/rear bracket	4.00	4	16.00
Total	--	--	125.00

Notes

- Any shortages may result in a customer complaint. However, it is the company's experience that only 25% of people complain when a component is missing.
- A customer complaint on a bag results in a complete bag being sent direct to the customer by return of post.
- Additional items are an extra cost to the company

Questions

Using the data above and in Table 2 (below), where the variation (+ or -) from a perfect bag is shown in the table, answer the following questions:

1 What is the cost of quality associated with the bag-filling machine?

2 What can be done to reduce the costs of quality associated with the bag-filling machine?

3 What would be the effect of adding 5 cream caps and 5 brown caps to each bag of components?

4 What elements of Dr Joseph Juran's theory of the Cost of Quality are involved in this example?

5 Comment on your answer.

Table 2 A random selection of 50 flat-pack 10/6F B component bags

Bag number	Bolts	Cams	5mm cap (cream)	5mm cap (brown)	Sink clips	Shelf support	F/rear bracket
1	+1	+1		+1			
2		+1		+2		+1	
3	+2	+1	+1			+1	
4	+1	+1	+2	+1			
5	+1	+1	+4	-2			
6	+1	+1	-2	-4			
7	+1	+1	-1		+1		
8	+1	+1	+1	+1			
9	+1	+1	+1	-1			
10	+1	+2		-2			
11	+1	+1		-1		-1	
12	+1	+1	+1	+1			
13	+1	+2					
14	+1	+1					
15	+1	+1	-1	+2			
16	+1	+1	-1				
17	+1	+1		-1	+1		
18	+1	+1	+1	+1			
19	+1	+1					
20	+1	+1		+1			
21	+1	+1		+1			
22	+2	+1		-1			
23	+1	+1	+5				
24	+2	+1	-1	-1			+1
25	+2	+1		-1			
26	+1	+1	+1	-1			
27	+1	+1	+3	+1			
28	+1		+1		+1		
29	+1	+1	+3	+1			
30	+1	+1	+1	-1			
31	+1	+1	+4		+1		
32	+1	+1	+2				
33	+1	+1		-1			
34	+1	+1				-1	-1
35	+1	+1	-1	+1			
36	+1	+1	-1		+1		
37	+1	+1	+1				
38	+1	+1	+3				
39	+2	+2		+1			
40	+2	+1					

Table 2 *(continued)*

Bag number	Bolts	Cams	5mm cap (cream)	5mm cap (brown)	Sink clips	Shelf support	F/rear bracket
41	+1	+1	+4				
42	+1			+2			
43	+1	+1	-1				
44	+2	+2	-1	+3			
45	+1	+1	+2	-1			
46	+1	+1	+1		-2		
47	+1	+1		+1			
48	+1	+1	+1	-1			
49	+1	+1	-1	-1			
50	+2	+1	+1				+2

Note	Plus (+) means more and Minus (-) means fewer components than is required in each component bag produced by the bag-filling machine at Pretty Kitchens.

Answers

1 What is the cost of quality associated with the bag-filling machine?

In order to calculate the cost of quality of the bagging machine a typical Operational Research approach can be adopted. An explicit statement of a set of definitions and assumptions are given to delineate the boundaries of the problem and a mathematical formula (a simple model) can be constructed and solved. Develop a spreadsheet to assist in answering the questions.

- *Definition of a Perfect Component Bag:* 'A component bag that contains exactly the right number of components (see Table 1, above), no extras and no missing components. Such a bag will not generate a customer complaint.'

- *Definition of a Faulty Component Bag:* 'A bag that has components missing and may result in a customer complaint'.

- *Assumption:* Additional components that cannot be used are not returned and are, therefore, a cost to the company.
- *Assumption:* Missing components that are not in a component bag are not paid for by Pretty Kitchens so they can be deducted from the number of extra components in each category but the bag is a Faulty Bag.
- *Assumption:* For faulty bags with missing components, only 25% of customers complain and are sent a replacement bag. (Given in the notes to Table 1).

Note   The faulty bags (missing components) which could generate a customer complaint are bags number: 5, 6, 7, 9, 10, 11, 15, 16, 17, 22, 24, 25, 26, 30, 33, 34, 35, 36, 43, 44, 45, 46, 48, 49 (ie 24 bags out of 50 bags in the sample).

Table 3 Extra components and missing components in the 50 bags in table 2.

Item	Cost (p)	Number in a bag	Total (p)	Extra parts minus missing parts in 50 bags	Cost (p) of extras in 50 bags
Bolts	1.50	30	45.00	57 – 0 = 57	85.50
Cams	3.00	8	24.00	52 – 0 = 52	156.00
5mm caps (cream)	0.10	30	3.00	44 – 11 = 33	3.30
5mm caps (brown)	0.10	30	3.00	21 – 20 = 1	0.1
Sink clips	2.28	2	4.56	5 - 2 = 3	6.84
Shelf supports	0.92	32	29.44	2 – 2 = 0	0.0
F/rear bracket	4.00	4	16.00	3 – 1 = 2	8.00
Total	–	–	125.00	148	259.74 (£2.5974)

Cost of Quality (COQ) can be calculated by constructing the model based on the definitions and assumptions.

COQ = Cost of   + Cost of   – Cost of   +Cost of   + Cost of
     replacement extra   missing   dealing with   Postage and
     bags   components components customer   Packing for
                               complaints   replacement
                                       bags

Some of these costs can be quantified, given the data in the case study, but others cannot be quantified. That is, we do not know the cost of dealing with customer complaints or the cost of handling the bags and postage and packing. This results in a modified cost of quality model as follows:

COQ   =   Cost of   + Cost of   – Cost of
                replacement   extra   missing
                bags   components   components

Cost of components
(extra minus missing
components) per 50 bags = £2.5974

Faulty Bags (per 50 bags) = 24 bags

Total cost (per 50 bags)   = Cost of components + Cost of replacement bags

Total cost (per 50 bags)   = £2.5974 + 24 Faulty bags x (£1.25) x 0.25 (ie 25%)
                            = £2.5974+7.50 = £10.0974

Total cost per week
(for 4000 bags)   = £10.0974 x 4000/50 = £807.792

Total cost per annum   =   £807.792x 52
                              =   £42,005.18

Comment: This is the salary of two Operatives or one middle/ senior manager.

As a Percentage of Turnover   =   (£42,005.184 / £20.4m) x 100 = 0.2059%

As a Percentage of Profit　　　=　(£42,005.184 / £1.3m) x
　　　　　　　　　　　　　　　　100 = 3.23%.

Both these figures look small and insignificant compared to the turnover of the company but saving £42,005.18 on one machine by making it deliver a perfect bag would be a very good saving indeed.

Further savings would be made on answering the estimated (ie worst case scenario) maximum number of 480 telephone calls per week or 24,960 telephone enquiries and complaint letters per annum plus the postage and packing for each replacement bag!

Number of Complaints　　　=　(52 weeks x 4000 bags/week
　　　　　　　　　　　　　　　　x 24/50 Faulty bags)
　　　　　　　　　　　　　　　　x 0.25
　　　　　　　　　　　　　　　　(25% complain)

Number of Complaints　　　=　24,960 per annum

In reality a smaller number of telephone calls and complaints are likely to be answered since customers will usually buy more than one flat pack kitchen unit and some additional components in some bags might make up for deficiencies in other bags. However, any substantial reduction in complaints would be a major saving in administration time and costs.

> **Note**　It could be argued that the number of customer complaints is a good Key Performance Indicator of quality, in this example, because it can be easily monitored and improvement activities will show rapid results if they are, or are not, successful.

2 What can be done to reduce the costs of quality associated with the bag-filling machine at Pretty Kitchens?

The component packs need some better way of preparation. Other approaches are:

- *Fix the Bagging Machine.* This might require a service contract with the manufacturer and there may be call out charges and the need for regular systematic inspections of the machine and samples of bags to be looked at. A cost benefit analysis would need to be done.

- *Buy a better bagging machine that is accurate.* This might also require a service contract with the manufacturer and there may be call out charges and inspection costs as above. A cost-benefit analysis would be required.

- *Subcontract out the component packs to a specialist packing company.* One single supplier being able to provide all the components for these packs is possible as there are specialist packaging firms available. So the approach might be to sub-contract out (the non-core business) of bag filling to another company specialising in the packaging of small components such as screws, caps and dowels etc.

- *Standardize the component pack.* It may be possible to stand-ardize the component pack for all types of flat pack kitchen units but only if this objective is made a requirement for any new designs being developed. These packs could then be called off in a 2-bin Kanban system from the packaging company if the production rate was fairly constant – which it is at 4000 bags per week.

- Put a problem-solving team on the problem and hope that quality can be improved by any of the ideas above or by some other method such as mistake-proofing (Poka yoke) or fail safe operation.

3 What would be the effect of adding 5 cream caps and 5 brown caps to each bag of components?

If we look at the table of contents from fifty bags (Table 2) we can see that a large number of mistakes (21 out of 24) are made by the machine during the process of putting the brown and cream 5 mm caps into the bags. A simple way to counteract this would be to set the bagging machine to add an additional 5 caps of each colour into the component bags. That is, the machine should be set to deliver 35 instead of 30 of each colour of caps in the bags. However this will increase the price of the extra components in fifty bags from £2.5974 to approximately £3.0974 (Table 4 below). But this will have the effect of reducing the number of customer complaints from 24 down to 3 for every 50 bags produced. Noting, that only bags numbered 11, 34, and 46 in Table 2, would be likely to generate a customer complaint. This will drive down the cost significantly and will also reduce the number of enquiries made by customers for extra bags and components.

This approach is a typical trade-off of costs of extra components versus costs of dealing with customer complaints, replacement component bags and all the costs associated with handling, packing and postage.

The calculations are as follows (see Table 4):

Table 4 Adding extra cream and brown 5mm caps (for 50 component bags)

Item	Cost (p)	Extra parts minus in 50 missing parts bags plus extra 5 caps in each bag	Cost (p) of extras in 50 bags
Bolts	1.5	57 – 0 = 57	85.50
Cams	3	52 – 0 = 52	156.00
5mm caps (cream)	0.1	44 – 11 = 33 +250=283	28.30
5mm caps (brown)	0.1	21 – 20 = 1+250=251	25.10
Sink clips	2.28	5 - 2 = 3	6.84
Shelf supports	0.92	2 – 2 = 0	0.00
F/rear bracket	4	3 – 1 = 2	8.00
Total	--	653	309.74 (£3.0974)

> **Note**   5 cream caps and 5 brown caps extra in a bag result in 250 caps extra of each colour cap in 50 bags.

Cost of components (extra minus missing components) per 50 bags is £3.0974.

Faulty Bags (per 50 bags) = 3 bags (bags 11, 34, and 46).

Noting that a bag with 5 extra cream and brown caps costs £1.26 (see table 5 below).

Total cost (per 50 bags)	= Cost of components + Cost of replacement bags
Total cost (per 50 bags)	= £3.0974 + 3x (£1.26) x 25% (ie 1/4)
	= £3.0974 + £0.945
	= £4.0424 per 50 bags
Total cost per week (for 4000 bags)	= £4.0424 x 4000/50
	= £323.3920
Total cost per annum	= £323.3920 x 52 weeks
	= £16,816.384

Table 5 Cost of a bag with 5 extra cream and 5 extra brown caps

Item	Cost (p)	Number in a bag	Total (p)
Bolts	1.5	30	45.00
Cams	3	8	24.00
5mm caps (cream)	0.1	35	3.50
5mm caps (brown)	0.1	35	3.50
Sink clips	2.28	2	4.56
Shelf supports	0.92	32	29.44
F/rear bracket	4	4	16.00
Total	--	--	126.00 (£1.26)

As a Percentage of Turnover = £16,816.384 / £20.4m) x 100
= 0.0824%

As a Percentage of Profit = £16,816.384 / £1.3m) x 100 = 1.2936%.

Number of complaints: = 4000 bags/week x 3/50 x 52 weeks x 0.25
= 3120 per annum
= 4000 bags/week x 3/50 x 0.25
= 60 per week

This is much easier to handle and costs Pretty Kitchens less than in the previous calculation and so could be a short-term solution to the problem of the bagging machine. It would buy the company time to sort the problem out rather than wasting money leaving the machine as it is.

The shortage of cream and brown caps in the bags leads to most of the problems with complaints at Pretty Kitchens (accounting for 21 out of 24 complaints from 50 bags). Simply adding some 5 extra cream and 5 extra brown caps to the bags eliminates a large number of customer complaints. Although, the theoretical cost of a basic standard bag which has the correct a number of components (including the extra cream and brown caps to eliminate the customer complaints) increases slightly from £1.25 to £1.26 because the cost of cream and brown caps is extremely small. However, the cost of extra components per 50 bags increases from £2.59 to £3.0974 approximately.

Overall, the cost of quality at the bagging machine has been reduced significantly by adding more cream and brown caps to each bag. This has reduced the cost of quality from £42,000 pa approximately down to £16,000 pa approximately due to the bagging machine. It has also reduced the number of customer complaints from 480 per week down to 60 per week. This is a marked improvement on the current situation in Pretty Kitchens. The knock-on effect of sending out replacement bags has been significantly reduced and is costing the company less than before and will have reduced the time and effort and the postage and packaging costs in replacing the bags.

However, in the longer term the bagging machine needs to be maintained, serviced, repaired, replaced or an alternative method found (eg a supplier of pre-packed components) for providing the component bags for the self-assembly kitchen units. These options should be investigated after a quality circle or quality improvement team has investigated the situation with this particular bagging machine.

This is the theoretical cost of a bag with 5 extra brown and 5 extra cream caps.

4 What elements of Dr Joseph Juran's theory of the cost of quality are involved in this example?

All of Dr Joseph Juran's Theory of the Cost of Quality are involved in this example but not all elements can be included in the calculations as there is not enough information concerning the costs of the receptionist's time in dealing with complaints, the operative's time in handling and packing a replacement component bag and the postage and packaging costs. However, some of these costs can be estimated from current pay rates and prices. It is possible that the actual cost of quality of the bagging machine could be as much as twice the calculated cost given here and perhaps as much as £100,000 per annum.

The Elements of the Theory of the Cost of Quality are: Control Costs (Prevention and Appraisal costs) and Failure Costs (internal failure costs and external failure costs). Waste in terms of: extra components, dealing with customer complaints, replacements, using management time to deal with problems and so on.

5 Comment on your answers

This type of problem and the response does not fit well with the idea of a high quality product or a Total Quality Management led company and may eventually damage the company's reputation. The company could be criticised for sending out a complete bag of components instead of an individual item.

This type of problem is ideal for a quality improvement team or quality circle to tackle on the shop floor. The amount of money that could be potentially saved is only a small fraction of the annual turnover of the company but could be equivalent to two operatives' wages for a year. If the receptionist and operative sending out replacement component bags is included there may be as much as £80,000 to £100,000 to be saved by fixing this problem (ie 'gold in the mine').

However, if several activities like this were carried out in various problem areas of the factory every few months or weeks the savings would potentially be quite large over a period of time. These savings would be year on year savings rather than year on year costs as is the current situation. This sort of quality problem represents what Joseph Juran called 'gold in the mine' and all such problems should be tackled to gain substantial savings for the company.

A more radical approach (ie cheaper) would be to have one person tackle this problem quickly once it is identified. This would involve a simple internal investigation of the following:

- *Age of the bag filling machine.* Is it new and under warranty and guarantee? If so call the manufacturers. Is it old? Does it have a service and maintenance contract? If so, call out the service engineer. Has it been serviced recently (a common cause of problems)? Where is the service history of the machine? Has this problem occurred before?

- *Decision on the future of the machine.* If the machine is old can it be repaired? What would that cost? How often does it require a service? Carry out a cost benefit analysis against the idea of purchasing a new machine. If the bagging machine is new why has the machine failed? Is it under warranty? Has it been properly maintained and serviced?

- *Buy a new machine.* Is this feasible? Carry out a cost benefit analysis versus maintaining the old machine.

- *Subcontract the bag filling.* Bag filling is not the company's 'Core Business' so find a bag filling specialists dealing with small components and ask for quotes for the job of filling 4000 component bags a week. Build in a penalty clause for any faulty bags and customer complaints. Evaluate the costs versus the existing costs and versus the costs of a repair, maintenance and service contract with the machine manufacturer.

At the end of such an analysis recommendations can be made to the senior management concerning the bag filling machine.

| Note | It is arguable that a sample of 50 bags from 4000 bags produced a week is not a representative sample. |

KTP tyres
The use of deseasonalization techniques in demand forecasting

Andrea Genovese and Mike Simpson

AUTHOR BIOGRAPHIES

DR ANDREA GENOVESE AND DR MIKE SIMPSON
ANDREA GENOVESE is a Lecturer in Logistics and Supply Chain Management at The University of Sheffield Management School.

Introduction

In a manufacturing context, demand forecasting can be seen as a proactive process of determining production needs. In other words, forecasting methodologies allow estimating what products are needed and in what quantities. For this reason, demand forecasting is a highly customer-focused activity that can act as a trigger for production-planning processes in make-to-stock environments. Within the wide range of available forecasting techniques, the one based on time series (or historical series) are particularly relevant. A *time series* or

Figure 1 Example of a time series with a strong (positive) trend component

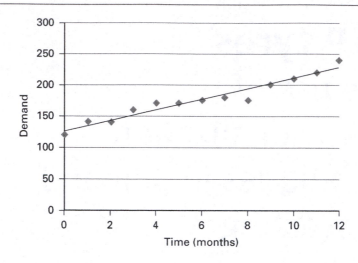

Figure 2 Example of a time series with a strong cyclic component

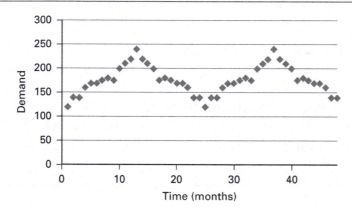

historical series $\{Y_i\}$ is a sequence of values $Y_1,..,Y_i,..,Y_n$ (representing, for instance, demand for a given product) sampled at regular intervals $T_1,..,T_i,..,T_n$ for a given time period. Several components can be identified in time series.

The *trend component* describes the *tendency* of the demand in the considered time interval. As an example, Figure 1 shows a time series with a strong and easily identifiable growing trend component.

Figure 3 Example of a time series with a strong seasonal component

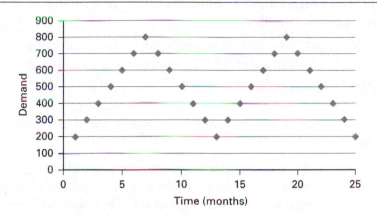

The *cyclic component* is due to typical variations over long time intervals (generally years), mostly related to business cycles. Figure 2 shows a time series with a strong cyclic component, in which it is possible to highlight a recurrent demand pattern, with a typical cycle length of two years.

Similarly, a *seasonal component* is due to typical behaviours within a year that become recurrent when observed on a time horizon of more years. Figure 3 shows a time series with a strong seasonal component, in which it is possible to highlight a recurrent demand pattern within a typical year, with a peak during summer months and a valley in the winter.

A *random component* is due to unpredictable variations that cannot be classified according to any of the categories listed above.

In the analysis of time series, the identification of trend components is highly desirable, as it allows predicting future demand tendencies through the use of statistical tools (such as regression models). However, in the presence of random, cyclical and seasonal components, the trend element may become less apparent. For this reason, it may be necessary to remove components whose origin may be traced back to a known and predictable pattern (such as seasonal or cyclical). In this context, the use of deseasonalization techniques can be very useful. The following case study illustrates an application of these techniques and an interpretation of the results they provide.

Useful definitions

- *Demand forecasting:* The process of determining future level of requests for products or services.

- *Time series (also, historical series):* A sequence of values $Y_1,..,Y_i,..,Y_n$ (representing, for instance, demand for a given product) sampled at regular intervals $T_1,..,T_i,..,T_n$ for a given time period.

- *Trend component:* The tendency of the demand in a considered time interval.

- *Cyclic component:* A component of time series due to typical variations over long time intervals (generally years), mostly related to business cycles and general economic conditions.

- *Seasonal component:* A component of time series due to typical behaviors (linked to seasons) within a year that become recurrent when observed on a time horizon of more years.

- *Random component:* A component of time series due to unpredictable variations that cannot be classified according to any of the categories listed above.

- *Deseasonalization:* In time series analysis, a methodology that allows the identification and the removal of the seasonal component from the data set.

Question

KTP is a company operating in the tyres industry. The company mainly manufactures tyres for agricultural machines (such as tractors and other types of equipment), with a special focus on tyres for vineyard tractors. The historical series of the company sales have been reported in the following Table 1. The company is not expecting major changes in the business climate and in industry operations in the short term.

In order to start the production-planning activity, the company wants to determine a reliable forecast for the overall demand for the next year. The company is somewhat aware of the seasonal nature of its business, but would like to get a clear assessment of the impact of this phenomenon on its sales.

Table 1 Historical series for KTP demand

Month	Year 1	Year 2	Year 3
January	7,400	7,700	8,400
February	6,100	6,600	7,100
March	8,800	9,800	10,500
April	10,500	11,200	12,400
May	12,600	13,800	15,100
June	16,500	18,300	19,900
July	19,900	22,500	24,200
August	21,600	22,800	24,800
September	19,300	20,500	21,900
October	13,600	14,900	15,900
November	9,800	10,600	11,300
December	10,900	11,700	12,700

Answer

The historical series provided by the company can be plotted as reported in Figure 4. It can be clearly seen that sales seem to have a seasonal pattern. This is to be expected, as the sales of tyres for agricultural machines are linked to seasonality in the agricultural industry and more intense usage of the machines in certain months of the year. Specifically, a peak is observed in summer months of each year.

Figure 4 Historical series of KTP sales

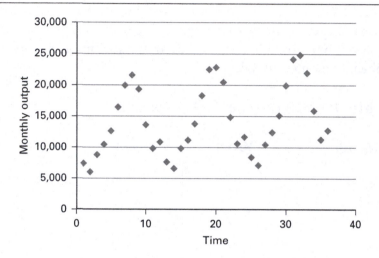

However, as revealed by Figure 5, the trend identification, in this case, is not straightforward. A trend line can be derived by using a simple linear regression model (using the appropriate function in MS Excel). However, the coefficient of determination R^2 (expressing the strength of the correlation between time and variations in demand) is equal to 0.09, representing a very low value (see Figure 5). While a growing tendency is identified, the low value of R^2 does not allow the company to use the trend line as a tool for determining a reliable forecast for the future demand.

Figure 5 Trend line for historical series of KTP sales

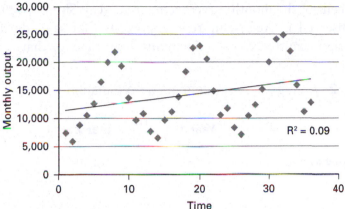

It is apparent that most of the variation in demand (apart from the identified growing tendency) is due to the seasonal pattern. For this reason, it may be useful to isolate the seasonal component from the historical series. This can be done through a very simple procedure.

First of all, for each year, the average monthly demand can be computed. Namely, this can be performed by obtaining the arithmetic average of all the sales values in a given year. The monthly average sales would represent, in an ideal scenario, the sales we could expect in each month if no seasonality could be observed in the demand. By defining as d_{ij} the demand value observed in the generic month i of the generic year j (and by assuming a time horizon of m years composed of 12 months each), the monthly averages sales for a given year j (defined as d_j) can be computed as:

$$\underline{d}_j = \frac{\sum_{i=1}^{12} d_{ij}}{12}$$

Results for this process are shown in Table 2. Subsequently, for each monthly sales value, the deviation from the monthly average d_j can be computed. This can be obtained by dividing each monthly sales value by the respective monthly average for the year under consideration, as shown in the following formula:

$$\delta_{ij} = \frac{d_{ij}}{\underline{d}_j}$$

Results are shown in Table 3. For instance, the value 0.57 observed in January in Year 1 means that sales during that month just equated 57 per cent of the monthly average for that year. Similarly, the value 1.65 observed in August in Year 1 suggests that sales during that month significantly exceeded the monthly average for that year.

Table 2 Average monthly demand determination

	Year 1	Year 2	Year 3
Monthly average	13,083	14,200	15,350

Table 3 Deviations from the averages

#	Month	Year 1	Year 2	Year 3
1	January	0.57	0.54	0.55
2	February	0.47	0.46	0.46
3	March	0.67	0.69	0.68
4	April	0.80	0.79	0.81
5	May	0.96	0.97	0.98
6	June	1.26	1.29	1.30
7	July	1.52	1.58	1.58
8	August	1.65	1.61	1.62
9	September	1.48	1.44	1.43
10	October	1.04	1.05	1.04
11	November	0.75	0.75	0.74
12	December	0.83	0.82	0.83

A look at the third column in Table 3 suggests that some typical behaviour can be identified across years. In other words, deviations do not happen by chance, but are a consolidated phenomenon. It is to be expected that in February sales values will be significantly lower than the monthly average (as deviation values are consistently in the range

[0.46, 0.47]); it seems to be normal to achieve a peak in sales during August (as deviation values are consistently in the range [1.61, 1.65]). This suggests that an indication of the *typical* expected deviation occurring in a given month i could be computed as the arithmetic average of the deviations observed in past years as:

$$\underline{\delta}_i = \frac{\sum_{j=1}^{m} \delta_{ij}}{m}$$

Values obtained from this procedure are shown in the following Table 4. These values can be assumed as seasonal indices, representing the *strength* of the seasonality effect in a typical month of a given year. A value close to 1 (as observable in May and October) suggests

Table 4 Seasonal indices

#	Month	Seasonal indices
1	January	0.55
2	February	0.46
3	March	0.68
4	April	0.80
5	May	0.97
6	June	1.28
7	July	1.56
8	August	1.62
9	September	1.45
10	October	1.04
11	November	0.74
12	December	0.83

that the seasonality effect in that month is negligible; values significantly lower than 1 (as observable in January, February and March) suggest that the seasonality has a negative effect on sales during those months; conversely, values significantly higher than 1 (as observable in the months from June to September) suggest that seasonality has a positive effect on sales during those months.

The computed seasonal indices can be utilized to *remove* the seasonal patterns from the historical series. Indeed, by dividing each monthly sales value from a given month i by the respective seasonal index δ_i, a deseasonalized time series can be obtained, according to the following formula:

$$\bar{d}_{ij} = \frac{d_{ij}}{\underline{\delta}_i}$$

Table 5 Deseasonalized historical series

#	Month	Year 1	Year 2	Year 3
1	January	13,413	13,957	15,226
2	February	13,132	14,208	15,284
3	March	12,898	14,364	15,390
4	April	13,130	14,005	15,506
5	May	12,951	14,185	15,521
6	June	12,870	14,273	15,521
7	July	12,751	14,417	15,506
8	August	13,300	14,039	15,270
9	September	13,324	14,152	15,119
10	October	13,058	14,306	15,266
11	November	13,174	14,249	15,190
12	December	13,162	14,128	15,336

Figure 6 Trend line for deseasonalized series of KTP sales

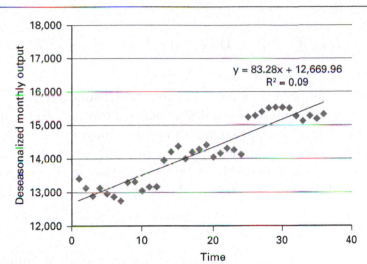

Results deriving from the application of this formula are reported in Table 5. A deseasonalized time series has been obtained: the effect of the seasonal component (represented by seasonal indices) has been removed from the original data. It is now possible to plot this deseasonalized time series, as shown in Figure 6. Having removed the seasonal component from the time series, the trend component is now more clearly identifiable: indeed, the R^2 coefficient is now equal to 0.86. This suggests that, besides the intrinsic seasonality of the sales at KTP, a growing tendency can be observed.

Given the very high value of the coefficient of determination, the trend line derived through a simple linear regression model represents a very good approximation of the deseasonalized sales; most of the variance in monthly values of sales is predictable by using the trend line, apart from some naturally occurring random variations.

For this reason, the trend-line equation can be utilized for predicting future demand values, assuming that the observed tendency will not change in the near future. This can be done, for a given month i of a given year j, by utilizing the following formula:

$$\bar{d}_{ij}^* = 83.28 \cdot [(j - 1) \cdot 12 + i] + 12669.96$$

Results of this process are shown in Table 6, with the Year 4 column (highlighted in bold) showing the predicted values. For instance, the predicted value for January (first month in the fourth year) has been obtained as:

$$\bar{d}^*_{1,4} = 83.28 \cdot [(4-1) \cdot 12 + 1] + 12669.96 = 15751$$

It has to be noticed, however, that this projection may have little meaning, as it is representing a *deseasonalized* forecast. To obtain an actual forecast d^*_{ij} for a given month i of a given year j, the effect of seasonality should be brought back in the time series. This can be easily done by multiplying the obtained forecasts for the respective seasonal indices, as shown in the following formula:

$$d^*_{ij} = \bar{d}^*_{ij} \cdot \underline{\delta}_i$$

For instance, the reseasonalized forecast for the month of January of Year 4 can be computed as:

$$d^*_{1,4} = \bar{d}^*_{1,4} \cdot \underline{\delta}_1 = 15751 \cdot 0.55 = 8690$$

Table 6 Deseasonalized historical series with prediction for Year 4

#	Month	Year 1	Year 2	Year 3	Year 4
1	January	13,413	13,957	15,226	**15,751**
2	February	13,132	14,208	15,284	**15,834**
3	March	12,898	14,364	15,390	**15,918**
4	April	13,130	14,005	15,506	**16,001**
5	May	12,951	14,185	15,521	**16,084**
6	June	12,870	14,273	15,521	**16,168**
7	July	12,751	14,417	15,506	**16,251**
8	August	13,300	14,039	15,270	**16,334**
9	September	13,324	14,152	15,119	**16,417**
10	October	13,058	14,306	15,266	**16,501**
11	November	13,174	14,249	15,190	**16,584**
12	December	13,162	14,128	15,336	**16,667**

Results of this process are shown in the following Table 7; the original historical series is then shown in Figure 7 along with sales predictions for Year 4 (highlighted in bold). It is possible to notice that predictions follow the similar seasonal pattern observed in the original time series. The reliability of the forecast is quite high, given the high coefficient of determination of the deseasonalized trend line that was used to derive the predictions; therefore the company can reasonably use this forecast in the short and medium term, provided that no significant changes will happen in the general business climate and in the operations of the industry.

Table 7 Historical series with predictions for Year 4

#	Month	Year 1	Year 2	Year 3	Year 4
1	January	7,400	7,700	8,400	**8,690**
2	February	6,100	6,600	7,100	**7,356**
3	March	8,800	9,800	10,500	**10,860**
4	April	10,500	11,200	12,400	**12,796**
5	May	12,600	13,800	15,100	**15,648**
6	June	16,500	18,300	19,900	**20,729**
7	July	19,900	22,500	24,200	**25,363**
8	August	21,600	22,800	24,800	**26,528**
9	September	19,300	20,500	21,900	**23,781**
10	October	13,600	14,900	15,900	**17,186**
11	November	9,800	10,600	11,300	**12,337**
12	December	10,900	11,700	12,700	**13,803**

Figure 7 Historical series of KTP sales with predictions for Year 4

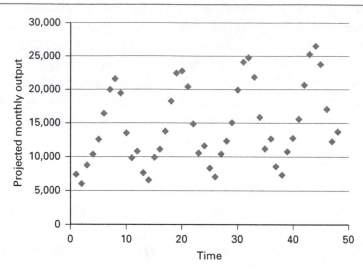

Conclusion

Sales predictions for Year 4 have been formulated for KTP Tyres. The application of the deseasonalization method (combined with the use of trend lines derived through simple linear regression models) provided a way to generate a reliable forecast that can be used by the company for the next year, provided that no major changes will happen in the industry and in the market. Indeed, the biggest limitations of forecasting methodologies based on trend-line approaches is the inability to detect turning points in phenomena (that may determine a change in the trend); for this reason, all the forecasts derived through similar procedures must be used with caution, and always be accompanied by an analysis of wider conditions.

Part two
Logistics and supply chain management

The logistics and supply chain management (SCM) section of this Collection contains 15 cases and extended exercises. There are three overarching themes presented in this section:

- Information technology and its use for improving supplier communications (case 2.2), the tracking and tracing of products (case 2.4) and enabling the performance of SMEs (case 2.7);
- The design of logistical networks including warehousing (case 2.1), retailing (case 2.5), and transportation planning (case 2.15); and
- Sustainability as it pertains to collaboration (case 2.3), fashion supply chains (case 2.9) and human resources in global supply chains (case 2.13).

Additional topics include and transportation related to ports (case 2.6) and third-party logistics service provider strategies (case 2.8); risk and resilience (case 2.11) and financial management and cost reduction (cases 2.10, 2.12 and 2.14). These themes and topics address the challenges noted in the introduction of increasing costs, the demand for quality of logistical and supply chain performance and service, the continuing globalization of supply and markets, risk, disruption and security, and the impact of logistics and SCM on the natural environment.

Professor David B Grant

The maintenance stores dilemma

A case study of Vortex, a maintenance stores operation

Gwynne Richards

AUTHOR BIOGRAPHY

GWYNNE RICHARDS is the Director of Apprise Consulting Ltd.

You are a logistics and warehousing consultant. You have just come out of a three-hour meeting with members of the management team of a maintenance stores operation in the UK. You also took a tour of the stores.

This is what the general manager told you as you were being shown around.

Introduction

Vortex, a manufacturer of hi-tech drilling equipment, has grown significantly over the past few years and it is now running out of storage space for its maintenance stores operation. The number of parts required to service and repair the company's equipment has increased substantially as new equipment and clients have been introduced and therefore space is at a premium.

This is borne out by the amount of floor space taken up by the storage of items ranging from large engines and drill bits, including metal suitcases containing repair equipment.

The engines and drill bits are banded onto pallets and are not stackable.

Returned equipment from various sites across the world are also stored on the floor close to the inbound area.

A second warehouse (Unit B), across the road from the main facility, also contains refurbished items whilst a third warehouse (Unit C), approximately 800 metres away, stores items that are yet to be refurbished together with items that, although deemed obsolete, have yet to be written off and removed. Some of these items are being cannibalized by the engineers on a regular basis.

The business philosophy of the company is to ensure that all their equipment, whether operated in the UK or abroad, has sufficient parts both local to the equipment and at the main warehouse to ensure minimum downtime. The main warehouse is utilized to replenish the local country warehouses and also to provide emergency cover for those parts that are not held at the local warehouses. A great deal of the company's success is based on a near 100 per cent up time for its equipment. However, the introduction of new equipment on a regular basis results in more hi-tech equipment being produced and therefore more sophisticated parts being required. These parts are produced both locally and in manufacturing sites in China, Brazil and Russia.

This can amount to 20 new lines each week as the machinery is very complicated and sophisticated.

In order to achieve competitive prices the procurement director needs to purchase large quantities from suppliers so as to obtain the best possible discounts.

The three directors are experienced in finance, engineering and procurement respectively.

In July 2004 TMS moved into a new warehouse and distribution centre. A 10-year lease was signed on the building. There is an additional plot of land adjacent to the warehouse on which an extension can be built. This will increase total space by at least 25 per cent and possibly up to 30 per cent. However, it will require an extension of the lease for at least a further 10 years. The other local stores sites are on short leases and the company can vacate easily by agreement and by giving three months' notice.

The stores

The stores area in Unit A has a floor area of approximately 3,000 square metres and a mezzanine floor at the far end of the warehouse opposite the inbound door. This is approximately 1,000 square metres and is reached by a set of stairs on the eastern side of the building. The warehouse has an internal height of eight metres to the eves. There is no sprinkler system installed.

A second structure of 1,000 square metres was constructed, with the landlord's permission, three years ago. This is accessed via a low tunnel (2.5 metres high) between the two structures. This also has a single door to the outside yard. The overall height of this structure is only 3.5 metres. This area is utilized for packing and despatch.

In total there is only one inbound door and one outbound door.

It was decided that the best configuration was to use Section 1 for inbound and to store all of the parts. Section 2 is used for packing, staging and despatch. Many of the replenishment orders for the local warehouses are held in this area until sufficient parts are ordered to fill a 20-inch container. Urgent orders are despatched either on a less-than-container load (LCL) basis or air freighted to the required destination.

Section 1 utilizes mobile shelving and standard shelving for the storage of the majority of the parts. These are situated both under the mezzanine and on the mezzanine itself.

A number of filing drawers are also utilized for the storage of very small parts such as nuts, bolts and washers.

Engineers and the localized stores are able to place orders for any quantities of goods. This often necessitates opening bags of screws to count out individual items.

The company operates a stock control system which is updated on a daily basis by manually keying in the quantities received and despatched.

Inbound

The inbound operation receives parts from a number of different suppliers. These are mainly delivered by parcel couriers; however, larger items and those parts manufactured in China, Russia and Brazil are received in 20-inch containers. On average the warehouse receives two containers per month. Some LCL traffic is also received.

Returns arrive on a regular basis although the warehouse is not always informed of their imminent arrival. These can remain in the inbound area for long periods awaiting decisions from quality control (QC) staff and the budget holders as to whether they should be transferred to the workshops for repair, sent to a third-party for repair, transferred to another working site or, if not able to be repaired, set aside for disposal.

All deliveries are checked against purchase orders. The inbound staff physically count each item and once checked the items are set aside either for put-away or are cross-docked and put in a cage awaiting despatch to the relevant country site.

A number of sites are in countries where the customs formalities take a significant amount of time and are very manual. Staff have to ensure that the paperwork is accurate and that all parts destined for a particular country have been labelled correctly and declared on the paperwork. This again takes a significant amount of time.

A large number of items have lot numbers, including screws and fasteners, which are all recorded. This has a knock-on effect on picking with individual lot ID numbers having to be picked. A receipt number from the system is entered onto the delivery note, dated and initialled.

Once the items have been picked the lot number integrity disappears as each individual item cannot be identified by lot number.

Storage

The location system in the warehouse is tied to individual products. There are over 15,222 stock lines on record but only 9,555 lines currently in stock of which only 60 per cent are 'live' – ie the part has appeared on at least one order in the past 12 months.

Every stock item has a fixed location.

Many of the fast moving parts are stored on the mezzanine floor in the filing drawers. This area has shelving and filing drawers which are used to store small parts. The shelving stores work-wear and PCBs in the main. There is available space both on the shelves and in the drawers; however, products are also left above the drawers because some of the allocated locations are not big enough to hold all the stock.

Unit B

This area is currently used to store pallets of lubricant, engineers' backpacks which have been purchased in bulk and items waiting for repair. It has been agreed not to renew the lease on this building which expires in June this year. The office area is used to store refurbished items and items awaiting repair.

Unit A repair area

This is located on the eastern side of the warehouse between the inbound shelving area and the stairs to the mezzanine floor.

It has some shelving but also utilizes the floor space in the centre of the warehouse. Items remain in this area until the repairs are authorized or labelled for disposal.

Warehouse office

This office is used by the manager but is also used for the storage of items such as work-wear, batteries and tools. It is located under the mezzanine floor.

Replenishment

This is carried out on an as and when required basis. As the location quantity falls below a certain level the stock control system produces a replenishment order. This can happen at any time during the day.

Outbound

Each order is picked individually through the use of a paper pick list. Orders are picked manually from the shelving and, depending on the item size, parts are put into trolleys, baskets or carried by hand. Order lead time could be up to five working days. During emergencies engineers were seen to enter the warehouse and pick their own items.

Orders for engineers' work-wear are received on a regular basis. These are shipped to the engineers' home addresses prior to them leaving for site.

Once orders have been picked they are checked, packed, all relevant documentation is produced and the items are either put into the static cages to be consolidated or stacked in the despatch area awaiting the arrival of the freight forwarder's vehicle to take them away to be loaded into a container.

The outbound staff spend a large percentage of their time producing export documentation and thoroughly checking the items prior to despatch. Hazardous products are sent off-site to be packed in crates.

Other information

There are no specific key performance indicators for the warehouse. For example, cycle count adjustments are how many lines are counted in total not how many errors are found; there are no measures around productivity.

The warehouse staff consists of 10 people. Overtime is being worked extensively and labour costs are way above budget. The mechanical handling equipment consists of two counter-balance forklift trucks and two pump-up trucks. Hours of work are from 6 am to 8 pm Monday to Friday with some overtime worked on a Saturday. This is a two-shift system.

One area of concern is the number of urgent requests received which has a detrimental effect on the warehouse operation. Staff are expected to respond immediately. Unfortunately this is not reciprocated when the warehouse require responses on what to do with items awaiting repair, disposal and the like.

Appendix A

Sketch of warehouse

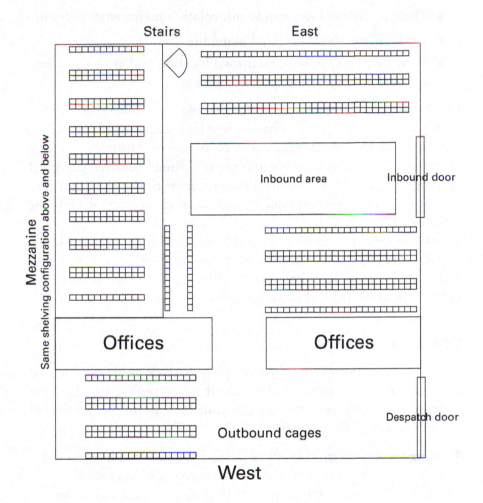

This case study is based on the writer's experience of working with a number of different clients over the years.

For reasons of commercial confidentiality the names of the companies and the data and specific situations have been disguised.

Vortex is a very successful company, but like many such companies its commercial expertise far exceeds its logistics performance.

Despite the new larger warehouse there are still some serious problems:

- There is a limited warehouse information management system.
- Stock information is entered manually.
- Some items do not have their own location and are located on top of the cabinets and mobile shelving.

By March 2013 these influences were having an adverse effect on the warehouse operations. Items had to be block stacked with all the attendant problems of damage and lack of safety. More importantly the warehouse was close to saturation as volumes received exceeded volumes despatched. Service to the engineers was also in decline and security was becoming an issue as higher-value products were being introduced.

It seems clear to you that the immediate priority is to increase the storage capacity and reduce block and floor stacking. But it is also important to consider what the warehouse policy should be in the light of the company's planned growth.

Questions

You have been engaged by the managing director as an experienced logistics consultant to solve the lack of space problem and to put forward a plan to cope with a significant increase in the number of sku over the next three years.

1 Using the information supplied detail the issues you have found that are causing problems for the company and produce a preliminary report detailing what steps you suggest should be taken to solve them.

2 What advice would you give the MD about expanding the size of the warehouse and extending the lease?

3 What other options are available to the MD?

Answers

1 Using the information supplied, detail the issues you have found that are causing problems for the company and produce a preliminary report detailing what steps you suggest should be taken to solve them.

Areas to concentrate on:

1 Items that are yet to be refurbished, together with items that, although deemed obsolete, have yet to be written off and removed.

Produce a plan to remove the obsolete parts as soon as possible.

2 In order to achieve competitive prices the procurement director needs to purchase large quantities from suppliers so as to obtain the best possible discounts.

Look for other suppliers where smaller quantities can be ordered or renegotiate with existing suppliers.

3 The three directors are experienced in finance, engineering and procurement respectively.

Look to employ an experienced supply chain director.

4 Engineers and the localized stores are able to place orders for any quantities of goods. This often necessitates opening bags of screws to count out individual items.

Ensure minimum-order quantities which equal a bag of screws, etc.

5 The company operates a stock-control system which is updated on a daily basis by manually keying in the quantities received and despatched.

Look to introduce a bar-code scanning operation or the use of voice technology to transfer data in real time.

6 Returns arrive on a regular basis although the warehouse is not always informed of their imminent arrival.

Improve the returns process so that there is full visibility.

7 All deliveries are checked against purchase orders. The inbound staff physically count each item and once checked the items are set aside either for put-away or are cross-docked and put in a cage awaiting despatch to the relevant country site.

Introduce a key performance indicator (KPI) for each supplier. Only check those suppliers where there are known issues; also new suppliers until you are certain that they are providing accurate deliveries.

8 During emergencies engineers were seen to enter the warehouse and pick their own items.

This should not be allowed under any circumstances.

9 There are over 15,222 stock lines on record but only 9,555 lines currently in stock of which only 60 per cent are 'live' – ie the part has appeared on at least one order in the past 12 months.

Discuss the disposal of the non-moving parts. Find ways to dispose of the products cost effectively such as returning them to the suppliers.

10 Every stock item has a fixed location.

Consider the introduction of random locations.

11 This office (the warehouse manager's) is used by the manager but is also used for the storage of items such as work-wear, batteries and tools. It is located under the mezzanine floor.

Re-locate the items to shelving or potentially invest in a carousel to hold the smaller, more expensive parts.

12 Orders for engineers' work-wear are received on a regular basis. These are shipped to the engineers' home addresses prior to them leaving for site.

Ship these items to the site with the parts orders as opposed to the engineers' homes.

2 What advice would you give the MD about expanding the size of the warehouse and extending the lease?

Suggest that building at present is not the answer. By introducing the above solutions and removing obsolete and non-moving stock there should not be a requirement to extend the warehouse for a number of years.

Introduce carousels, use random as opposed to fixed locations and erect racking to take a number of pallets that are currently stored on the ground.

3 What other options are available to the MD?

One potential solution would be to outsource the operation to a third-party logistics company.

Other potential areas

Introduce training into the warehouse.

Communication in business practice
Its central role in supply chain management

Xia Zhu

AUTHOR BIOGRAPHY

XIA ZHU is a Senior Lecturer in Marketing at Sheffield Hallam University.

Introduction

Wonder Trade is a small company in PTfield that makes metal trolleys. They have been dealing with CPaints (a paint supplier) for eight years. CPaints is a large reputable company. A representative from CPaints rings Wonder Trade about once every two or three months to check whether everything is running smoothly or not. In a period of eight years, Wonder Trade has seen a representative from CPaints only once. The last representative who rang is the fourth representative that Wonder Trade has spoken to during the eight years. The representative that Wonder Trade originally met left a long time ago. Wonder Trade never receives any information of any special offers.

Flow of information

Eight months ago, Wonder Trade placed an order with CPaints who promised a delivery in two days' time. On the supposed delivery date, the production planning manager of Wonder Trade rang CPaints asking about the delivery. CPaints said that the delivery was going to be made the next morning. CPaints did not inform Wonder Trade about whether the order had been despatched or the delivery had been delayed. Wonder Trade would have appreciated CPaints calling to explain that the delivery was going to be one day later.

Six months ago, Wonder Trade placed another order with CPaints who agreed that the customer would collect the paint themselves. Wonder Trade sent a driver to CPaints at 8 o'clock in the morning to collect the paint. Wonder Trade's driver had to wait there for three hours because the paint would not be ready until after 11 o'clock. Andy (the logistics controller of Wonder Trade) said: 'It cost us time and money – a driver, a wagon, and a unit, three hours lost. CPaints could have rung us that morning and said this paint was not going to be ready until 11 o'clock. We could then have made alternative arrangements: rang the driver and sent him somewhere else instead.'

Sharing information

Three months ago, Wonder Trade delivered steel parts to CPaints to be powder coated. The finished parts were shipped as deck cargo to a factory on an island in the middle of the Indian Ocean. Wonder Trade's customers complained about the quality after they received the items: they were rusty. Wonder Trade sent complaints to CPaints for investigation. The customer service manager responded to Wonder Trade's complaint that the steel parts came in a poor state, and the pre-treatment was not good enough. No information had been given as to what would happen to the items after they left CPaints. Having spent six weeks as deck cargo on a ship, the steel parts received the best salt spray test in the world, and they went rusty. The customer service manager further explained that if Wonder Trade had told CPaints that the items were to be shipped out to the Indian Ocean by the cheapest method, deck cargo on a ship, CPaints would have immediately known that the powder coating they offered was inadequate. The customer service manager of CPaints commented: 'We make different finishes on one product: this will last a year; that will last five years; those will last ten years, at different prices. I am offering you this paint finish and that is the effect. If you need something else to be done, this is our offer.' Wonder Trade was not aware of different offers available. Wonder Trade were unhappy about the investigation and said: 'Our customers are very upset and they should not be affected.'

Keeping promises

More recently, Wonder Trade was very frustrated with an enquiry they sent to CPaints. The enquiry was sent to CPaints on a Monday for a quote of price and delivery on a metal finishing job with a deadline of the following Thursday. On the following Thursday at 12.50, Andy (the logistics controller of Wonder Trade) rang CPaints about the quote. A lady at CPaints promised that she would ring Andy back in half an hour. But after 40 minutes, at 13.30, nothing had happened. Andy rang her back but had to speak to somebody else, because the lady he spoke to was not there and her colleague explained that she always had lunch between 13.00 and 14.00. To Wonder Trade, CPaints was trying to avoid giving them an answer because they did not have one, instead of being honest and telling them, 'I am trying to get an answer and I will ring you back as soon as I can'. On the other side, Wonder Trade's contract manager was sitting in a meeting with a client who was going to spend £300,000 on a job and wanted to know when he was going to get his metal trolleys. The contract manager was waiting for the answer from Andy. Andy was going to ring the contract manager at 13.30, because the lady from CPaints had said that she would ring him at 13.20 with an answer. Wonder Trade's contract manager was in an awkward position because he has not heard from Andy. When Andy finally got on the phone, the lady from CPaints promised again that she was going to ring Andy at 8.30 the next morning. At 8.45, Andy had to ring her because she has not phoned him but she was not there because she did not start work until 9.00. Andy ended up getting hold of her at about 9.15 in the morning and complained about how CPaints treated him as a customer.

Wonder Trade made the decision that they were not going to deal with CPaints anymore, and went on various websites to search for alternative suppliers.

Disclaimer

This case recounts a real-life business situation. For reasons of commercial confidentiality the names of the companies and the data and specific situations have been changed.

Questions

1 Identify obstacles to coordination in supply chain management.

2 What is the role of communication in a business-to-business context?

3 What is the impact of communication in supply chain management?

4 How can communication be improved in a business-to-business context?

Answers

1 Identify obstacles to coordination in supply chain management.

- the number of people involved in business practice;
- not knowing to whom one is speaking;
- the lack of information sharing;
- not understanding customer needs and requirements;
- irresponsiveness;
- dishonesty and not keeping promises.

2 What is the role of communication in a business-to-business context?

Communication is crucial for exchanging information in a timely manner in order to facilitate business interactions such as placing or tracing orders, checking the progress of jobs, delivery time, requesting an urgent delivery, arranging a vehicle for delivery or negotiating price.

3 What is the impact of communication in supply chain management?

- Communication is linked to buyer and supplier performance. Information sharing influences the collaboration in a buyer–supplier relationship. Suppliers' work is dependent on the information that customers provide. The flow of information impacts on suppliers' as well as on customers' production and planning.

- Good information exchange can reduce the complexity of processing orders, facilitate job completion, provide assurance to customers of the orders undertaken and smooth the business process.

- Suppliers communicate with customers to express care and support. Firms are likely to have more frequent communication with their best customer than an average buyer.

- Overall, communication impacts on the customer experience, and can be viewed as a potentially powerful tool for relationship management.

4 *How can communication be improved in a business-to-business context?*

- Face-to-face communication: face-to-face communication is highly valued by both suppliers and customers as it enhances mutual understanding.

- Frequency of contact: the frequency of communication depends on customer needs. Neglecting customers and insufficient communication may cause business-to-business relationships to deteriorate.

- Sharing information: the amount of information customers share with suppliers impacts on suppliers' service to customers.

- Responsiveness: customers' demands for suppliers to be responsive are due to a domino effect, ie the customers' clients are waiting for an answer which is based on upstream suppliers' reply.

- Accessibility: being able to get hold of supplier employees instead of having to go through an automated menu system on the telephone.

- Honesty: customers appreciate suppliers being open and honest with customers, such as admitting the impossibility of meeting the deadline that customers want. Customers need suppliers' accurate and honest information in order to plan production, and it has a domino effect on customers' clients.

Collaborative distribution considering economic and environmental performance

Vahid Mirzabeiki

AUTHOR BIOGRAPHY

DR VAHID MIRZABEIKI is a Senior Research Fellow at the Supply Chain Research Centre of Cranfield School of Management, Cranfield University.

Introduction

Green logistics, as the integration of environmental thinking into all the processes of logistics and transportation of cargo through the distribution networks, is becoming increasingly important in the strategy planning of logistics companies. In the most developed countries, road is the dominant transport mode and therefore it shapes a significant part of the overall environmental impact of logistics.

Increasing the filling rate of trucks is a very effective sustainability improvement, as it can create both environmental and economic benefits for the performance of the companies. The environmental results of improving utilization of vehicles, ie by sending consolidated shipments to multiple destinations rather than single shipments to each of them, include reducing emissions, traffic level and noise pollution.

Consolidating shipments can lead to reducing the total number of running kilometres by trucks and also the amount of CO_2 emissions. Shared deliveries can provide advantages for the transport providers and also for the companies whose freight is consolidated; ie the transport provider can offer them a relatively lower price for the consolidated transportation because by doing this they can save full truckloads. It means that they can allocate the saved truck to another trip, and make more profit.

Company

The company Craft Gardening Equipment (CGE) is a supplier of gardening equipment, with its central distribution centre in Cologne, Germany. Their customers are retailers of building and gardening products located in different European countries including Austria, the Czech Republic, Italy and Poland.

Strategic decisions made by the managing board of the company have emphasized making the operations of the company more efficient and also more eco-friendly by reducing the amount of emissions through their distribution network. The managing board believes that such an improvement will not only lead to savings on the cost of transportation, but it will also improve their reputation in the market as a socially responsible company. The company has identified logistics as a department that has potential for a high level of contribution to the new strategy. An obvious action to be taken by the logistics department for contributing to the strategy is improving the filling rate of the trucks, ie reducing the empty space on the trucks transporting the products of the company from their central distribution centre in Cologne to their customers in European countries. The management group believes that even if the logistics department is currently performing well, there is still potential for improvements. Such improvements would be very important, as they have the potential to advance both the environmental and financial performance of the company.

Discussion

After reading the description above, assume that you are the manager of the logistics department of CGE, responsible for arranging all the logistics operations of the company. When planning for the requested improvements to your department, you should start doing some analysis to find appropriate solutions contributing to the strategy of the company. Looking into the shipments list for a specific period of time as a sample should provide a general picture of the current situation of the logistics department regarding the filling rates of the trucks. You are therefore provided Excel sheets containing the data about the shipments in the time period 3–10 January 2014. It is a good sample as the transport in this period is very similar to the average weekly shipments during the year. This data is available in Table 1 in the appendix. In the table you have a list of the shipments from the central distribution centre of the company located in Cologne to different cities in Austria, Italy, the Czech Republic and Poland. Destinations are indicated by the names of the countries, cities and their zip codes. For every shipment the specification of the freight including the weight, volume and length of the freight is indicated. The last column in the table indicates the category of the freight: express shipments, consolidated cargo (when the cargo of the company is consolidated to the cargo from another company being shipped to an area near the destination), full truckloads (FTL) and less-than-truckloads (LTL) cargo.

Freight forwarders are contacted to arrange the shipments of the FTL and LTL cargo, and therefore the logistics department of CGE has the responsibility for administrating these shipments, saving the logistics costs for the company. The express deliveries, including small items to be delivered very fast, are sent by the post company. Planning and operating the consolidated deliveries is outsourced to a third party logistics service provider, as they can arrange the consolidation of shipments because they have many other customers to consolidate their cargo to CGE's freight.

By looking into the data you should provide answers to the questions in the following section, regarding the potential improvements that you can make to your logistics operations.

When making any decision, you should always bear in mind your main commitment as the manager of the logistics department to the

Table 1 Shipments list

Shipping date	Departure location		Destination location Country/zip code/ city		Nr of pallets	Nr of packages	Weight (Kg)	Volume (m³)	Load length (m)	Type of shipment
03.01.2014	DE 51105 Cologne	AT	9500	VILLAC	24	0	3,998.10	31.56	9.6	LTL
03.01.2014	DE 51105 Cologne	AT	6300	WÖRGL	20	4	3,952.90	29.9	8	LTL
03.01.2014	DE 51105 Cologne	AT	2700	WIENER NEUSTADT	26	3	5,032.80	40.01	10.4	LTL
03.01.2014	DE 51105 Cologne	AT	8042	GRAZ OST	27	4	5,735.70	40.97	10.8	LTL
03.01.2014	DE 51105 Cologne	AT	1030	VIENNA	23	2	5,058.80	36.61	9.2	LTL
03.01.2014	DE 51105 Cologne	AT	8295	ST. JOHANN IN DER HAIDE	4	1	471.5	7.99	1.6	Consolidated
03.01.2014	DE 51105 Cologne	AT	8753	FOHNSDORF	21	1	4,317.60	29.93	8.4	LTL
03.01.2014	DE 51105 Cologne	AT	1220	VIENNA	36	1	7,131.10	63.84	14.4	FTL
06.01.2014	DE 51105 Cologne	AT	8051	GRAZ-NORD	0	2	10.5	0.12	0	Consolidated
06.01.2014	DE 51105 Cologne	AT	1220	VIENNA	2	1	162.5	0.72	0.8	Consolidated
06.01.2014	DE 51105 Cologne	AT	8054	GRAZ - WEST	0	1	4.6	0.04	0	Consolidated
06.01.2014	DE 51105 Cologne	AT	8431	GRALLA	1	0	37.8	0.45	0.4	Consolidated
06.01.2014	DE 51105 Cologne	AT	6020	INNSBRUCK	1	2	402.1	1.11	0.4	Consolidated
06.01.2014	DE 51105 Cologne	AT	7344	STOOB-SUED	0	1	0.92	0.01	0	Consolidated
06.01.2014	DE 51105 Cologne	AT	2500	BADEN	0	4	23.5	0.24	0	Consolidated
06.01.2014	DE 51105 Cologne	AT	7501	UNTERWART	1	1	87.6	0.43	0.4	Consolidated
06.01.2014	DE 51105 Cologne	AT	1030	VIENNA	0	2	22.1	0.14	0	Consolidated
06.01.2014	DE 51105 Cologne	AT	9029	KLAGENFURT	0	5	21.2	0.25	0	Consolidated
06.01.2014	DE 51105 Cologne	AT	9800	SPITTAL/DRAU	1	0	79	0.58	0.4	Consolidated
06.01.2014	DE 51105 Cologne	AT	8431	GRALLA	32	4	5,514.30	51.22	12.8	FTL
06.01.2014	DE 51105 Cologne	AT	6460	IMST	16	2	3,581.30	24.83	6.4	LTL

Table 1 (continued)

Shipping date	Departure location		Destination location Country/zip code/ city		Nr of pallets	Nr of packages	Weight (Kg)	Volume (m³)	Load length (m)	Type of shipment
06.01.2014	DE 51105 Cologne	AT	9300	ST. VEIT	12	3	2,876.20	18.23	4.8	LTL
06.01.2014	DE 51105 Cologne	AT	9800	SPITTAL/DRAU	15	4	3,433.60	21.87	6	LTL
06.01.2014	DE 51105 Cologne	AT	6380	ST. JOHANN I.T.	15	1	3,386.50	21.96	6	LTL
06.01.2014	DE 51105 Cologne	AT	6020	INNSBRUCK	34	3	6,644.90	55.65	13.6	FTL
06.01.2014	DE 51105 Cologne	AT	9029	KLAGENFURT	33	2	6,237.90	51.86	13.2	FTL
06.01.2014	DE 51105 Cologne	AT	8054	GRAZ - WEST	38	0	7,524.90	62.36	15.2	FTL
07.01.2014	DE 51105 Cologne	CZ	470 01	CESKA LIPA-LADA	0	1	17.4	0.07	0	Consolidated
07.01.2014	DE 51105 Cologne	AT	2334	VOESENDORF	0	1	7	0.06	0	Consolidated
07.01.2014	DE 51105 Cologne	AT	2700	WIENER NEUSTADT	1	0	123	0.41	0.4	Consolidated
07.01.2014	DE 51105 Cologne	AT	8330	FELDBACH	0	1	6.4	0.06	0	Consolidated
07.01.2014	DE 51105 Cologne	AT	8295	ST. JOHANN IN DER HAIDE	1	0	82.6	0.29	0.4	Consolidated
07.01.2014	DE 51105 Cologne	AT	9400	WOLFSBERG	24	2	4,871.70	37.41	9.6	LTL
08.01.2014	DE 51105 Cologne	CZ	796 07	PROSTEJOV	0	2	24.7	0.09	0	Consolidated
08.01.2014	DE 51105 Cologne	CZ	143 00	PRAHA - 4	1	0	61.3	0.36	0.4	Consolidated
08.01.2014	DE 51105 Cologne	CZ	301 01	PLZEN	1	0	101	0.64	0.4	Consolidated
08.01.2014	DE 51105 Cologne	AT	6300	WÖRGL	1	2	60.4	0.62	0.4	Consolidated
08.01.2014	DE 51105 Cologne	AT	9500	VILLAC	1	0	72.1	1.73	0.4	Consolidated
08.01.2014	DE 51105 Cologne	AT	9400	WOLFSBERG	3	0	348.7	6.3	1.2	Consolidated
08.01.2014	DE 51105 Cologne	AT	6380	ST. JOHANN I.T.	1	0	46.9	1.73	0.4	Consolidated
08.01.2014	DE 51105 Cologne	AT	6020	INNSBRUCK	6	2	836	13.88	2.4	Consolidated
08.01.2014	DE 51105 Cologne	AT	6460	IMST	1	0	72.1	1.73	0.4	Consolidated
08.01.2014	DE 51105 Cologne	AT	6300	WÖRGL	3	0	273.5	4.46	1.2	Consolidated

Table 1 *(continued)*

Shipping date	Departure location		Destination location Country/zip code/ city		Nr of pallets	Nr of packages	Weight (Kg)	Volume (m³)	Load length (m)	Type of shipment
08.01.2014	DE 51105 Cologne	AT	1220	VIENNA	6	0	710.8	12.16	2.4	Consolidated
08.01.2014	DE 51105 Cologne	AT	8295	ST. JOHANN IN DER HAIDE	0	1	12.6	0.18	0	Consolidated
08.01.2014	DE 51105 Cologne	AT	1030	VIENNA	4	1	591.9	7.48	1.6	Consolidated
08.01.2014	DE 51105 Cologne	AT	8042	GRAZ OST	2	0	228.8	3.41	0.8	Consolidated
09.01.2014	DE 51105 Cologne	AT	1030	VIENNA	2	0	265.7	1.58	0.8	Consolidated
08.01.2014	DE 51105 Cologne	IT	41100	MODENA (MO)	0	1	2.49	0	0	EXPRESS
08.01.2014	DE 51105 Cologne	AT	7501	UNTERWART	0	1	1.99	0	0	EXPRESS
08.01.2014	DE 51105 Cologne	CZ	400 04	TRMICE	0	1	5.2	0	0	EXPRESS
09.01.2014	DE 51105 Cologne	AT	9029	KLAGENFURT	7	1	717.4	11.47	2.8	Consolidated
09.01.2014	DE 51105 Cologne	AT	7501	UNTERWART	4	3	780.5	10.76	1.6	Consolidated
10.01.2014	DE 51105 Cologne	AT	8051	GRAZ-NORD	9	0	1,072.70	14.11	3.6	LTL
10.01.2014	DE 51105 Cologne	AT	8054	GRAZ - WEST	6	2	884.6	14.74	2.4	Consolidated
10.01.2014	DE 51105 Cologne	AT	8431	GRALLA	5	1	661.9	10.92	2	Consolidated
10.01.2014	DE 51105 Cologne	AT	9500	VILLAC	0	1	17	0.13	0	Consolidated
10.01.2014	DE 51105 Cologne	AT	9800	SPITTAL/DRAU	0	1	17	0.13	0	Consolidated
10.01.2014	DE 51105 Cologne	AT	8431	GRALLA	1	0	71.5	0.72	0.4	Consolidated
10.01.2014	DE 51105 Cologne	AT	9300	ST. VEIT	0	1	17	0.13	0	Consolidated
10.01.2014	DE 51105 Cologne	AT	9400	WOLFSBERG	0	1	17	0.13	0	Consolidated
10.01.2014	DE 51105 Cologne	AT	6380	ST. JOHANN I.T.	1	0	55	0.58	0.4	Consolidated
10.01.2014	DE 51105 Cologne	AT	6020	INNSBRUCK	1	0	105	0.67	0.4	Consolidated
10.01.2014	DE 51105 Cologne	AT	8753	FOHNSDORF	4	0	411.1	5.28	1.6	Consolidated
13.01.2014	DE 51105 Cologne	AT	6460	IMST	1	0	71.5	0.67	0.4	Consolidated

Table 1 (*continued*)

Shipping date	Departure location		Destination location Country/zip code/ city		Nr of pallets	Nr of packages	Weight (Kg)	Volume (m³)	Load length (m)	Type of shipment
10.01.2014	DE 51105 Cologne	AT	6300	WÖRGL	1	0	55	0.58	0.4	Consolidated
10.01.2014	DE 51105 Cologne	AT	2700	WIENER NEUSTADT	5	0	441	7.3	2	Consolidated
10.01.2014	DE 51105 Cologne	AT	1220	VIENNA	1	0	55	0.38	0.4	Consolidated
13.01.2014	DE 51105 Cologne	AT	1030	VIENNA	1	0	105	1.44	0.4	Consolidated
13.01.2014	DE 51105 Cologne	AT	8042	GRAZ OST	1	0	55	0.58	0.4	Consolidated
10.01.2014	DE 51105 Cologne	AT	8051	GRAZ-NORD	1	0	1,020.30	0.79	0.4	Consolidated
10.01.2014	DE 51105 Cologne	AT	8431	GRALLA	1	0	1,020.30	0.79	0.4	Consolidated
10.01.2014	DE 51105 Cologne	AT	7344	STOOB-SUED	1	0	1,020.30	0.82	0.4	Consolidated
10.01.2014	DE 51105 Cologne	AT	7501	UNTERWART	1	0	1,020.30	0.79	0.4	Consolidated
10.01.2014	DE 51105 Cologne	AT	7210	MATTERSBURG	0	1	6.3	0.02	0	Consolidated
10.01.2014	DE 51105 Cologne	CZ	779 00	OLOMOUC	3	0	690.1	3.27	1.2	Consolidated
10.01.2014	DE 51105 Cologne	CZ	735 64	Havirov	1	0	58	0.69	0.4	Consolidated
10.01.2014	DE 51105 Cologne	PL	43-100	TYCHY	0	1	11.8	0.34	0	Consolidated
10.01.2014	DE 51105 Cologne	PL	52-326	WROCLAW	0	2	16.78	0.77	0	Consolidated
10.01.2014	DE 51105 Cologne	PL	02-180	WARSAW	0	2	14.8	0.68	0	Consolidated
10.01.2014	DE 51105 Cologne	PL	02-801	WARSAW	0	3	24.2	0.72	0	Consolidated
10.01.2014	DE 51105 Cologne	PL	03-576	WARSAW	1	0	43	1.44	0.4	Consolidated
10.01.2014	DE 51105 Cologne	PL	31-876	KRAKOW	0	2	16.7	0.88	0	Consolidated
10.01.2014	DE 51105 Cologne	PL	80-298	GDANSK	0	3	24	1.26	0	Consolidated
10.01.2014	DE 51105 Cologne	PL	30-663	KRAKOW	0	1	14.7	0.5	0	Consolidated
10.01.2014	DE 51105 Cologne	PL	20-329	LUBLIN	0	2	16.7	0.48	0	Consolidated
10.01.2014	DE 51105 Cologne	PL	25-558	KIELCE	0	1	11.8	0.34	0	Consolidated

customers of the company, ie delivering the products on time and in the right amount and quality. In order to keep the level of service standard, your alternative suggested improvements are not allowed to result in a delivery time of more than 5 days later than what is stated in the table.

There are different types of trucks used for road freight transportation in Europe. You can obtain information on their types and sizes by referring to the websites of some of the main European logistics companies, like DHL or DB Schenker for example. Try using the search words 'loading space' or 'truck types' on Google or on the companies' websites.

'Euro pallets' are typically used for shipments (1.2 m (length) × 0.8 m (width)). The height is dependent on the cargo. Note that for this type of cargo, the pallets are non-stackable, ie they cannot be placed on top of each other in order to prevent potential damage to the packages.

Feel free to make reasonable assumptions when you think that some specific information for providing answers to the questions is missing.

Questions

1 Calculate the average percentage of the volume-wise filling rate of your trucks, considering that the type of trucks used for the FLT, LTL and consolidated transport is the mega trailer with dimensions of 13.6 m (L) × 2.45 m (W) × 3 m (H), and a capacity of 90 m^3 of cargo volume.

2 What types of solutions do you suggest for improving the filling rate of the trucks?

3 Assuming that for every kilometre of transportation, the amount of CO_2 emissions for the empty mega trailer truck is 0.77 kg/km and for the full truck is 1.10 kg/km, how much are your CO_2 emissions savings by implementing your suggested improvement measures? (You can assume a linear relation between the filling rate of the truck and the amount of emissions generated by it in terms of kilograms.)

4 How much will the company save in terms of transportation cost by implementing your suggested improvement measures for the shipments in the given time period?

5 You will probably have heard about the triple-bottom-line model (3BL) for sustainability in supply chain and logistics management, describing the sustainability in three dimensions of society, environment and economy. The core discussion regarding 3BL is that the sustainability strategies implemented by the companies last a long time and become a part of their overall strategy, if they bring financial benefits to the company, besides the social and environmental benefits. Can you explain how the 3BL aspects of the logistics sustainability performance are improved here by clarifying and explaining the benefits of such a logistics improvement for the economy of the company, for society and for the environment?

Answers

1 Calculate the average percentage of the volume-wise filling rate of your trucks, considering that the type of trucks used for the FLT, LTL and consolidated transport is the mega trailer with dimensions of 13.6 m (L) × 2.45 m (W) × 3 m (H), and a capacity of 90 m³ of cargo volume.

Create an Excel sheet based on the available data. For each of the shipments divide the volume of the cargo by the capacity of the trucks. Multiply this number by 100 to find the percentage of the filling rate for that shipment. Calculate the same number for the whole rows of the table. By using Excel calculate the average of the filling rates of the shipments.

For example, if we have a cargo that has the weight of 5,700 kg, volume of 41 m³ and length of 10.8 m, the volume-wise filling rate of the truck is: $41/90 = 0.45 = 45\%$.

2 What types of solutions do you suggest for improving the filling rate of the trucks?

You should consider the technical limitations, eg the size of trucks you are using and the limitations for placement of the pallets on each other. Your commitment to your customer for on-time deliveries in the right amount and quality is the most important aspect to be considered.

In considering all these limitations, be aware that heavy and low volume cargo are always the best match to be consolidated with light and high volume items, eg cotton and steel go well with each other.

Therefore you need to calculate the density of the cargo (the ratio of weight/volume) and then if possible try to consolidate the high-density cargo with the low-density cargo to get the highest possible level of filling rate on your trucks. You can use different types of standard trucks for freight road transportation in Europe as a solution for improving your filling rate, but you should always consider that having frequent transportation of smaller trucks, even with a higher filling rate, might be more expensive for your company in the long term, as you will be charged more for the fixed cost of every trip and also you might produce more emissions since you are increasing the running kilometres of your vehicles.

3 Assuming that for every kilometre of transportation, the amount of CO_2 emissions for the empty mega trailer truck is 0.77 kg/km and for the full truck is 1.10 kg/km, how much are your CO_2 emissions savings by implementing your suggested improvement measures? (You can assume a linear relation between the filling rate of the truck and the amount of emissions generated by it in terms of kilograms.)

The amount of emissions per kilogram for the mega trailer used for the transportation of the cargo mentioned in the suggested answer for question above (45% full truck) is calculated as:

$$X = .45 \times (1.1 - 0.77) + 0.77 = 0.92 \text{ kg/km}$$

By multiplying this number by the distance to the destination in kilometres, you will find the amount of emissions in kilograms for this trip.

If you suggest using smaller trucks, then the amount of emissions per kilometre will be relatively lower. You can find information on the amount of emissions by kilometre for different types of trucks on their manufacturers' websites. Therefore try to use those real numbers for your calculations.

After making your suggested solutions you can then calculate the savings on your CO_2 emissions.

4 How much will the company save in terms of transportation cost by implementing your suggested improvement measures for the shipments in the given time period?

When pricing for transportation, logistics companies usually consider the weight of the cargo, but they always consider the volume (the space taken by the cargo) and the loading metre or LDM (area on the floor of truck occupied by the pallet) in their calculations as well. Therefore, by converting the volume and the LDM into weight, they have three size dimensions of the cargo in kilograms. They charge the company based on the largest number in kilograms among these three dimensions.

For example, a full load of cotton might be light in terms of weight but it will occupy almost the whole space of the trucks. Therefore when it comes to space-taking cargo (cargo with low density), then the freight companies convert the volume of the freight to weight by multiplying it by a number which varies for different companies (eg 200 is used frequently).

Another dimension they consider when pricing for transportation is based on the loading metres (LDM), which is a criterion for measuring the surface of the truck occupied by the cargo. They use this criterion because if you do not use the height of the truck, ie when loading non-stackable cargo, they make sure that you are charged for the whole space in the truck because you have made it non-usable anyway. For example, if you have a Euro pallet, with dimensions of 1.2 m × 0.8 m, then the area occupied on the floor of the truck by this pallet is 1.2 × 0.8 = 0.96 m² divided by the width of the truck (2.4 m for standard truck). Therefore the LDM for a Euro pallet becomes 0.96/2.4 = 0.4 loading metres. This number is multiplied by the constant (eg 1000) to be converted into weight in kilograms. Therefore a non-stackable Euro pallet will be calculated as 0.4×1000 = 400 kg.

Create an Excel sheet based on the available data. For each of the shipments assess the volume, weight and LDM of the cargo, and identify which one is the largest, to be considered as the amount of cargo when calculating the cost.

As mentioned before, you can convert the volume and LDM to weight as: 1 m³ = 200 kg, 1 LDM (load metre) = 1000 kg.

For example, if we have a cargo that has a weight of 5,700 kg, volume of 41 m³ and length of 10.8 m the logistics company makes these calculations to identify which weight is to be selected when charging you:

The size of the cargo in terms of weight: 5,700 kg
The size of the cargo in terms of volume: 41×200 = 8,200 kg
The size of the cargo in terms of LDM: 10.8×1000 = 10,800 kg

Therefore the LDM size of the cargo is the largest among all the three size measurements and the size of cargo is calculated based on this size.

When calculating the price you will be charged for transportation, usually companies have tables that indicate prices per distance and weight of cargo. You can use the table below, which is a very simplified form of such tables, to make your calculations easier. Note that for every country in Europe there are different transportation prices but to make your calculations easy, you can use the same price throughout the whole Europe in this case.

Table 2 Price of transportation for the company based on distance and weight of cargo (the prices are fictional and the table is a simplified version of the ones used by transport companies).

	Less than 500 km	500–1000 km	1000–1500 km
Less than 1000 kg	126	147	156
Between 1000–8000 kg	1130	1450	2314
More than 8000–16000 kg	2003	2570	4099

Therefore, for the cargo mentioned above, assuming that it will travel to a destination that is located 800 km away, the price of transportation will become €2,570.

You can make these calculations for all the shipments easily by creating the formulas in Microsoft Excel.

You can calculate the cost of transportation based on your suggested solution. To present your results, create a table as below and compare your solution (to be) to the current situation (as is), in terms of number of FLTs, distance travelled by trucks, emission, cost of transport and filling rate.

Table 3

Situation	As is	To be	Difference
Number of FLTs			
Distance (km)			
Emission (kg)			
Cost of transport (€)			
Filling rate (%)			

5 You will probably have heard about the triple-bottom-line model (3BL) for sustainability in supply chain and logistics management, describing the sustainability in three dimensions of society, environment and economy. The core discussion regarding 3BL is that the sustainability strategies implemented by the companies last a long time and become a part of their overall strategy, if they bring financial benefits to the company, besides the social and environmental benefits. Can you explain how the 3BL aspects of the logistics sustainability performance are improved here by clarifying and explaining the benefits of such a logistics improvement for the economy of the company, for society and for the environment?

The answer is related to your suggested solution, which you should have summarized in the table used for answering the previous question. In your table you should identify how much you have saved on CO_2 emissions and how much savings you have made on transportation costs for the company. If you have only made savings on the cost of transportation while producing more emissions, then you are not improving the environmental performance of the company. On the other hand if you are making environmental savings while increasing the transportation cost of the company, or making late deliveries to your customers, then your solution is not going to be acceptable to the managers of the company.

The best solutions are the ones that lead to both environmental and economic improvements at the same time. But in the real world it is not always very easy to create such situations. Discuss.

Data sharing between supply chain actors
Advantages and disadvantages

Vahid Mirzabeiki

AUTHOR BIOGRAPHY

DR VAHID MIRZABEIKI is a Senior Research Fellow at the Supply Chain Research Centre of Cranfield School of Management, Cranfield University.

Introduction

There is high demand for continuous and on-time delivery of car-body components to the manufacturing lines of car-assembly factories, due to the short buffer time between arrival of products to the car factory and usage of them in their manufacturing lines. It leads to high-speed lean production, by reducing the total inventory cost of the products. If the car-body components arrive late to the assembly factory, the company can risk late delivery of the finished car to the final consumer, causing negative financial consequences. This can be a serious risk for the reputation of a car-manufacturing company in the very competitive automotive market.

In the case of railway transportation in automotive supply chains, when a train departs from a car-body components factory to a car assembly factory, the different partners in such a logistics network should collaborate. Such supply chain partners include the senders and receivers of the products, transportation companies, third-party logistics providers, government authorities and other types of stakeholders of the supply chains depending on the type of products and the logistics networks. Each of these partners or organizations is interested in monitoring the condition and location of different levels of transported objects on the train, as their moving assets. These objects include the rail wagons, containers inside the wagons, racks and pallets inside the containers, and the products inside the racks and pallets.

Track and trace (T&T) is a function that enables companies to know the location of the objects, their movement history and even their condition. When T&T applies to the movement of objects between multiple supply-chain partners, eg railway transportation of car-body components in this case, it requires the collaboration of supply chain partners in the form of sharing hardware, software and data. This case study investigates the body components supply chain of Volvo cars in Sweden and illustrates how collaborative T&T might take place between the stakeholders of an automotive supply chain.

Volvo's collaborative T&T system

The Volvo Car Corporation has started using a collaborative radio frequency identification (RFID)-enabled T&T system in order to monitor the location of their cargo, shipped from their body components manufacturing factory in Olofström in southern Sweden to its car assembly factories located near Gothenburg, a city in the west of Sweden.

This T&T system is built on the foundations of an RFID data-capturing and sharing system designed to control the usage and wear-and-tear of the rail tracks in the Swedish railway network. It was created and is managed by the Swedish Transport Administration which is the government authority that owns the country's railway infrastructure. The Swedish Transport Administration has installed

RFID readers alongside the railway tracks to enable T&T of rail wagons owned by transport operators. To enable the system to work, the rail wagons are equipped with a uniquely coded RFID tag. The system stores the RFID event data captured by the readers from the RFID tags of wagons of railway transportation companies. Whenever a wagon passes by the RFID reader captures data including the time, the date, its location and its direction. Every RFID reading station on the railway network has sensors that check the temperature of the axles and wheels of the wagons to check that they are running under safe conditions. By combining the RFID data of each wagon and the data from the sensors, the technical condition of each wagon can be monitored individually.

The data captured is stored in a central database owned by the Swedish Transport Administration and it can be shared or made accessible through the internet. This data is integrated with the data collected by the RFID readers inside the production facilities of the body components factory in Olofström and the car assembly factory in Gothenburg, thus enabling T&T of rail wagons through the whole Volvo Cars body components supply chain. In other words, by doing this, the required data for enabling the function of the T&T system is fed into the system by readers of different organizations, at different locations through the supply chain. Figure 1 illustrates the information architecture of the Volvo Cars collaborative T&T system. As you

Figure 1 The information architecture of the Volvo Cars body components supply chain

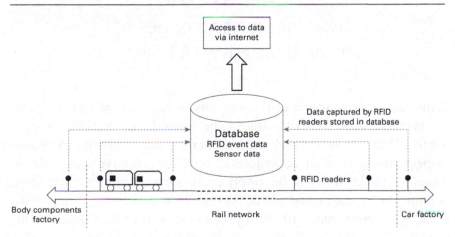

can see, the data captured by the RFID readers of different organizations in the supply chain are stored in a central database owned by the Swedish Transport Administration. This data can be shared via the internet with any user, for example the Volvo Cars body components and the Volvo Cars assembly factories and the logistics company, GreenFreight.

Such methods of T&T are expected to replace the current tools and methods of using email, fax, and barcode readers. An example of the data that is shared on the internet for T&T of shipments of wagons for the users in this supply chain is illustrated in Table 1.

Table 1 RFID information from the rail wagons available on the internet for the users.

Location (RFID reading station)	Date/time	Direction	Wagon ID
Olofström (Volvo body components factory)	2014-11-05, 12:40	North	15689
Halmstad	2014-11-05, 15:30	South	25689
Varberg	2014-11-08, 9:25	North	19856
Gothenburg (Volvo Cars assembly factory)	2014-11-08, 10:30	South	27854

CASE STUDY
Advantages and issues of the collaborative T&T system

This case is an example of the inter-organizational information systems projects based on data sharing between the partners of a supply chain. There are many such projects in different industries. A shared aspect among all of these projects is that they can have many advantages for the business of the supply chain partners but there are some significant obstacles and issues that make implementing them difficult. As a result, many of these projects stay at pilot stage, without being implemented on a large scale basis and utilized to maximize commercial returns for the companies.

The Volvo Cars T&T project is currently at the pilot stage where the organizations are studying the potential advantages that the system can bring to their business, before investing further time and money on developing it.

Assume that as a project manager from one of the organizations involved in this supply chain, or as a consultant, you are asked to provide an analysis of the solutions and methods that can help to bring the potential advantages of the system into practice and can help to overcome the obstacles of developing the project further. The advantages and issues will be questioned in the next section.

You need to balance your solutions by considering the perspective and the interests of the individual organizations involved in the supply chain, and also by bearing in mind the general goal of the supply chain, which is on-time and accurate delivery of Volvo car-body components to the Volvo car assembly factory. Your solutions and suggestions should be feasible, so feel free to get help from other information including interviewing experts, reading academic/industrial articles and project reports, and reviewing the information available on company websites regarding the success and failures they may have add when dealing with similar projects. Make reasonable assumptions when necessary to provide your answers.

Questions

1 Within such a logistics network, which moving objects (wagons, containers, racks, pallets and products) are each actors interested in tracking and tracing?

2 If the Swedish Transport Administration decides to commercialize the data stored in its central database and indicates prices to the other partners of the supply chain, how can the value of this T&T data be measured by Volvo Cars and GreenFreight? What are the reasons for this level of value? How much do you think the companies are willing to spend to have access to the T&T data? As a manager, propose a method for cost/revenue analysis to identify the value of T&T data of this system. Compare the level of value of T&T data for different organizations.

3 When initiating the project, the Swedish Transport Administration expected the system to be of help in making savings for transport operators by enabling them to reduce the cost of their maintenance operations. The idea was that by doing some software engineering an individual profile for each wagon could be established, identified by its unique RFID code, which would enable the measurement of the accurate number of kilometres it has been running and provide data regarding the temperature of its wheels and axles. This would thus enable GreenFreight to carry out condition-based wagon maintenance instead of periodic maintenance. As a project manager, what type of changes will this bring to GreenFreight and also to its relationships with other companies that are involved in the maintenance operations?

4 GreenFreight believes that this system provides the fundamentals necessary in making transport administration and transport documentation automatic. Do you have any suggestions on how this system can be used to enable automatic transport administrative processes? Suggest two examples of transportation documents that can be produced using the RFID readings?

5 In this case Volvo Cars needs to install RFID readers inside its facilities and the transport companies should install RFID tags on their wagons, which are costly. There are costs associated with the integration of their information systems into the new shared system, educating users as well as other relevant expenses which are involved in making the system work. In such inter-organizational projects, one issue is that the level of cost each partner bears for making the system run is not correlated with the level of benefits they receive from the shared system. What solution can overcome this issue?

6 An important issue regarding the projects that necessitate the sharing of some levels of data is trust, ie the willingness of the companies to share their commercial information which is directly or indirectly released through sharing RFID event data. How can this problem be resolved? What can companies do to mitigate the potential risks involved in releasing their confidential data?

Answers

1 Within such a logistics network, which moving objects (wagons, containers, racks, pallets and products) are each actors interested in tracking and tracing?

In this case the wagons are owned by GreenFreight, therefore they are interested in knowing where the wagons are located and if they are in a good mechanical condition. Volvo Cars, which includes the body components factory and the car assembly factory, are interested in knowing the location of their products. Therefore, Volvo Cars are interested in tracking and tracing the cargo including the containers containing the pallets and racks of the body components.

2 If the Swedish Transport Administration decides to commercialize the data stored in its central database and indicates prices to the other partners of the supply chain, how can the value of this T&T data be measured by Volvo Cars and GreenFreight? What are the reasons for this level of value? How much do you think the companies are willing to spend to have access to the T&T data? As a manager, propose a method for cost/revenue analysis to identify the value of T&T data of this system. Compare the level of value of T&T data for different organizations.

The value of the information is measured by identifying the functionality or usefulness of it for the companies. The advantages that the data produced by the system can bring to the companies should be considered.

In this case, GreenFreight can offer better service levels to their customers by providing RFID T&T data which is much more accurate compared to their traditional T&T methods. Therefore, managers of GreenFreight should analyse how much their customers are willing to pay for such information. The cost of buying this data from Swedish Transport Administration should be compatible with the revenue that selling the data to their customers will bring to them. For Volvo Cars the RFID T&T data can help them make the process of receiving the products at the car assembly factory more efficient, eg by saving the waiting time of the unloading equipment and personnel when receiving the cargo at the car assembly factory. Also it might help their risk management, eg when their cargo has been delayed because of an accident somewhere on the railway. By identifying the benefits of the system for their company, they can estimate the price that they are willing to pay to Swedish Transport Administration for the RFID T&T data. The data has more value for the company that benefits the most from it and therefore this company should be willing to pay more to have access to this data.

3 When initiating the project, the Swedish Transport Administration expected the system to be of help in making savings for transport operators by enabling them to reduce the cost of their maintenance operations. The idea was that by doing some software engineering an individual profile for each wagon could be established, identified by its unique RFID code, which would enable the measurement of the accurate number of kilometres it has been running and provide data regarding the temperature of its wheels and axles. This would thus enable GreenFreight to carry out condition-based wagon maintenance instead of periodic maintenance. As a project manager, what type of changes will this bring to GreenFreight and also to its relationships with other companies that are involved in the maintenance operations?

Considering the high cost of maintenance of rail wagons this might be a huge financial benefit for GreenFreight, but it should always be remembered that the feasibility of bringing technical solutions to the companies does not necessarily guarantee their fast adoption. In this case, the perspective of GreenFreight and also the companies who are involved in their maintenance operations should be considered. Careful thought should be given to how this new solution intended to enable condition-based maintenance can guarantee the safety of rail wagons, taking into account the regulations for standards of wagons and their spare parts. In this case, GreenFreight probably needs more time to analyse and coordinate such issues with their maintenance service providers.

4 GreenFreight believes that this system provides the fundamentals necessary in making transport administration and transport documentation automatic. Do you have any suggestions on how this system can be used to enable automatic transport administrative processes? Suggest two examples of transportation documents that can be produced using the RFID readings?

In order to come up with accurate answers to this question the process of administration and documentation of the cargo should be mapped carefully. When setting up the train departure, documents designed to marshal the train, including information about the sequence of wagons, their identification and their contents, can be generated automatically without lots of manual data entry into the information system which is time-consuming. Proof-of-delivery documents can also be generated automatically by the system when the cargo passes the last RFID reading station inside the car assembly factory.

5 In this case Volvo Cars needs to install RFID readers inside its facilities and the transport companies should install RFID tags on their wagons, which are costly. There are costs associated with the integration of their information systems into the new shared system, educating users as well as other relevant expenses which are involved in making the system work. In such inter-organizational projects, one issue is that the level of cost each partner bears for making the system run is not correlated with the level of benefits they receive from the shared system. What solution can overcome this issue?

Cost sharing is a common issue in many logistics networks that demand collaboration of multiple-organizations for implementing a shared information system. In this example the cost of installing RFID readers and other hardware and software settings is not that high for the companies, considering their financial strengths. But the existence of a governmental umbrella organization – the Swedish Transport Administration – which has made the huge investment on installing RFID sensor-reading stations is very important as a facilitator of running the project.

6 An important issue regarding the projects that necessitate the sharing of some levels of data is trust, ie the willingness of the companies to share their commercial information which is directly or indirectly released through sharing RFID event data. How can this problem be resolved? What can companies do to mitigate the potential risks involved in releasing their confidential data?

In this case trust is not mentioned by the managers as an issue, considering the non-competitive nature of the supply chain partners, aiming to deliver the products on time to the car assembly factory in a collaborative manner. However, in many other industries especially when competitor organizations have to share data, this issue becomes very sensitive since some sales volumes (and therefore indication of financial performances) can be deduced from the analysis of the RFID data. It is a barrier for implementing many such inter-organizational information systems. In some cases the companies revise the data before sharing it or exchanging it with their competitor companies, to make sure that their confidential data is protected.

Supply chain design for e-retailers

Vahid Mirzabeiki

AUTHOR BIOGRAPHY

DR VAHID MIRZABEIKI is a Senior Research Fellow at the Supply Chain Research Centre of Cranfield School of Management, Cranfield University.

Introduction

Internet retailing has been growing steadily during the last decade. There are companies who sell their products only online via their websites, whilst others have the option of internet selling as an alternative to selling products in their physical stores.

E-retailing has advantages compared with traditional retailing. One of its benefits is reducing retailing store-keeping costs given the high expense of having stores in popular areas of crowded cities.

On the other hand, when selling products online, the responsibility for on-time delivery of the product to the customer is carried by the e-retailer. Therefore, the delivery time of the product being shipped to the customer is an important customer-service aspect that should be controlled by e-retailing companies. High volumes of returned items, especially footwear and items of clothing, is another issue that also needs to be addressed by the e-retailing sector.

E-retailing demands more planning and control of logistics operations in both directions towards the consumers and coming back from them, and logistics is vital for the profitability of these companies.

Companies adopt different strategies regarding inventory allocation of products available in their e-stores to keep standard delivery times acceptable to customers. Some of the companies prefer to have all the items in their warehouses, and ship them to the customers directly. Others, to decrease their tied-up capital, prefer to source the items from their third-party suppliers after they've received the orders from the customers.

Companies

In the next section you will be provided with a brief introduction to the supply chains of two e-retailers that have slightly different supply chain strategies. After reading the introductions you should answer the questions in the following sections regarding the advantages and issues related to the supply chain design adopted by these two companies.

When providing answers feel free to use your own experience of online shopping. You may also refer to company websites, read academic or practical journal articles, or interview people who have knowledge of the logistics planning of e-retailing companies.

Company 1: Fabulous

With their headquarters in Germany, Fabulous is a multi-national company selling footwear, clothes and fashion items for men and women. The company sells its products via its website and its markets have expanded through Western and Northern Europe which include Germany, Austria, Switzerland, France, Belgium, Sweden, Denmark, Finland, Norway and the UK.

The company stocks all the items in their warehouses and shipments to customers are made from there. The customers in Germany, Austria and Switzerland are served from Fabulous's central warehouse in Germany. The company owns a number of local distribution centres and warehouses in Europe and the customers in the other European countries receive their items shipped from those local warehouses. The delivery time from order to collection for German customers is up to 48 hours and for customers in Austria and Switzerland is between 5 to 11 days.

The company provides a price list for delivery of the items depending on the size of the package and whether the customer has requested a fast delivery. Customers in Austria and Switzerland are charged an extra shipping fee if they request shipment to arrive within 48 hours from the order time. The items are delivered to post offices or grocery stores in the consumer's neighbourhood, to be collected.

Company 2: OrangeClick

OrangeClick is an e-retailer of home furniture, fashion items for men, women and kids, and leisure items. The company is Swedish but operates in Norway, Denmark, Finland and Russia. They have a larger variety of stock keeping units (SKUs) compared to Fabulous.

The products are listed on the company's website as well as in catalogues that are delivered for free to households in cities, as advertisement.

The company has two separate channels for shipping the ordered items to the customers. A group of items are available in the central warehouse of the company located in mid-Sweden. Another group of items are shipped directly from the suppliers of OrangeClick to consumers.

Delivery time for the items shipped from the OrangeClick's central warehouse is between 2 to 5 days. For the items ordered from the suppliers, the delivery times varies between 5 to 12 days.

Questions

1 Draw a simple process map of the flow of the items from the central warehouses/suppliers to the collecting point of the customers. Compare the differences between the process maps of Fabulous and OrangeClick. Look at your process maps. What are your suggestions to decrease the total delivery time of items to the customers?

2 Refer to the supply-chain design of OrangeClick. What is the trade-off between having the products available in the central warehouse, and shipping them directly from suppliers, in terms of

delivery time, especially when a customer orders a combination of items that are stocked in the warehouse with items that are stocked in the suppliers' warehouses? What are the pros and cons related to each of these strategies for the company and for the customers?

3 Which items are better shipped directly from the supplier and which ones should be available in the central warehouse of OrangeClick, considering the different specification of items such as their value, size and frequency of orders?

4 Assuming that you are responsible for planning the supply chain, where would you locate Fabulous's central warehouse for customers in Germany, Austria and Switzerland, considering that the demand from the cities in these three countries is related to the population numbers of the cities?

5 Is knowledge about the demographics of the population of the market countries important when identifying the location of the central warehouse, assuming that you are in the stage of designing the supply chain of the company and you need to forecast the demand?

6 The percentage of returned items is higher for e-retailers compared to traditional retail stores. What are the reasons for this higher level of returns? What are the impacts of product return on logistics costs? How can the companies decrease these percentages? Add the processes of reverse logistics onto the process maps of the companies you designed.

7 Some of the logistics companies have installed pack stations in the streets of populous cities, which are automated machines that have a number of boxes used to house parcels for collection and return. They are always available, 24 hours a day. How do these pack stations affect customers and transport companies in the e-retailing sector?

Answers

1 Draw a simple process map of the flow of the items from the central warehouses/suppliers to the collecting point of the customers. Compare the differences between the process maps of Fabulous and OrangeClick. Look at your process maps. What are your suggestions to decrease the total delivery time of items to the customers?

On your process map include all the processes that are included in the total delivery time. The processes might include order processing, packing, labelling, shipping, delivery by transport companies (including processes such as terminal operations and warehousing), and then the waiting time in the grocery store or post office.

One way of improving the items delivery process to customers can be reducing the waiting time of the items in the central warehouse before being delivered. Shipping the items with express delivery services, which usually cost more than normal deliveries can also be a solution. Increasing the availability of the items to the customer after being delivered to the collection points is another way of getting the ordered items sooner to the customer. This can be achieved with increased collaboration between the logistics companies and the grocery stores across different locations or by using automated pack stations where customers can pick up products 24 hours a day.

2 Refer to the supply-chain design of OrangeClick. What is the trade-off between having the products available in the central warehouse, and shipping them directly from suppliers, in terms of delivery time, especially when a customer orders a combination of items that are stocked in the warehouse with items that are stocked in the suppliers' warehouses? What are the pros and cons related to each of these strategies for the company and for the customers?

For customers placing an order of multiple items, some of the items might be shipped from the central warehouse, whilst others might be shipped from the suppliers, thus resulting in them receiving their items in different packages on different days.

By arranging direct shipments from the suppliers, OrangeClick reduces the capital tied up in their warehouse, related to buying and storing items. They also reduce their warehousing cost by decreasing the size of their storage area. On the other hand, they have less control of inventory level and product availability for their customers.

3 Which items are better shipped directly from the supplier and which ones should be available in the central warehouse of OrangeClick, considering the different specification of items such as their value, size and frequency of orders?

Usually the items that are ordered frequently, the ones that are not very expensive and products that do not occupy lots of space are the ones that should be available in the central warehouse. The high-price items increase the tied-up capital of the company and large items increase the logistics and warehousing cost of the company.

4 Assuming that you are responsible for planning the supply chain, where would you locate Fabulous's central warehouse for customers in Germany, Austria and Switzerland, considering that the demand from the cities in these three countries is related to the population numbers of the cities?

By making the assumption that the demand from the cities is related to their population numbers, the more populous cities of Germany, Austria and Switzerland have a higher demand for products. Therefore, the central warehouse used for shipping the products to these three countries should be at the demand centre of these three countries. Use the single location centre of gravity algorithm to determine the demand centre:

$$X = \frac{\Sigma(x_i D_i)}{\Sigma D_i} \qquad Y = \frac{\Sigma(y_i D_i)}{\Sigma D_i}$$

Where: x_i = the horizontal distance coordinate for city i
y_i = the vertical distance coordinate for city i
D_i = the demand for products to be delivered to city i

You can consider a location as the point 0 on your map ($x = 0$, $y = 0$) and then identify the location of the cities related to this point in terms of miles or kilometres. Considering that the demand from each city is correlated to the population of the city you can consider the demand as $D_i = P_i \times Q$ when P_i is population of city i and Q is a constant demand per special number of population in the three countries. Therefore the formula for identifying the centre of gravity becomes:

$$X = \frac{\Sigma(x_i P_i Q)}{\Sigma P_i Q} = \frac{\Sigma(x_i P_i)}{\Sigma P_i} \qquad Y = \frac{\Sigma(y_i P_i Q)}{\Sigma P_i Q} = \frac{\Sigma(y_i P_i)}{\Sigma P_i}$$

To simplify your calculations you can pick the three most populous cities of each of the three mentioned countries.

5 Is knowledge about the demographics of the population of the market countries important when identifying the location of the central warehouse, assuming that you are in the stage of designing the supply chain of the company and you need to forecast the demand?

Demographics of population are very important when forecasting the demands from a market. Accurate information about the age, sex, level of income of people, etc. is a key aspect in designing the supply chain, including identifying the appropriate location for the central warehouse of the company. As an example, a young population that has high buying power will of course raise more demand for fashion items compared with an older population with lower levels of income. There are many other aspects that should be considered when identifying the location of the facilities of a supply chain, including the price of land, or other fixed and marginal costs of operation of a warehouse in different locations.

6 The percentage of returned items is higher for e-retailers compared to traditional retail stores. What are the reasons for this higher level of returns? What are the impacts of product return on logistics costs? How can the companies decrease these percentages? Add the processes of reverse logistics onto the process maps of the companies you designed.

One reason can be the lack of close customer experience when shopping online, especially when it comes to clothes or footwear. Sometimes the ordered size does not fit the customer or sometimes the material of the items isn't the customer expected. Usually the customers are not asked to pay for returning items, therefore the reverse logistics costs are paid by the e-retailer.

The companies can reduce the cost of reverse logistics in the first instance by designing better websites that provide more accurate and tangible information about their products. Also they can make their reverse logistics systems more efficient.

When drawing the steps of reverse logistics on your process map, consider the point at which the customer leaves the item to be collected as the beginning and the central warehouse of the supplier's warehouse as the ending point. Draw the reverse logistics process for both Fabulous and OrangeClick and compare the reverse logistics of the two companies by considering the costs of operations.

7 Some of the logistics companies have installed pack stations in the streets of populous cities, which are automated machines that have a number of boxes used to house parcels for collection and return. They are always available, 24 hours a day. How do these pack stations affect customers and transport companies in the e-retailing sector?

Such pack stations increase the availability of the items for collection by the customer as they give service to registered customers 24 hours every day. The customers do not need to consider the opening hours of post offices or grocery stores for collecting or leaving items.

The transport companies might reduce their transportation costs by replacing their post offices with these automated pack stations which are less costly in the long term and do not need employees to be available there for giving and receiving items. You can explore the other effects of the pack stations for e-retailers and consumers by researching appropriate cases and reports online.

Delays entering a container port
A logistics bottleneck

Brian Lawrence

AUTHOR BIOGRAPHY

BRIAN LAWRENCE is Lecturer in the School of Management at the Assumption University in Bangkok, Thailand.

Introduction

Service speed is a major criterion for operations in container terminals. This case is an examination of the entry-gate operation for container trucks at a shipping container yard at a port in Australia, to find out how to reduce the unacceptable queuing time. A bottleneck is caused by most trucks arriving at the terminal in the same time period, and having to endure the lengthy inspection and registration process because of inadequate staffing and too few truck lanes.

Three alternative scenarios are proposed for the port management company to solve this problem. The first emphasizes adding gates and staff. The second focuses on changing the staff lunch-break times. The third concentrates on redesigning the work flow. Significant criteria are: waiting time, resource utilization, costs and process cycle time. These criteria were used to compare the as-is situation and the three scenarios to select the most appropriate.

The company

Lozziestistics plc is the Australian subsidiary of an international container terminal operating company. It is an agent for shipping lines that handles container cargoes and operates container storage, for both outgoing exports for delivery to container ships and incoming imports from ships for delivery to customers. Lozziestistics' core business is the management of port facilities for entry to the terminal and for temporary storage yards, consisting of:

- Gate operation: operating the checking and registration point at the entry gate for empty and full containers on trucks, and at the exit gate for trucks collecting empty and full containers to take away to customers.

- Yard operation: managing the temporary storage of empty and full containers, and providing powerful cranes for lifting and lowering containers from/to trucks within the terminal yard.

The problem

In 2014, the average volume of cargo handled within Australia was 30,000 containers per month. Container volume has grown in the past couple of years, and Lozziestistics must improve the speed of its port operation, to enhance the quality of customer service and manage the increasing demand volume effectively and efficiently.

The increase in the number of containers carried by trucks entering the port has caused traffic congestion inside and outside the terminal. Most of this congestion is caused by full container trucks queuing for the entry-gate process. Drivers have to waste their time, which adversely affects their work schedule. The long queues often produce heavy traffic in nearby roads.

There are two types of processing a container full of cargo, carried on a truck:

1 Entry-gate exports (EXP): this is the process of collecting containers from customers' factories, transporting them to the port by truck, and going through the entry-gate formalities to the storage yard, for eventual uploading into a ship.

2 Entry-gate imports (IMP): this is the process of a truck going empty through the entry gate to collect a full container that has arrived at the port by ship, for eventual transportation to a customer.

All trucks wanting to enter the container terminal queue in four lanes 1, 2, 3, 4 ready to be called to stop at one of the two gates for inspection. Lanes 1 and 2 go either side of Gate A. Lanes 3 and 4 go either side of Gate B. Bottlenecks happen in these four lanes leading up to the gate barrier. For EXP, once at an actual gate, the truck and its container are inspected, pay a fee, move into the container yard, have a giant crane lift the container off, then move out of the yard through an exit gate and into the street. For IMP, the process is similar except that the truck goes through the gate empty, to have a crane lower an incoming full container onto the truck, which then, after customs and security checks, moves out of the terminal through an exit gate and into the street.

The two gates together can cope with 480 trucks per day, but higher than that causes delays during the peak period. The number of trucks entering through the gates varies daily, ranging from 390 on four off-peak days to 540 on three peak days (Tuesday to Thursday). IMP trucks average 5,250 a month, and EXP 8,220 a month. This is beyond the efficient capacity of the gate process.

Each truck inspection and registration then takes at least ten minutes before further steps. A great number of export containers (EXP) arrive in the same period, which is shortly before the container ship's final time for loading. This peak period is Tuesday to Thursday, as the main weekly ship final loading time is Friday evening. The situation is further exacerbated by half the gate staff taking a one-hour meal break, followed by the other half, which means that for two hours the gates are only half staffed.

If this gate process does not improve, some trucks and their full containers will be too late for the ship's departure. The ship often has to wait, or sail without a complete load of containers, thus losing income and angering truck drivers, owners and cargo owners in Australia and at destination ports waiting for the containers to

arrive. If the ship does wait beyond its official departure time, this
affects its scheduled arrivals and departures at subsequent ports,
again to the anger of many parties. This traffic congestion is a critical
issue for Lozziestistics and for shipping lines, for loading and unloading ports, and for customers.

There are four steps for terminal entry:

1 Inspection (which takes on average six minutes).

2 Registration and document checking (which takes on average
four minutes).

3 Planning where to drop off the container within the terminal
(which takes on average two minutes).

4 The actual drop-off (which takes on average three minutes).

The bottleneck usually occurs during the first two steps or the first
ten minutes of waiting time.

It is difficult to move out of a lane, so a breakdown adds to the
congestion until mechanics can manoeuvre and tow the faulty truck
through a security emergency entrance at either sides of the gates for
repair. The main problem, however, is that the actual process at the
terminal requires some time to perform each step, especially the initial inspection process. The inspection is conducted in an assigned
area. These lengthy processes, to which must be added the waiting
times, cause traffic problems in the lanes up to the gates, so that the
whole operation has significant delays. One major reason for the
lengthy process at the port is safety and security checks, especially in
the first inspection process.

Within the container yard, lifting a container from a truck is done
by a top loader crane, which grabs the top edges of the container,
operated by a driver high up in the cab. This takes a very short time,
but the process is a smooth one only if there are enough cranes and
the cranes are ready. There is a separate rail checking process as container trains enter the terminal through a separate gate so sometimes
the top loader crane is needed for an arriving container train.
Therefore, sometimes the equipment level is not enough to support
full container-gate operations, causing delay.

Efficiency criteria for gate operations

Maximizing the productivity of the handling of containers is a key performance and efficiency indicator. Gate-operation productivity is measured by throughput, the number of container trucks moving through a lane and gate per hour, and the total time a truck spends in a terminal. The performance of staff is measured by the number of trucks dealt with per hour. Gate productivity itself can be improved by capital investment in buildings and equipment, and staff resources can be improved by the number of staff hired as well by the training offered to them. However, external factors like the arriving container volumes and ship schedules are not usually alterable by the port.

Attempts to improve container entry at ports

Most ports with an entry problem are able to improve operation time and reduce waiting time. Delays at the entrance gate in a US port were solved by extending the gate-operation hours and installing an appointment system for trucks. However, the appointment system caused a problem in the next operation because of the variability of other transactions and the operators' lack of planning skills.

In another port, two solutions were considered to reduce congestion. One was to increase the number of gates. The other was a truck arrival appointment system. Another port concentrated on service time but rejected improvement which would incur construction costs of more gates and lanes.

Yet another port tried to reduce truck turnaround time and costs by increasing the number of lifting cranes and using a truck appointment system. An interesting idea was to look at both the land side of the terminal and the ocean side, but this also led to extended gate hours and a gate appointment system.

Lozziestistics' suggested solutions

To find solutions Lozziestistics used a simulation technique to construct a queuing model. Computer simulation enables the analysis of data regarding data processes and can generate solutions without having to physically experiment with real trucks at the gate, which might take many days during which waiting times are exacerbated. The simulation used the following steps to model the as-is situation and possible alternatives, having collected data and opinions from gate and terminal staff, and truck drivers:

Step 1: Truck arrives at the terminal.

Step 2: Truck moves to the terminal gate for inspection. There are two gates and they can accommodate a maximum of four trucks at one time. Staff write container numbers, seal the number and condition of the container on a special form, and give it to the driver. If the container is damaged, it will be rejected and the driver has to take it a special repair area, and return for checking again once repairs have taken place.

Step 3: The truck driver submits the special form and customs documents to the gate staff and pays the gate charge. The staff check the documents. If the documents are correct, they will update the data in the computer system and give an approval sticker to the driver. If the document is incomplete or has an error, the truck has to move beyond the gate for the driver to revise the documents. Then the driver walks back to gate staff for recheck approval. The number of damaged containers is quite low at 1 per cent. Poor or missing documentation accounts for about 2 per cent of trucks. Together, those 3 per cent interrupt the smooth flow of trucks and gate checks by creating extra work for staff.

Step 4: The truck moves to contact yard staff for instructions on where they should park their trucks for the lifting crane. Yard space is crowded, and empty containers are in stacks, sometimes eight high. There is little space for trucks moving to their assigned position.

Step 5: The truck moves to the position for the container to be lifted from the truck.

Step 6: The truck moves on and exits the terminal; the end of the process.

The company's gate service is in operation 24 hours every day. It has two 12-hour shifts, day and night. There are 32 staff involved: eight inspectors check the container condition and record it on a special form; four survey staff also survey the container, record it, write the container number and seal number on the special form (full containers are sealed shut so that tampering or pilferage are obvious at specific stages of the journey); eight gate staff enter container details into the computer system, check documents and collect the gate fee; four yard staff plan the exact lifting position beneath a crane; four yardmen stand by to signal and direct the truck driver; and finally another four yardmen control the heavy cranes that lift the containers from the truck and then move on rails to the temporary storage area.

Three alternatives for improvement

Simulation created the as-is situation and these three alternatives:

1 Add an extra gate (with its two lanes) and more staff.
2 Change the meal-break times of gate staff.
3 Redesign the gate entry process, by combining inspection and registration, and increasing the number of survey staff.

Alternative 1: add an extra gate and staff

This needs two staff: one an inspector, the other a gate staff.

Table 1 Waiting time result by adding a gate and staff

Scenario	Resource		Simulation result	
	Inspector	Gate staff	Average waiting time (minutes)	Average number of trucks in queue
1	8	8	10	5
2	9	9	8	4
3	10	10	4	2

The first scenario is the as-is present state in the simulation model, with an average waiting time of ten minutes, and an average of five queuing trucks.

The second scenario adds a gate, an inspector and one gate staff. In this case, the average waiting time decreases by two minutes, and the average number of queuing trucks decreases by one.

For the third scenario, two inspectors and two gate staff are added to the team with the extra gate in operation. This reduces the average waiting time to four minutes, which is four minutes less than scenario 2. The average number of queuing trucks reduces to two, which is two less than scenario 2.

Scenarios 2 and 3 are both better than the as-is situation.

It seems that the more additional staff used, the lower the waiting time at the bottleneck. But this method could increase the average waiting time beyond the gate in the yard as more trucks move into the yard and that would not impress truck drivers in the long run.

Alternative 2: changing the staff break schedule

Currently, gate staff take a complete break to eat. Two staff in each position at a gate have the same break time. These periods produce the longest waiting time for trucks, as some gate staff disappear for two hours.

For the day staff, two inspectors and two staff at Gate A break from 11.00 to 12.00. The other team of two and two at Gate B break between 12.00 and 13.00. The night staff take their break 12 hours after the day staff. Break times of other staff are similar, but they are on permanent standby.

A new break schedule would spread these break times, with one inspector and one staff breaking from 11.00 to 12.00, the next pair from 11.30 to 12.30, the next pair from 12.00 to 1300 and the final pair from 1300 to 14.00 (the night team would have their break 12 hours later in the same fashion.) So, there would be four overlapping breaks, each for two people, spread over three hours instead of two hours.

The simulated resulting average waiting time would be seven minutes (compared with as-is ten), and the average number of queuing trucks would be four (compared with as-is five). However, actual truck arrival time is volatile. And a specific break time would often have to be disregarded, as the operations time is also unpredictable in practice.

Alternative 3: redesigning the process at the bottleneck

The aim is to reduce the cycle time. In a new process flow, the inspection, checking of documents and paying would be done concurrently. This would save time as truck drivers do not need to wait for the inspection before checking and paying. Truck drivers would go to the gate immediately after receiving their special forms. With this method the special form would need to be issued at the first step. This new design would need four additional staff to issue the special forms.

With the redesign, average waiting time results of the new process flow would be six minutes (ten in as-is). Average number of queuing trucks in the queue would be three (five in as-is). Average cycle time would be ten minutes (thirteen in as-is). Cycle-time reduction would also increase the truck service capacity.

Cost

There is a final factor: cost. The first alternative which adds four staff has the highest cost, US$5,100 for adding two staff, or US$7,000 for adding four staff. These costs include extra gate facilities and office supplies. There is no increased cost for the second alternative. In the third alternative, the extra cost is US$1,200 for the extra four survey staff.

Questions

1 Which of the alternatives would you choose, and why?

2 Can you think of other alternatives?

3 It seems like a simple problem. Why do you think it was not immediately tackled and solved?

Answers

1 Which of the alternatives would you choose, and why?

- Average waiting time and number of queuing trucks is lowest in the first alternative. As these are the most obvious features of the congestion problem, this method would seem the most effective solution. In the second alternative, waiting time is slightly decreased from as-is but higher than the others. In the third alternative waiting time is the highest of the three.

- Average resource utilization of staff in the first alternative is the lowest because of increased staff numbers. Resource utilization in the second and third alternatives is not much different from the as-is current situation.

- Cycle time is reduced in the third alternative.

- Cost of the third alternative is lower than the first alternative. The first alternative needs the highest investment, and could later create more costs, for such items as repairs.

- The first and third alternatives are useful for improving the container gate process. The first alternative is useful for reducing the truck waiting time at the bottleneck. The third alternative does not reduce as much waiting time as the first one but it does reduce cycle time.

- Therefore, the third alternative is the recommended method. It can be applied with less cost than the first alternative. This redesigned process can be installed almost immediately. Also, it is the only method that reduces the cycle time because the operational flow is improved by operating two activities concurrently. The reduced cycle time also increases the truck capacity (less waiting and process time releases trucks for more journeys).

- Finally, any change to the gate process must be carefully considered for its consequent effect on the whole terminal. Ignoring this is a fundamental flaw in these alternatives. Quicker gate entry would reduce the trucks' waiting time, but that merely moves the wait to the congested container yard. Tell that to the management! Remind them that every system is connected to other systems (systems theory).

2 Can you think of other alternatives?

- It would be worth considering using more than one alternative such as combining the first one and the third one. The process flow would be adjusted to reduce the cycle time; meanwhile opening more gates and adding more staff would reduce the waiting time. It would increase the efficiency of Lozziestistics' service performance.

- Have a computer check-in, like airlines. That could save time at the gate. Container ships do that, with an electronic list of cargo items (known as a bill of lading), and ports demand approaching ships email that to the port authorities. The proliferation of smartphones and tablets should extend to the truck drivers.

3 It seems like a simple problem. Why do you think it was not immediately tackled and solved?

People can sometimes be complacent critics. They are often content to criticize but don't take the initiative or take responsibility for taking actions and hope others will do something instead. They might say that managers wouldn't listen or perhaps they don't trust their relationship with the gate staff in the first place, fearing voicing their concerns would result in their being made to wait longer or being told that the required documents aren't correct. It needs observant, responsibility-taking people at all levels who are often impartial, operating within an atmosphere of trust, to counter these negative unhelpful attitudes.

Note	I am grateful to K Sutijit Sugandhavanija for permission to use some of her research material.

Drivers and barriers in implementing information management systems in European micro enterprises
Empirical evidence from a success story

Francesco Pomponi, Lorenzo Coccia and Arvind Upadhyay

AUTHOR BIOGRAPHIES

FRANCESCO POMPONI is a Research Associate at the University of Cambridge, Centre for Sustainable Development.

LORENZO COCCIA is an IT consultant with experience in various industries such as transportation, manufacturing and gambling. He is currently working in the consumer goods industry within the Kantar Retail group XTEL S.r.l.

DR ARVIND UPADHYAY is Senior Lecturer in Logistics and Supply Chain Management at Brighton Business School.

Introduction

Small and medium-sized enterprises (SMEs) represent 99 per cent of companies across Europe, providing two-thirds of the jobs in the private sector and contributing to more than half of the total value created by EU businesses. Furthermore, European SMEs have been described as the backbone of the economy for the leading role they play in wealth, economic growth, innovation, and research and development (R&D).

Specifically, 90 per cent of European SMEs are characterized by employing less than ten people, what is known as a micro enterprise. Such realities are extremely cost-sensitive; investments have to be planned extremely carefully due to tight financial resources. In this respect, advancement in information and communication technologies (ICTs) often come long after the acquisition of more strategic, and more urgent, assets, such as machinery, skilled workforce, marketing and sales support. In addition to limited resources, the lack of technological competence appears to be the other main reason that hinders a wider adoption of ICTs among SMEs.

Despite the steadily growing pace with which ICTs have developed over the last decades to facilitate business processes and organizations as a whole, the micro enterprises of the European Union (EU) have benefited little in this area. However, there is another side of the coin. Indeed, not only do micro enterprises lack financial and technological resources to fully benefit from ICTs but also ICTs companies often exclusively target big firms as customers due to higher chances of success of their investments and strategic planning.

In such a context, those micro enterprises willing to invest in ICTs and advance their technological levels to benefit from the great potential that computer science has to offer are often left without viable ways forward from the market. This case study addresses such a shortcoming by presenting a success story of a micro enterprise that effectively achieved a high level of technological advancement in information management and business processes support.

CASE STUDY
Edilglas

Overview

This case study is based on the authors' consultancy work done for Edilglas, an Italian SME competing in the flat-glass business. The company is involved in both the construction and interior design sectors, thus having an extremely diverse clientele. Additionally, it works with and for other companies, both bigger and smaller in size, and private customers, such as home owners. Not only does such a diverse clientele imply significantly different jobs size, but also requires an almost opposite approach in the information flow from the company towards the customers. More specifically, when dealing with other companies that already know what they want and also when and how, information is to be kept to the minimum.

Generally, incoming orders are followed by outgoing confirmations to the customers, and then the job is passed onto the manufacturing department. On the other hand, private customers are often a lay audience, which needs to be informed about glass, its great potential, and its few limitations. The process with private customers is therefore much longer and much more communication-laden then the one with other companies. Often, technical staff need to visit the private customer's residence, try to explain the feasibility of different solutions, get a gist of what the budget is going to be like, and then make an estimate. It is very unusual that the first estimate fully meets the customer's expectation. More often, it represents the starting point of a long communication in which the original solution is amended, revised, made cheaper and – eventually – agreed upon. Once the estimate satisfies both Edilglas and the customer an agreement is signed and the job is again passed onto the manufacturing department.

Edilglas does the vast majority of the manufacturing activities inhouse although some expensive glass treatment processes are outsourced. Finally, once the manufacturing is completed, customers are informed they can collect their products or, more often, the next and last phase, that is installation of the product, takes place. All of these processes, stages, communications and agreements were almost fully and completely paper based. More specifically, estimates were type-written in a word-processing software but, once printed, they could only be traced by retrieving the hard copies stored and filed in the company's archive.

The IT solution: a multi-dimensional support system (MSS)

High uncertainty about the business's needs and how and where IT solutions should be supporting business processes represent two key risk factors in implementing a support system in a small company. Although there is no doubt about the potential benefits that adopting IT enterprise solutions would bring to the business, such a dramatic change may not be well accepted and understood by small businesses where there is a long-lasting tradition of trusting human actions and, consequently, a strong reliance on manual processes.

Such a social aspect needs to be carefully dealt with. Top-down solutions implemented by IT consultants with the aim of revolution-izing and digitalizing a company's approach to information manage-ment have far too often proved doomed to fail. There is, indeed, the constant and underlying risk of a financial investment that could be neither understood nor eventually used by the people it has been de-signed for. People, or more appropriately users, thus play a crucial role and their continuous involvement – as far as their technological literacy allows – is essential. In other words, an efficient and effective communication between IT professionals, project managers and the relevant stakeholders is of paramount importance, and it has been our constant aim throughout the consultancy project.

Suffice to say, all of these aspects are combined with high levels of technological complexity for an IT project that bears significant un-certainty about business requirements and a fairly strict and low budget.

Given the context explained above, we decided to properly tackle such constraints and difficulties by managing the project through the adoption and the implementation of an incremental Agile approach. Specifically, we used a Lean Software Development (LSD), which is part of the Agile methodology. As per any Agile approach the main goal is to release a small increment of functionalities to gather early feedback and eventually refine requirements for the next increment. In the case of Edilglas, we worked very closely with all the stakeholders, involving them in discussions for each small increment. As shown in the flow chart of the adopted approach (Figure 1) we focused only on the current iteration at hand, ignoring any other requirements coming from new functionalities that were to be developed at a later stage.

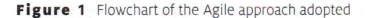

Figure 1 Flowchart of the Agile approach adopted

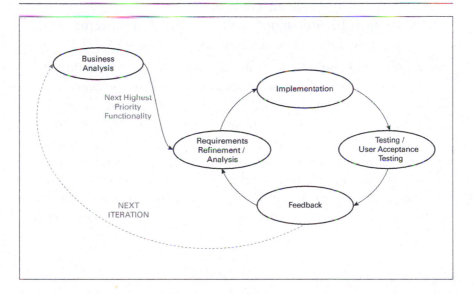

Such a structured methodological approach allowed us to delay both the analysis and implementation of additional modules/functionality until the relevant and related business needs and requirements were well defined. Furthermore, we engaged deeply with the company's stakeholders to make sure that each and every function had clear proven benefits, and well-understood expectations, prior to its implementation. By using an LSD terminology, we aimed to address and satisfy two chief principles: namely: 'Eliminate waste' and 'Decide as late as possible'. Such an approach allowed us to keep control over the budget and reduce risks of major changes at later stages, on one side, and to increase the business value of each new function without introducing any overhead in the transition from the manual to the automated workflow, on the other side.

The potential overhead represented a crucial part of the prioritization and design. Whereas big firms often strongly rely on strictly defined processes, small businesses need more flexibility in workflows to handle different scenarios coming from different type of customers or different size of jobs, such as the specific case of Edilglas explained in the introduction. Therefore, our main goal was to design the MSS around real scenarios and tangible business needs. We even redefined alternative workflows in order to avoid, as much as possible, strict standard processes that would produce overhead's in the workflow without producing any significant benefit.

MSS has then been designed with a modular architecture, which covers the following areas of the business:

- *Estimates* (Figure 2): As a first module it brought significant support to the estimation process, considering the previous adopted solutions to use MS Word files. There are clear benefits in moving to a centralized and automated estimation system. First, all the data produced by an estimate are indexed and gain effectiveness. Estimates can be further categorized by the product type, customer type, status or even the stage within the production cycle (eg whether it actually got confirmed and therefore triggered an order to the manufacturing department).

Figure 2 Screenshot of the estimates list

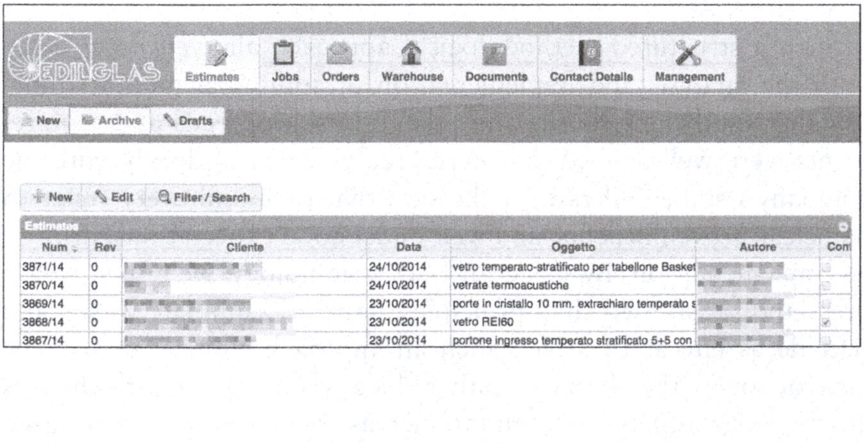

- *Jobs* (Figure 3): This generally represents an actual order to the production department. Here all the information regarding production is then collected allowing accurate metric measurement about the time spent in each phase of the production.

Figure 3 Screenshot of the jobs list (top) and a specific sample (bottom)

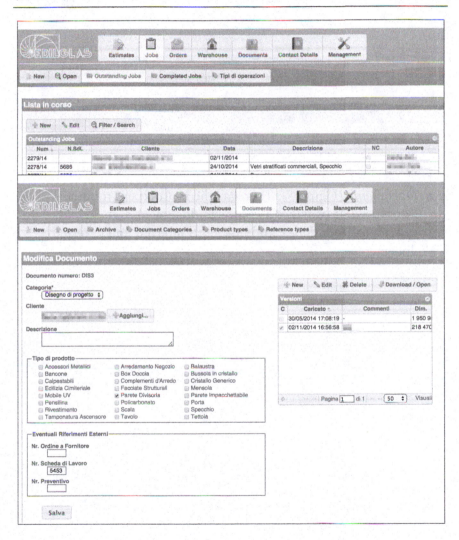

- *Orders* (Figure 4): Similarly to the estimations module, our solution also provided a module to handle all the orders to suppliers, storing, clustering, and automating relevant information.

Figure 4 Screenshot of the orders list

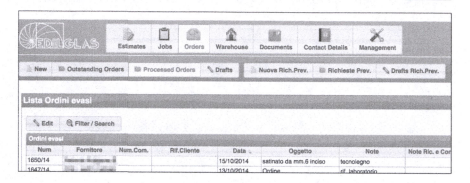

- *Documents* (Figure 5): This was the most recent module introduced. It provides a complete document management system, to store, index and link both internal and external documents.

Figure 5 Screenshot of the documents list (top) and a specific sample (bottom)

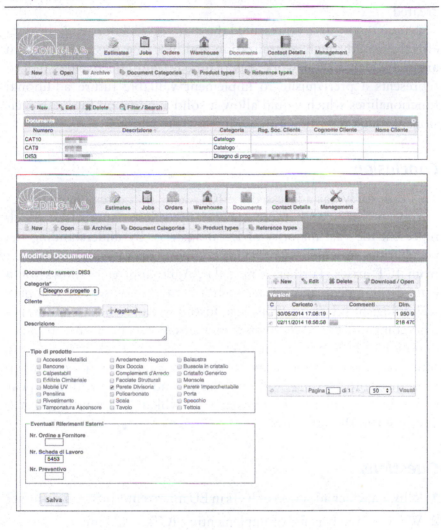

The modular architecture that we designed and developed eased the incremental approach and as the main goal provided dynamic interconnections between different entities across different modules. More specifically, as an example, an estimate could generate an order to the manufacturing department and have additional satellite documents like technical drawings, records for the quality assurance certification, pictures of the final product, and the like. At the same time, due to explicit requests made by the company, the office department has free flexible entry points along the standard workflow. For instance, the estimate can be skipped and an order to production directly created.

The company data represented the main drive. Improving the data effectiveness through centralization and indexing was the main aim around which all our work was planned. Data effectiveness indeed represents a prerequisite to implement valuable future additional functionalities which would allow a solid support on business decisions through reporting, forecasting and predictions.

Conclusion

This case study has addressed the ICT delay that often characterizes European SMEs and, more specifically, micro enterprises which represent the vast majority of EU industries. By understanding the peculiarities in which a particular company operates, a true benefit from ICT arises. Further, a modular, Agile approach allows for a lean development and implementation of otherwise too complex technological solutions whilst also instilling an IT culture in the specific company. EU SMEs would immensely benefit from a broader adoption of ICTs but the intrinsic characteristics of their success are often also the main impediments to doing so. In this respect, much more needs to be done and modularity and customization appear to be the two chief dimensions around which such a technological development should grow.

Questions

1 Why is a wider adoption of ICTs in EU micro enterprises important?
2 What are the benefits of implementing ICTs in EU micro enterprises?
3 How can a lean and flexible approach maximize the synergies between ICTs and EU micro enterprises?
4 What are the possible ways to identify business needs and prioritize accordingly?
5 What are the advantages of customization and modularity in designing ICT solutions?

Answers

1 Why is a wider adoption of ICTs in EU micro enterprises important?

EU small and micro enterprises represent the real backbone of the European economy. It is therefore crucial that these firms are enabled to compete on a global basis and benefit from the advancement in technology that have become available on the market over the last decade. A broader adoption of ICTs would enable European SMEs to spend less time on value-less information creation, storage, management and retrieval, thus allowing them to focus on the core elements of their business that determine their competitive advantage. Furthermore, and more importantly, IT solutions are key to effective strategic decisional support in environments such as the SMEs where information is often highly fragmented and of little significance since it lacks a broader and aggregated view of the company as a whole. Although this approach would ideally lead to sophisticated forecasting and prediction, it nonetheless immediately allows for efficient support in monitoring. Specifically, it gives the opportunity to base company decisions on hard data and facts rather than the entrepreneur's experience which often leads major decisions. Edilglas benefited greatly from the possibility to access information as aggregated or as detailed as necessary in terms of estimates, sales, orders, supplies, quality reports, and the like. For instance, estimate analyses allowed the company to get the gist of how many estimates actually turned into jobs and what are the common underlying features of those which do not. Additionally, by reducing clerical work, ICTs free some significant financial capacity to invest in strategic assets, such as new and more advanced machinery or skilled human capital. In a broader perspective, a structured and automated approach to information management also significantly benefits the effectiveness of an information life cycle. More specifically, human errors are reduced, undesired biases in prioritizing some pieces of information over others are eliminated and the risk of losing important documents overcome.

2 What are the challenges of implementing ICTs in EU micro enterprises?

In a context where the majority of EU SMEs are often family-owned with ten or less employees, effective communication and interpersonal relations play a crucial role. In other words, people need to be at the centre of the process. IT solutions need to be taken out of their complex, often 'geeky' context, and brought back into their practical applications and usability to the company's stakeholders. IT consultants need to make the extra effort to understand the specific constraints and peculiarities of each and every SME they deal with. This is the only way through which business needs can be truly understood and then supported and informed by the power of ICTs. Additionally, due to the extremely diverse panorama of European SMEs, it is extremely unlikely that a blanket approach can be replicated over and over across different companies. Such a need to tailor the IT solution to each specific circumstance represents an additional challenge to fully exploit potential synergies.

3 How can a lean and flexible approach maximize the synergies between ICTs and EU micro enterprises?

An Agile and lean approach to IT solutions development arguably represents the most sensible way to bring ICTs into European SMEs. Specifically, such a methodology permits the breaking down of a bigger technological project into smaller, more manageable and less costly sub-tasks that can be effectively dealt with in turn. The resulting process is therefore faster, less bulky, and allows to some extent mistakes and setbacks without necessarily hampering the whole process. Furthermore, the feedback/feed-forward Agile cycle gives the opportunity to isolate specific functions and implement them individually without, however, eliminating the possibility of intervention on the IT solution as a whole. Such an incremental process generates an additional benefit. Specifically, SMEs often lack any form of IT culture, which in turn does not allow them to foresee and understand what benefits an IT system could actually bring about. With the Agile/lean methodology, SMEs are introduced little by little to them. They eventually tend to revise their sometimes radical views on what the priorities are, often understanding that their initial idea of a blackbox IT solution needs to be revised and restructured along with time according to how the IT company culture settles, develops and evolves.

4 What are the possible ways to identify business needs and prioritize
  accordingly?

In the specific case of European SMEs a deep understanding of the
specific context is undoubtedly necessary by the IT consultants. We
found that the most effective way to do so is through a survey, or a
field study. Indeed, when the IT department members spend some
time with the company stakeholders, holding informal interviews
with them and registering their needs and wants, the risk of misun-
derstanding is kept to a minimum. We have also identified that flow-
charts, process maps and visual representations of the IT solution
that is to be implemented are the best media to show, share and discuss the specific ICT with the company as a whole.

5 What are the advantages of customization and modularity in designing
  ICT solutions?

In times of such economic uncertainty, like those we currently live in,
business needs change very frequently. This is even truer for EU SMEs
that are characterized by a flexible approach to manufacturing, which
allows them to attempt to target new markets and/or customers more
easily than big industries. In such an evolving context, the support
required from ICTs varies constantly and, to some extent, significantly. In our specific experience with Edilglas, several follow-ups
were needed to include, amend or adapt specific modules according
to the evolving business requirements. With a non-customized, rigid,
black-box IT solution this would have not been possible, thus greatly
limiting the support ICTs could give to Edilglas.

Growth strategies of logistics service providers

A RBV perspective on the logistics industry

Christian König and Nigel Caldwell

AUTHOR BIOGRAPHIES

CHRISTIAN KÖNIG is a PhD candidate in Operations Management at Heriot-Watt University.

DR NIGEL CALDWELL is Associate Professor in Logistics at the School of Management & Languages at Heriot-Watt University.

Introduction

Recently, the logistics industry has experienced significant growth as a result of continuous outsourcing activities by manufacturers, producers, wholesalers and retailers from all industries. Trends such as global sourcing, increasing supply chain complexity in terms of the number of suppliers and buyers, worldwide relocation of production plants and the global nature of e-commerce increases the need for sophisticated logistics solutions. The emergence and the development of third-party logistics (3PL) providers have therefore attracted attention from practitioners and scholars across different disciplines. For more information on the market size and numbers, there are a couple of annual studies available online such as the 'Top 100 in European Transport and Logistics Services' by Fraunhofer SCS and the annual 3PL study on the state of logistics outsourcing by Langley and CapGemini.

The purpose of this case study is to examine the different roles and capabilities of logistics firms in order to understand their future development and strategic growth. In particular, a resource-based approach explains the role of logistics in the strategy of a firm. The resource-based view (RBV) of the firm, as introduced by the strategist Jay Barney in 1991, represents a theoretical lens that explains how an organization cannot only maintain its competitive advantage but also outperform its competitors and finally achieve a sustained competitive advantage, based on their strategic capabilities of exploiting and accessing bundles of resources.

Useful definitions

- *Strategic outsourcing:* The strategic arrangement and rearrangement of a firm's boundaries towards the achievement of a competitive advantage. Central questions are identifying what functions of a firm contribute to its core competences, and then decide on outsourcing non-core activities. Further questions will then include how to outsource these non-core activities in terms of governance mechanisms.

- *Resource-based view (RBV):* A resource-based approach or RBV of the firm underpins the exploitation of a firm's tangible and intangible resources and strategic capabilities as the central and sole source for its competitive advantage. A sustained competitive advantage can therefore be achieved and explained by the scarcity of a firm's resources.

- *Logistics providers:* Any firm that undertakes peripheral and non-core activities such as transportation, warehousing, material handling and packaging for a manufacturer, producer or retailer. Logistics services are the most likely activity to be outsourced and the providers for such services build short-term or long-term relationships with the focal firm.

- *3PL:* Third-party logistics firms provide peripheral services that include parts or all of the customer's supply chain activities.

- *4PL:* Fourth-party logistics firms provide more value-adding services to a customer's entire supply network, including activities such as procurement, financing, consulting and technology integration. The ultimate aim of 4PL services is to provide supply chain wide and integrated solutions.

Applying the lens of RBV to logistics outsourcing

According to RBV, a sustained competitive advantage is explained by the leveraging effect of scarce firm-specific resources, which are bundled and accessed through interorganizational relationships. The exploitation of these bundles of resources therefore relates to the firm's performance and strengthens its core competences.

Resources in the context of logistics comprise physical assets, that is tangible resources such as warehouses, transportation vehicles and equipment in order to provide a distribution and sourcing network, as well as human assets, that is intangible resources such as knowledge and skills of both top management and operational employees. RBV assumes that these idiosyncratic resources do not add any value outside the core capability of the firm's boundaries. Hence, the necessary capabilities and resources to pursue effective logistics operations determine the strategic importance and length of a partnership between a service provider and the focal firm.

However, the bundle of services provided by third parties does not necessarily need to be complex or of much strategic importance for the focal firm; moreover, third parties can also be used as tools or one-time providers for services. Less important or peripheral and rather modular logistics activities that are not a firm's core capability such as simple transportation and warehousing services, however, can be operated more efficiently by third parties, due to economies of scale and scope, as well as their internal knowledge and experience within these operations and the industry they are operating in.

RBV proponents suggest it can be applied to the choice of the right governance form and can explain the decision to move from outsourced market transactions (where strategic importance of capabilities is low), to a hierarchical governance form using a service provider of logistics systems (where strategic importance of capabilities is higher), and towards the form of logistics systems integration (where strategic importance of capabilities is highest).

Various examples from the industry

This is an authentic case study but based on a composition of various clients the authors have worked with. For reasons of commercial confidentiality the names of the companies and the data and specific situations have been disguised. The findings are based on interviews that were conducted with mid-level and C-level managers across various firms that offer logistics services across Europe. The present case study does not focus on a particular industry per se but emphasizes more on the understanding of service provision and logistics capabilities across various industries.

Furthermore, this case study builds on common definitions of a logistics firm. Most cases or textbooks also differentiate three types of logistics firms such as carriers, intermediary firms and 3PL firms, in order to understand the different logics of such firms and their interdependence based on the firms' network capabilities and scope of operations. This case study, however, evaluates and differentiates between logistics operators (also referred to as transportation carriers), third-party logistics providers (3PL) and fourth-party logistics providers (4PL), based on their distinct capabilities of exploiting and accessing logistics resources.

Logistics operators and transportation carriers

Standardized transportation activities represent the most common services that are offered by any logistics firm. Such firms act as transportation carriers and offer very basic and less strategic operations that are not integrated in any wider supply chain context. These carriers execute simple transportation processes between a manufacturing or production plant to a customer's warehouse or any other retail facility. The requirements and specifications of these transactions are very low and do not ask for any specific assets or equipment. In most cases these logistics services only requires physical and human assets in the form of transportation vehicles without specific requirements, and human capital in the form of drivers and industrial employees in a warehouse. A small number of staff handle and coordinate the clients' orders and enquiries, and allocate the company's equipment in order to gain best vehicle and staff utilization. The strategic capabilities, drawing on the resource-based constructs, is therefore very low for standardized outsourcing activities. The exploitation of assets such as vehicles and other transportation equipment is done to an extent that can easily be copied by competitors that have access to the relevant resources. Hence, the resources are not scarce and valuable on their own. In contrast, there are high maintenance and running costs, such as fuel, insurance and labour costs.

Consequently, logistics operators or transportation carriers operate in a highly competitive market environment, based on the low market entry barriers. RBV suggests that only resources that are valuable, rare, inimitable or non-substitutable will contribute to a firm's sustained competitive advantage. Hence, carrier firms do not necessarily possess or can exploit any other forms of bundles of resources or services that limits their ability to increase their performance or profit margins.

Third-party logistics (3PL) providers

Logistics processes that are more complex in their nature such as distribution networks and integrated warehousing activities represent the service offerings of third-party logistics (3PL) providers. Here, the frequency of operations and services is not predictable; and high uncertainty in demand and capacity allocation defines the nature of these activities. The required capabilities, however, for these transactions are of less strategic importance for the focal firm's competitiveness. Mostly producers or manufacturers of industrial goods, whose core competence is not the logistics function, consider integration with a dedicated 3PL provider in order to fulfil their logistics requirements. Examples are retailers or supplier firms for industrial organizations. The 3PL companies provide a specific network and bundle of services to their customers, resulting in longer-term contractual relationships. Investments into the provision of distribution networks in terms of facilities, vehicles and equipment is very high, and the providers benefit from economies of scales and economic synergies.

Hence, transaction costs are high, given that the individual requirements are very specifically tailored to the customers and involve long planning and training time. Renegotiation and monitoring is a big part in the contractual relationships. Also the effective use of information technology has been proven to be a crucial factor of a successful relationship. Taking all these determinants into account makes it very difficult, costly and time consuming to switch suppliers or providers. Outsourcing the logistics function but maintaining an integrated relationship in terms of communication and data exchange therefore represent the hierarchical governance form for these 3PL transactions.

Again, the strategic importance for logistics activities increases with the nature of the provided services or product of a focal firm. Short lead times and availability issues such as it is present in the food and the oil and gas industries determine the governance structure of logistics transactions. Even so the specification of certain activities, such as transportation, storing and handling of the goods, is comparatively low, an efficient operation determines the competitive advantage of a focal firm. Tangible and intangible resources can be of high value, if they are exploited in an adequate way, business relationships and reputation can be barriers to entry or the rerendering of a contract. Hence, 3PL providers are in a slightly better position than transportation carriers regarding competitors. Also, the uniqueness of the logistics network capabilities and tangible resources, such as special tank trailers and warehousing facilities, can guarantee that the transactions are non-substitutable for other firms.

Fourth-party logistics (4PL) providers

The highest form of complexity is present when the number of partners in a network increases, and operations include transactions across different functions such as procurement, replenishment and distribution. These complex supply structures appear when multinational organizations organize the replenishment and delivery of industrial and commercial goods to their global customers, retail stores or end consumers. Increasing complexity requires an efficient coordination of all activities along the supply chain. 4PL providers offer integrated solutions with the aim of full visibility and flexibility, incorporating all supply chain and logistics functions such as distribution, warehousing, financing, ordering and inventory management. The very high complexity of operations and adaptation of information technology systems to coordinate multiple partners and processes results in very high specifications for these transactions. Due to extremely long planning and induction times, the transaction costs increase and the integrators for these systems aim to overcome the opportunistic behaviour of individual partners. Individual organizations or managers can be better controlled and dealt with due to the provision of fully visible supply-chain-wide operations. Strategic capabilities for these transactions are very high as the 4PL firms provide not only a bundle of different services but also exploit the necessary resources by subcontracting and building alliances with other logistics partners. 4PL providers usually do not possess all of the required equipment by themselves but are still capable of providing integrated solutions to their customers. Particularly in fast-moving consumer goods (FMCG) sectors like the fashion retail industry, where fast-changing consumers' behaviour and requirements force customers to use fourth-party providers.

Discussion and managerial implications

Where simple market transactions are carried out by transport carriers or logistics operators with their own vehicle fleet and warehousing facilities, operations are very modular and the strategic importance very low. Outsourcing these functions only for the sake of transporting products does not add any value, and results in a simple short-term dyadic market relationship. Where logistics activities are more integrated with an external 3PL provider and the relationship extends a simple market transaction, the strategic importance increases. Hence, highly integrated relationships encompass more than simple transportation and warehousing processes. Where an integrator of logistics or 4PL provider controls and organizes the entire chain of partners and activities, both transaction specification and strategic capabilities are far higher than for any other function within an organization. Continuous adaptive solutions.

The presented case study has several implications. First, while considerable research on logistics outsourcing has focused on the perspective of the focal firm in terms of supplier selection and cost benefits, RBV contributes by identifying and classifying different logistics transactions themselves and switching the focus towards the provider site. Second, we found that logistics operations and the extent of their implication to the overall performance of a focal firm's supply chain have not been fully understood among both providers and users of such services. Even though most providers tailor their services to the specific requirements of their customers, the integration, especially regarding information technology and data exchange, is often a source of dissatisfaction for all partners. Third, the interviews showed that there is an increasing demand for integrated solutions, as customer requirements and environmental uncertainty significantly impact on the need for adapted solutions in order to maintain a sustained competitive market position.

Questions

1 What strategic capabilities does each category of logistics firms appear to have?

   a) logistics operators;

   b) 3PL firms;

   c) 4PL firms.

2 What are the different capabilities each category would have to grow or acquire to move from

   a) logistics operators to 3PLs?

   b) 3PL firms to 4PL firms?

3 How would performance be measured among

   a) logistics operators?

   b) 3PL firms?

   c) 4PL firms?

Answers

1 a) What strategic capabilities do logistics operators appear to have?

Logistics operators represent the simplest form of logistics activities. Due to their very basic and standardized operations, their strategic capabilities are limited to mostly physical assets and tangible resources such as transportation units, warehousing facilities, truck drivers, and industrial staff and employees. Most capabilities are not particularly scarce or valuable by themselves, which results in a highly competitive market environment. Market-entry barriers are also very low due to the easily accessible and inimitability of resources.

However, logistics operators appear to excel in the exploitation and accessibility of these very basic resources and assets, which then defines and contributes to their competitiveness. So basically it is not the resources alone but the operators' capabilities of exploiting them in the most effective and efficient way (such as benefiting from economies of scale) that makes a difference.

1 b) What strategic capabilities do 3PL providers appear to have?

3PL providers represent a more complex and integrated form of logistics activities. The 3PL firms provide rather advanced resources that include entire distribution networks, warehousing and consolidation facilities mostly on a national or European-wide level. Furthermore, 3PL firms possess established relational capabilities and a strong organizational structure. These relationships with other 3PL firms or smaller-scale operators allow them to benefit from economies of scale and scope. Also, the capabilities are less asset focused but emphasize the exploitation of knowledge and human capital or similar intangible resources.

1 c) What strategic capabilities do 4PL providers appear to have?

4PL providers represent the highest form of logistics and supply chain integration. Even though this concept is rather vague and abstract, 4PL firms operate on a purely strategic level of an organization and control and manage supply chain wide decision making. Their capabilities therefore do not include any physical or tangible assets, such as warehouses or transportation units. Moreover, their focus is mostly on the integration of information technology, that is the alignment of goals and the provision of solutions. Hence, the most important capabilities are integration capabilities and the ability to increase supply chain visibility.

2 a) What are the different capabilities each category would have to grow or acquire to move from logistics operator to 3PL providers?

Logistics operators must increase their relational capabilities in order to increase their operational scope to a more national level. Actions could include joining any European or global logistics networks and partnerships. Alternatively, the acquisition and development of own assets such as vehicles and office locations will increase their level of responsibilities. However, all actions are associated with high costs. The costly and expensive nature of logistics assets and equipment does not represent a very good return of investment ratio.

2 b) What are the different capabilities each category would have to grow or acquire to move from 3PL providers to 4PL providers?

3PL firms could increase their impact on customers and extend their scope on a more supply chain wide level by offering a broader range and bundle of services. The key here would be to provide a combination of various activities and operations that are linked together. For example, in addition to the warehousing activities, 3PL firms can easily offer distribution, replenishment, material handling and packaging services to the same customer. It is important, however, that services are offered to the same core customers in order to increase the dependability and gain trust over time. Eventually, 3PL providers will be able to provide more strategic and consulting advice and move away from the provision of physical assets to the development of knowledge and know-how.

3 a) How would performance be measured among logistics operators?

Measuring transportation and warehousing performance is limited to very basic and conventional objectives such as on-time delivery, vehicle utilization ratios, pallets or products throughput and warehouse turnaround times. There is actually no need and no requirements from the industry or customers to include more sophisticated performance objectives. Measuring performance is too costly, and given the basic nature of the operations, monitoring is done on a very low level. Performance within transportation carriers is mostly limited to operational efficiency including ratios that determine empty running, fuel consumption, driving hours, and so on.

3 b) How would performance be measured among 3PL providers?

Monitoring and measuring 3PL services could be done via more sophisticated tracking and tracing technologies, as well as event scanning, and providing information on the entire network performance. Here, the focus must lie on combining and integrating information and data (such as shipment volume, size, numbers and times) from various transportation carriers or other sub-tier providers. These measurement objectives will ultimately lead to a supply chain wide transparency from the point of origin to the point of consumption. However, implementing such objectives is highly complex due to the heterogeneity of information and systems requirements from different partners and suppliers along the supply chain.

3 c) How would performance be measured among 4PL providers?

Monitoring and performance measurement on a supply chain and supply-network-wide level certainly raises issues and challenges that are due to the complexity and interaction of multiple suppliers and customers. However, the main focus should be on adapting a customer-centric perspective. Ultimate performance objectives address the end consumers' needs and quality expectations. The challenge for 4PL firms is to provide the platforms and IT capabilities in order to guarantee transparency over all activities that go beyond the conventional transportation and warehousing links but also include the condition of products and goods at any time at any stage in the supply chain or the product life cycle. Most 4PL firms provide customer-specific performance indicators that are highly customized and can be accessed from any place in the world.

CASE STUDY 2.9

Managing sustainability in the fashion supply chain

Operationalization and challenges at a UK textile company

Piyya Muhammad Rafi-Ul-Shan,
Patsy Perry and David B Grant

AUTHOR BIOGRAPHIES

PIYYA MUHAMMAD RAFI-UL-SHAN is a PhD student at the Logistics Institute, Hull University Business School. Research areas include supply-chain risk management, sustainable supply-chain management, agile and responsive supply chains, and the garment and fashion industry.

DR PATSY PERRY is a Lecturer in Fashion Marketing in The School of Materials at The University of Manchester. Her research interests include corporate social responsibility in fashion supply chains, and she has published a number of book chapters and academic journal papers in this area.

PROFESSOR DAVID B GRANT is Professor of Logistics at Hull University Business School. His research interests include logistics customer service, satisfaction and quality, retail logistics, and sustainable logistics and supply-chain management. He has over 175 publications including *Sustainable Logistics and Supply Chain Management* and *Fashion Logistics* for Kogan Page.

Introduction

The fashion industry has a high environmental impact in terms of its carbon, water and waste footprint, and is therefore facing increased pressure from multiple stakeholders to balance environmental, social and economic needs – the three tenets of the triple bottom line (or TBL). Production of the most popular fibre, cotton, entails high use of water and chemicals such as pesticides and fertilizers during the plant-growth phase, with further heavy use of chemicals, water and energy during the textile-production phases of dyeing, drying and finishing. Furthermore, intensifying competition in the fashion market has led to pressure for low-cost products and short lead-times. To address these pressures, vertical disintegration has become commonplace with textile and garment production activities typically outsourced to lower labour-cost countries in the developing world. However, this strategy has resulted in complex globally dispersed fashion supply chains, with potentially negative impacts for people and the planet. The transportation of fashion products from developing countries where goods are produced to developed countries where goods are sold has a negative environmental impact in terms of carbon emissions. In addition to environmental issues, the fashion industry also faces criticism regarding social issues of worker exploitation in its global production networks. The fashion industry's worst industrial disaster to date occurred in Bangladesh in April 2013, where poor building safety standards led to the collapse of the Rana Plaza garment factory and resulted in the loss of life of over 1,100 workers producing garments for global fashion retailers. These issues have resulted in an increased focus on sustainability issues in the fashion industry. However, the challenge for fashion businesses lies in how sustainability can be incorporated into an industry sector where the critical success factors are cost efficiency and effectiveness.

Sustainability in fashion supply chains

Currently, there is no unified and universally accepted definition of the concept of sustainability or its operationalization. Complexities in integration of its elements, interconnectedness, the interests of different stakeholders and multiple interpretations have made it into a buzzword. The two most prominent and frequently cited definitions of sustainability are those of sustainable development and the triple bottom line. Sustainable development aims to meets the needs of present without compromising the needs of the future generations, thus ensuring a better quality of life for present and future generations. The triple bottom line consists of three interconnected pillars: people (social), planet (environment) and profit (economic). It aims to measure the social and environmental performance of a company over a period of time, as well as its economic performance.

People: The social perspective of sustainability places emphasis on humanitarian-related issues in global supply chains, such as poverty and income inequality, access to health care, water and sanitation, education, and developing solutions to globalization and economic development. Fashion companies may introduce ethical codes of conduct to address social issues such as child labour, working hours and conditions, health and safety, wages and freedom of association in supplier facilities.

Planet: The environmental perspective of sustainability focuses on the effective management of physical resources and ensuring consumption below their natural reproduction level or according to the availability of substitutes or alternatives. Ecosystem biodiversity, limits to growth and natural capital are the tenets and key concepts of this perspective, which places emphasis on physical limits to the planet as a resource provider, as well as accommodator of waste and industrial discharge. Fashion companies may introduce initiatives to prevent and control pollution, such as environmentally friendly dyeing and finishing processes, responsible disposal of waste and use of bio-degradable raw materials.

Profit: The economic perspective of sustainability emerged from economic growth models and macroeconomic aspects of business entities. It places emphasis on industrial activities, pollution by business operations, resource use and the impact of business activities on the population. This perspective concerns the economic benefit of the business to society as a whole, not simply internal profit.

What is implied in sustainability, biologically, is the avoidance of extinction and ensuring the organism lives to reproduce. Economically, sustainability implies avoiding major disruptions, disasters, collapses and vulnerabilities by hedging against instabilities and discontinuities.

Sustainability thus concerns longevity and continuity. Sustainable actions are taken today in the hope that they will lead to future survival.

Sustainable supply chain management can be defined as the strategic integration of social, environmental and economic goals in organizational business processes to improve the long-term economic performance of the company and its supply chain. However, recent trends such as outsourcing, globalization, advances in infrastructure and information technology, cheap labour and raw materials have resulted in increased supply chain vulnerability, fragility and likelihood of operational disruptions in fashion supply chains. Increasingly, companies are being held responsible for environmental and social impacts of not only their own operations but also those of their supply chain partners; this has led to an extended supply chain responsibility for managing sustainability. Therefore, it is imperative for fashion businesses to understand sustainability, integrate it into their strategy and ensure good management thereof for supply chain continuity and to avoid business disruption or failure. Within the fashion industry, companies may incorporate specific sustainable practices such as use of organic or renewable fibres, recycling of fibres and garments, use of natural or low-impact dyes, designing longer-lasting products instead of fast fashion, use of Fairtrade raw materials and fibres, implementation of ethical labour practices in supplier facilities, reducing energy consumption and water consumption, reducing packaging. The following initiatives are examples of sustainable actions that fashion companies may take to manage sustainability:

- Preparing a sustainability report, such as Marks & Spencer's annual Plan A report.

- Reducing waste, such as H&M's global garment collection initiative to allow consumers to return used clothing to store for responsible disposal.

- Reducing use of energy resources by using a more efficient energy system such as Inditex's use of motion detectors to automatically turn off lights in low-traffic areas within its eco-model store in Barcelona.

- Using fuel-efficient vehicles for transportation, such as Clipper Logistics' use of electric vehicles to make deliveries to stores in London's Regent Street.

- Constructing green buildings, such as Brandix's world-leading platinum-rated LEED certified green apparel factory in Seeduwa, Sri Lanka.

- Developing partnerships with NGOs, such as Greenpeace or Labour Behind the Label.

- Designing products that consider the environment, such as Patagonia's use of recycled and organic fabrics.

- Being proactive and anticipating regulatory changes.

- Seeking certifications, such as SA8000, ISO140001 or ISO50001.

- Enhancing worker-based programmes, such as Gap's PACE (Personal Advancement & Career Enhancement) programme.

However, the fashion industry is notorious for its high product variety, short product life cycles and unpredictable demand. Cost and lead-time pressures are combined with a complex and geographically long supply chain, which presents a clear challenge to the implementation of sustainability. Managing sustainability is therefore highly complex, multi-perspective and problem oriented. The following case study of a UK knitwear manufacturer and retailer illustrates some of the challenges to sustainability faced by companies in the fashion sector.

CASE STUDY
Company A

Company A is a UK-based designer knitwear manufacturer and retailer, originally established as a domestic textile manufacturer during the eighteenth century but now involved in global outsourcing and retailing activities of own-brand products as well as contract manufacturing for other fashion brands. The company counts some of the world's top fashion brands among its customers and most of its products are made of the finest natural fibres, such as merino wool, cashmere and the world's top-quality cotton. While raw material production takes place in China and Italy, almost all garment manufacture takes place at the company's UK factory.

Operationalization of sustainability in company A

Company A incorporates a number of sustainability initiatives into its business operations in order to support ongoing business longevity and growth, as well as environmental and human resource protection.

Building partnerships with relevant stakeholders and creating a supportive organizational culture is important for the operationalization of sustainability within the business. The company strongly believes in partnerships and therefore has entered into a number of partnerships with supply chain partners, NGOs, universities and industry bodies in order to improve their knowledge of sustainability issues and best practice. Proactive, pre-emptive, whole-process supply chain and right first time thinking cultural initiatives are being introduced to manage sustainability more effectively.

To support business longevity and pre-empt supply chain disruptions, the sourcing team sets up long-term contracts for raw material supply continuity and to take advantage of average prices. Contracts are rechecked and renegotiated in case of any discrepancies or if suppliers deviate from what was already agreed. Buying in bulk is also preferred to save cost. In order to overcome capacity problems and shortage of a technically skilled workforce, the company has introduced apprenticeships and some major initiatives to cross-train the workforce. Currency hedging, use of certified and approved supply chain partners, agencies, forums, factories and materials are also used as sustainability risk management tools to prevent supply disruptions.

Within the UK factory, the company has set up a works council as a regular forum for employees to raise issues with management and thus address the social perspective of sustainability. For overseas supplier factories, the technical manager makes regular visits to identify and audit sustainability risks.

As a premium fashion brand and supplier, Company A conforms to strict EU legislation regarding use of chemicals, dyes and other environmental issues when importing raw materials into the UK for garment production. Being proactive in anticipation of regulatory changes as well as cost increases, it is investigating alternatives and substitutes for restrictive and expensive substances, materials and processes in order to comply with laws and regulations and to save cost. It also adopted the Toyota Production System model of lean manufacturing to reduce waste in the UK factory and thereby achieve cost savings as well as reducing environmental impact. The product design phase is seen as crucial in identifying sustainability risks, so senior management meets designers to discuss and identify sustainability risks before garments go into production.

Challenges to sustainability in company A

Despite the development of a number of initiatives to address sustainability issues in the business, Company A sees a number of challenges to improving its performance in managing sustainability risks, outlined as follows:

- The company's small size and stagnant growth – therefore, it lacks resources to recruit a dedicated sustainability manager and instead relies upon its technical or sourcing managers to manage sustainability issues.
- Lack of a dedicated team or champion who looks solely at sustainability, generates information and is ultimately responsible to manage such issues.
- Old technology, factory and infrastructure and inability to invest in more modern, efficient and environmentally friendly technology and processes.
- Lack of sustainability knowledge and a short-term view of the business.
- Lack of visibility and control of the whole supply chain.
- An unwanted move to fast fashion and increasing number of own-brand collections to respond to intensifying competition in the market, which increases the risk of supply chain vulnerability, fragility and likelihood of operational disruptions.
- An ageing working force, stagnant culture and no newness coming into the factory, which results in a lack of new ideas for overcoming the barriers to sustainability.

Questions

1 What do you understand by the term 'sustainability'?
2 What are the key sustainability challenges in the fashion industry?

3 What are the challenges to managing sustainability in fashion supply chains?

4 How does Company A incorporate sustainability into its operations?

5 What are the barriers to managing sustainability for Company A?

6 How could the company overcome these barriers?

Answers

1 What do you understand by the term 'sustainability'?

Sustainability can be defined from two perspectives. First, to be capable of being sustained. Sustainability is about ensuring sufficient resources remain for future generations, and to ensure longevity, continuity or survival in the future. Second, to be capable of being maintained at a steady level without adverse impact on environment or causing ecological damage. Sustainable development is defined as development that meets the needs of present without compromising the needs of the future generations, ensuring a better quality of life for people today and tomorrow. The triple bottom line (TBL) view of business emphasizes the interconnectedness of people, planet and profit. This implies that social and environmental sustainability initiatives, in order to be successful, should be considered in conjunction with economic and long-term corporate sustainability.

2 What are the key sustainability challenges in the fashion industry?

In terms of the environment, the fashion industry makes high use of water and chemicals such as pesticides and fertilizers during the plant-growth phase, with further heavy use of chemicals, water and energy during the textile-production phases of dyeing, drying and finishing. The transportation of garments from developing country producers to developed country sales markets results in a high carbon footprint.

In terms of people, the fashion industry faces criticism for of worker exploitation in its global production networks. Production is outsourced to developing countries to take advantage of lower labour costs, but standards may be lower than in developed countries and the sweatshop problem may arise.

3 What are the challenges to managing sustainability in fashion supply chains?

Cost and lead-time pressures often take precedence over sustainability. For example, the examples of actions that fashion companies may take to improve sustainability require upfront investment. A complex and geographically long supply chain makes it difficult to have full visibility and control of sustainability issues throughout the supply chain.

4 How does Company A incorporate sustainability into its operations?

- Building partnerships with relevant stakeholders and creating a supportive organizational culture is important for the operationalization of sustainability within the business.
- Set up long-term contracts for raw material supply continuity and to take advantage of average prices, supporting business longevity and pre-empting supply chain disruptions. Currency hedging, use of certified and approved supply chain partners, agencies, forums, factories and materials are also used as sustainability risk-management tools to prevent supply disruptions.
- Set up a works council in UK factory as a regular forum for employees to raise issues with management and thus address the social perspective of sustainability.
- Make regular visits to identify and audit sustainability risks in overseas supplier factories.
- Conform to EU legislation regarding use of chemicals, dyes and other environmental issues when importing raw materials into the UK for garment production. Being proactive in anticipation of regulatory changes as well as cost increases, it is investigating alternatives and substitutes for restrictive and expensive substances, materials, processes in order to comply with laws and regulations and to save cost.
- Adopt the Toyota Production System model of lean manufacturing to reduce waste in the UK factory and thereby achieve cost savings as well as reducing environmental impact. Identify sustainability risks in product design phase, so senior management meets designers to discuss and identify sustainability risks before garments go into production.

5 What are the barriers to managing sustainability for Company A?

- The company's small size and stagnant growth – therefore, it lacks resources to recruit a dedicated sustainability manager and instead relies upon its technical or sourcing managers to manage sustainability issues.

- Lack of a dedicated team or champion who looks solely at sustainability, generates information and is ultimately responsible to manage such issues.

- Old technology, factory and infrastructure and inability to invest in more modern, efficient and environmentally friendly technology and processes.

- Lack of sustainability knowledge and a short-term view of the business.

- Lack of visibility and control of the whole supply chain.

- An unwanted move to fast fashion and increasing number of own-brand collections to respond to intensifying competition in the market, which increases the risk of supply chain vulnerability, fragility and likelihood of operational disruptions.

- An ageing workforce, stagnant culture and no newness coming into the factory, which results in a lack of new ideas for overcoming the barriers to sustainability.

6 How could the company overcome these barriers?

This question is not specifically covered in the case but is an opportunity for students to move beyond the case and consider how supply chain or management concepts they may have learnt previously could help the company overcome barriers to managing sustainability. For example:

- Build a continuous improvement culture and promote team-working within the business in order to address sustainability issues despite the company's small size and lack of a dedicated sustainability champion.

- Keep quality as a priority to avoid further shift into fast fashion.

- Develop closer trading relationships (perhaps technology-enabled) with suppliers to increase visibility and control of the supply chain.

- Develop sustainability knowledge by using existing bodies and forums for guidance and information, eg EU legislation, SEDEX, Better Cotton initiatives guidance, ISO 14001 (environmental management) and ISO 26000 (social responsibility) guidance. These sources are easily accessible online and free to download.

- Be more proactive and prepared for future critical issues by developing a longer-term sustainability strategy for the business.

Further activity

Ask students to research examples of other fashion retailers or brands (large or small) that have undertaken one or more of the suggested initiatives to help manage sustainability. Discuss how they have achieved this and what have been the benefit(s) to the business as well as to society and the environment.

Supply chain dreams and nightmares

The risks of unmanaged cost reduction

Gerard Chick

AUTHOR BIOGRAPHY

GERARD CHICK is Chief Knowledge Officer at Optimum Procurement Group. He has considerable experience working with some of the keenest minds at the most senior level in supply management today. He is regularly invited to make keynote presentations and deliver workshops on strategic procurement issues to senior executive teams across the world.

Introduction

Driving cost out of the supply chain has kept businesses on their toes for the last 30 years, but in doing so many have incrementally increased their exposure to risk; sometimes to catastrophic levels. This may be expected in situations of pure cost reduction with no regard to product quality or service delivery, but even some of the *wunderkind* of procurement, who recognize that cost reduction can be allied to innovation and competitiveness, have not been immune to this folly. One classic and high-profile case which I'm exploring in this paper is Boeing. With a globe-spanning supply chain, the Boeing 787 Dreamliner became the fastest-selling aircraft in aviation history. Boeing's share price skyrocketed and the C-suite received their bonuses. Procurement supporting the business at its best and the work was done, or was it?

Background

On 10 November 2013, a 787 Dreamliner flight operated by Japan Airlines developed a problem with its battery – the latest in a spate of problems plaguing Boeing's 787 aircraft. A cockpit indicator in the aircraft pointed to a problem with the battery connected to the aircraft's auxiliary power unit. The 787 Dreamliner was developed by leading airplane manufacturer the US-based Boeing Airplane Company (Boeing). The 787 Dreamliner was Boeing's modern jet in which the aircraft manufacturer used new technology to cut the cost of fuel used for operating the plane by 20 per cent. To reduce weight and improve fuel efficiency, the aircraft manufacturer used carbon-fibre materials and electronic systems with more powerful generators and higher-energy lithium-ion batteries.

Boeing's 787 Dreamliner was expected to be a game-changer for the commercial airline industry. According to public sources, although nearly 900 aircraft have been sold, Boeing's profitability came into question as the organization's far-reaching global supply chain began to quickly suffer fatigue. The 787 dream was to systematically reduce development time from typically six to four years and cut associated costs from around \$10 billion to \$6 billion. The result has been catalogued more like a nightmare. The project is reported to be billions of dollars over budget and three years behind schedule.

Let's examine the back story. Reports say that the 787 was Boeing's response to losing market share to Airbus in the late 1990s. It decided to innovate with a new aircraft that would generate revenues by creating value for customers in two ways:

- First it aimed to improve the passenger travel experience. Using a composite material in the 787 allowed increased humidity and pressure to be maintained in the passenger cabin, which offered substantial improvement to the flying experience.

- Second, the lightweight composite materials would enable the 787 to fly non-stop to and from anywhere in the world.

At the heart of the problem is Boeing's mimicry of other organizations 'best practice' (supported by experts).

Best practice No. 1

Boeing used the 'Dell Model' – Dell developed a direct-sales model and its 'build-to-order/configure-to-order' approach to manufacturing – and applied it to the project's funding model.

Boeing aimed to improve value for their customers, the airlines themselves, through improvements in operational efficiency. These would offer the airlines fuel savings of 20 per cent for comparable flights and their cost per-seat-per-mile would be 10 per cent lower than for any other aircraft currently in service. Boeing's innovative composite based fuselage would reduce maintenance and replacement costs to the airlines too. So far, a supply chain sourcing dream: true innovation, requiring sourcing and procurement at its best to turn blueprints into a commercial reality.

The nightmare seemingly began because of critical errors of judgement regarding both the outsourcing and offshoring of the project. Industry researchers are now saying that Boeing's attempt to minimize financial risks by maximizing the number of its development partners has had the opposite effect: outsourcing on the scale they did – 80 per cent, including large complicated componentry – actually increased the risk of project management failure.

The 787 involved not merely the outsourcing of a known technology; rather. it involved major and unproven technological innovation. Would the carbon-fibre composite survive the rigours of long distance flying? Could lithium-ion batteries, with a reputation for overheating and causing fires, be safely used? No one seemed to know and the interactions among these novel technologies, introduced simultaneously, exponentially increased the risk of wicked and as yet unforeseen problems.

The risks generated by the introduction of these several innovations then demanded a *greater* involvement by the OEM (the original equipment manufacturers) in the development and manufacture of the aircraft; yet, Boeing opted for less, delegating much of the detailed engineering and procurement to sub-contractors. This resulted in a burgeoning list of problems which then compounded a massively delayed project with freefalling costs.

Procuring a complex product system such as a commercial airliner involves a necessary degree of business process outsourcing (BPO), simply because one business may well lack the expertise in-house to cover all areas. In cases such as this the 'detail' that must be built into the outsourcing model is as complex as the final product is. And yet in this case Boeing significantly increased the amount of outsourcing for the 787 compared with their previous manufacturing of earlier planes – by as much as 70 per cent.

Moreover, it didn't approach outsourcing its operations and manufacture as a risky necessity; rather, it enthusiastically embraced it as a means of reducing costs and time of development. The dream was to build a supply chain that was going to keep manufacturing and assembly costs low, while spreading the financial risks of development to their suppliers.

Experience tells us that cost-cutting in this way via BPO both domestically and overseas without a specific focus on mitigation or elimination of predicted costs and risk creates an environment for them to materialize and multiply.

Even with proven technology there are major risks in BPO. Frequently components won't fit together during final assembly – the maxim is that the performance of the prime manufacturer can never exceed the capabilities of the *least* proficient of the suppliers. Costs do not vanish merely because the work is out-of-sight. In this case with untested assembly processes and new technology they had to endure a biblical scale of additional costs which should have been planned for at the project's outset. 'Make versus buy' decisions have to be based on complete assessments of all potential costs. Outsourcing also requires considerable additional up-front effort in planning to avoid situations such as major sub-assemblies not fitting together at final assembly and suffering increased cost and the loss of any advantage gained at the design stage. A telling fact is that Boeing outsourced the engineering and construction of the plane long before the product was defined and the costs established and understood.

The project's risk profile was magnified by the adoption of a new assembly outsourcing model too. Traditionally Boeing integrated and assembled different parts and subsystems produced by its suppliers in-house but this supply chain was to be based on a tiered structure that would allow the OEM to foster partnerships with 50 or so tier-1 strategic partners.

These strategic partners were to be the integrators; assembling different parts and subsystems produced by the tier-2 and tier-3 suppliers. Before long, it became apparent that some of their tier-1 partners didn't have the knowledge or experience to develop different sections of the aircraft or to manage their tier-2 suppliers. To regain control of the process, they had to buy one of the key tier-1 suppliers (Vought Aircraft Industries) and supply expertise to the others. Boeing then also had to pay their strategic partners compensation for potential profit losses stemming from the delays in production. As result the Dreamliner project went billions of dollars over budget; its delivery schedule has been pushed back at least seven times and the first planes were delivered more than three years late, with Boeing's reputation tarnished.

Best practice No. 2

Boeing attempted to mimic Toyota's tiered outsourcing model. This enabled the company to develop new cars with shorter development cycle times relying on a trusted group of partner firms for around 70 per cent of production.

It's a good idea in principle but key elements of the Toyota model appear to have been overlooked by Boeing. Toyota maintains tight control of the overall design and engineering of its vehicles, only outsourcing to suppliers who have proven track records in delivery based on time, quality, cost reduction and continuous innovation.

Adopting a tiered outsourcing model in this way but only paying scant regard to the values and practices on which it rests does not work. Poorly designed contractual arrangements create perverse incentives to work at the speed of the slowest supplier, providing penalties for delay but no rewards for timely delivery. The model requires the lead company to work closely with its suppliers and respond to concerns with integrity and respect, rather than putting this to one side in a file marked too difficult.

Another critical aspect here is offshoring. Some degree of offshoring is an inevitable aspect of manufacturing a complex product system such as a commercial airliner. Some expertise exists only in certain geographies for an assortment of reasons for example, the capacity to manufacture lithium-ion batteries lies outside the US. However more than 30 per cent of the 787's components came from outside the US, radically more than the 5 per cent for their hugely successful 747.

In principle there is nothing wrong with offshoring, but long supply chains create additional risks and mitigating them requires substantial and continuous communication between the buying and supplying organizations, often requiring on-site involvement, thereby generating additional cost. Not planning these communications or direct involvement results in additional cost and increased risk.

Boeing introduced a web-based communications tool called Exostar through which suppliers were encouraged to input project data and information regarding the progress of their work. The tool was to provide supply chain visibility, improve control and integration of critical business processes, and of course reduce development time and cost.

But the Orwellian black box failed. Without having first fostered trust in the supply chain, to expect suppliers to input accurate and timely information is a big ask. The result of a communications breakdown is that neither tier-1 suppliers nor Boeing were aware of or able to address fast-developing problems. Boeing's deep reliance on technologies contrasts sharply with agile practices of supplier relationship management where continuous face-to-face communications ensures that everyone is on the same page.

Ambitious projects with extraordinary risk require a leadership team with a deep understanding of end-to-end supply chain management. A diverse team with deep-smarts has the expertise and ability to anticipate and mitigate wide array of risks. In Boeing's case it is on record that instead of involving the employees in the decision-making process regarding these critical activities, they took a unilateral approach, which backfired, as labour relations broke down due to the outsourcing and offshoring decisions resulting in a costly strike. Effectively a combination of the risks outlined above constituted a threat to Boeing as a going concern.

Proximity of the leadership to manufacture

And where was the C-suite while these risks were being suffered? This is an interesting question in itself. In conjunction with the 787 decisions being made Boeing moved headquarters from Seattle to Chicago, for the leadership to be seen as neutral among the various divisions of Boeing, scattered throughout the US. The management didn't want to be bothered with, as Forbes reported it, 'how-do-you-design-an-airplane stuff', or to be involved in boring meetings with Boeing's key customers (airlines) who came to Seattle.

So while the CEO was in Chicago, strategizing about the future of Boeing the rest of the business back in Seattle were making the big decisions that would determine whether there even would be a firm to strategize about in the future.

Ultimately the Boeing case is an example of where, in a cost reduction focus, a business falls prey to two myths of supply chain management:

1 The first is economies of scale; the lure of cost savings through mass production in vast specialist factories. But of course they can't because all of the unanticipated costs noted earlier; carriage and transport costs, ramify the possibility and consequences of mistakes, the mopping up through rework and dealing with snagging and other problems relating to work being carried out incorrectly. Not to mention the knock-on costs both up and downstream and finally the management costs of sorting it all out. These circumstances cause economies of scale to lose their meaning, becoming diseconomies.

2 The second myth is the blind obedience to the promises of free-market fundamentalists. Corporations habitually overestimate the coordinating power of markets – and thus the attractiveness of the short-term benefits of offshoring/ outsourcing to low cost countries – while underestimating the increased importance of organization in this model.

Conclusions

So is it any wonder that the Dreamliner has turned into a nightmare for Boeing and the airlines that paid a list price of more than $200 million per aircraft? Whilst it suffered problems typical in new aircraft, such as brake malfunctions and computer glitches, it was the incidents such as the battery fire in Boston and the emergency landing by the All Nippon Airways flight bound for Tokyo that led the Federal Aviation Administration to ground the fleet. It is these incidents that have really unpacked the scale of supply chain misjudgement in this project.

The management principles here point to the need for supply chains that are as short as possible in both time and distance. Small and local – whether for police stations and GP practices to banks and computer firms' call centres – almost always beats large and remote in the balance of cost and risk. Expertise needs to be upfront, immediately at hand, whether on the production line or the phone, where it can respond to customers immediately.

The University of Cambridge Institute for Manufacturing published a report a little while ago; its title *Making the Right Things in the Right Place* says it all: in a globalized, virtual world, location and supply chain decisions are more critical not less. Given the turbulent ride experienced in this project, the grounding of the aircraft was in many respects inevitable for a project marked by missed opportunities, narrow vision, and ultimately dreams deferred.

The case is structured to help achieve the following:

- To develop an understanding of the importance of innovation in the aerospace industry and how Boeing managed their supply chain to develop a product that was hailed as a major innovation.

- To examine the reasons for the post-launch problems faced by the 787 Dreamliner.

- To carry out some analysis regarding the pros and cons of outsourcing in aviation.

- To explore ways in which Boeing could have better used their procurement and supply-management team to avoid their ultimate nightmare scenario.

Questions

1 How did Boeing manage their supply chain to facilitate innovation in the development of a new product?

2 What are the reasons for the problems that appeared post-launch of the 787 Dreamliner?

3 What are the pros and cons of outsourcing in the aviation industry?

4 How could Boeing have used its procurement and supply chain management team to avoid their ultimate nightmare scenario?

Answers

1 How did Boeing manage their supply chain to facilitate innovation in the development of a new product?

The company used the Dell Model (for building computers from OEM supplied parts) to build a new aircraft from new materials. There is no such thing as best practice, as issues vary between companies, industries, sectors, geographies and cultures. Boeing should have used their internal knowledge and experience to guide the activity they were engaged in. Where innovation was required they needed to consider the OEMs as partners and experts in their own right when it came to the deployment of the product or service they supplied to Boeing.

2 What are the reasons for the problems that appeared post-launch of the 787 Dreamliner?

In this case study, the reader will be able to discern that working with suppliers face to face and collaborating throughout the process will mean everyone is on the same page. The 'virtual' nature of much of the relationship management meant that things conspired to go wrong all at the same time, post-launch.

3 What are the pros and cons of outsourcing in the aviation industry?

Outsourcing is risky as you are moving your operations out of the business. Additionally your brand and reputation gets put into the hands of the service provider you have outsourced the work to. So if it is late or poorly executed you bare the risk and the consequences. Go back through the text and extract the pros and cons for Boeing you can find.

4 How could Boeing have used its procurement and supply chain management team to avoid their ultimate nightmare scenario?

Boeing took a lazy attitude to manufacturing a new aircraft, in a new material. They made too many assumptions about what the various outcomes of their decision-making processes would be. They asked consultants to choose and deploy procurement models for them rather that utilize their hard-earned experience. The mind-set of the project was one of 'short-term' cost reduction rather than a long-term strategy to manufacture a game-changing aircraft.

Uncertainty, disruption and resilience

Severe flooding in Bangkok and its effects on supply chains

Brian Lawrence

AUTHOR BIOGRAPHY

BRIAN LAWRENCE is Lecturer in the School of Management at the Assumption University in Bangkok, Thailand.

Introduction

You are an experienced supply chain specialist, just recruited to management status by a Singapore firm which has bought a factory in an industrial estate in north Bangkok. The CEO, a Singaporean, paid a bargain price because the mega-floods of 2011 had closed this factory for a month. He wants you to research what happened, identify the risks and prepare a business continuity plan so as not to be caught in a similar situation.

You discover the following abbreviated report based on research by a previous employee who was studying for a master's degree in supply chain management.

This research report explores the impact of a calamity to businesses in Thailand. Foreign firms operate alongside local firms (often foreign–local partnerships), whose supply chains are within Thailand but also cross boundaries. In 2011 there was disastrous flooding in industrial sites in north Bangkok, due to monsoon rainfall accumulating as the river flowed south, and through the capital, to the sea. The government flood control centre was flooded, and moved to the old airport, which also became flooded. Overflow from the swollen river was allowed to flood the northern suburbs and industrial sites so that the central commercial district could be saved. Many parts of Bangkok are below sea level and sinking, drained by a network of canals feeding into the river.

Research report

Introduction

Thailand is an attractive factory location for foreign investors, and several industries use it as their production hub for the region. This paper presents empirical data on how some firms dealt with Thailand's worst flooding in 70 years, and their attempts at resilience.

Literature review

Risk is the probability of experiencing a less than desirable event that affects one or more parties within a supply chain (Schlegel and Trent, 2012). Globalization is a key driver of complex supply chains. Unexpected events disrupt these trading webs. Failure to deliver to the customer is an uncertainty, whose causes include irregular weather conditions (Ho *et al*, 2005).

Resilience is the ability to recover from disruptions of any type (Schlegel and Trent, 2012).

To manage supply chain vulnerability, firms must plan for resilience and continuity, yet studies show that many organizations have not done this (Christopher and Peck, 2004).

Sheffi (2007) stated that enterprises can create resiliency through 'redundancy' or through 'flexibility'. *Redundancy* (slack resources) provides 'shock absorbers' through extra inventory, spare capacity, redundant suppliers, and product designs not dependent on a specific supplier (Tang, 2006). However, Chongvilaivan (2012) warned that redundancy through extra inventory and suppliers could be prohibitively costly. *Flexibility* is achieved through standardized facilities and processes, interchangeable parts and products, concurrent processes, postponement, alignment of procurement strategy with supplier relationships and collaboration (Sheffi, 2007). Resilience implies flexibility and agility: its implications extend beyond process redesign to fundamental decisions of sourcing and the establishment of more collaborative supply chain relationships (Christopher and Peck, 2004). Creating flexibility through information exchange and collaboration with trading partners is crucial to resilience against high-impact low-probability shocks such as floods (Chongvilaivan, 2012).

Interestingly, Waters (2011) combines the methods suggested for redundancy and flexibility and calls them ways of increasing agility (such as spare capacity, back-up systems, stocks of finished goods, holding cash reserves, postponement and short lead times).

Srivantaneeyakul (2011) argued the need for disaster-management planning. Emergency supply must be planned in advance, and so precisely that the logistics will be able to plan for the right time and the right capacity to handle those supplies. Each missing link in the supply chain will affect the rest. So each link needs a plan to handle unexpected crises. It is called a business continuity plan (BCP). This identifies the organization's exposure to threats, synthesizes hard and soft assets, and provides for effective prevention and recovery. Designing a plan would take around 6–12 months, and would involve all units. It is the last survival kit of the company. Five to seven steps are needed:

1 project plan;

2 risk analysis;

3 business impact analysis;

4 recovery strategy;

and then developed through:

5 training;

6 testing;

7 maintenance.

Despite the obvious need for a continuity plan in these risky times, most research shows that the majority of firms do not have one. There is always tomorrow for planning – but sometimes, tomorrow becomes today. One example of poor planning is the lack of IT continuity plans and insufficient risk avoidance. So much information is now stored in computer systems, not necessarily backed up or protected by more than a firewall. Yet hacking becomes bolder, even reaching the US president and the Pentagon. Research shows that 90 per cent of companies that lose their data in a disaster are out of business within two years.

Flood challenges

The World Bank (2012) estimated that the Thai flood in 2011 cost US$46.5 billion in economic losses, making it one of the costliest recent natural disasters. The floods had a severe impact on the private sector, especially manufacturing, which represents 38.5 per cent of Thailand's GDP and is one of the main drivers of Thailand's exports. The majority of manufacturers (about 70 per cent) are in five flood-affected provinces. Floods affected seven industrial estates and 66 out of 77 provinces.

The floods affected over four million households and 13 million people; 2,329 houses were completely destroyed, while 96,833 houses were partially damaged; 657 people died. Unemployment followed due to the closure of many factories. It was feared that the national economy was threatened through reduced investor confidence, which could lead to more unemployment. Enterprises faced serious challenges to survive such an unexpected disaster.

Methodology

Semi-structured interviews were conducted with managers working for firms affected by the floods. These interviewees were randomly chosen from graduate student-employees studying an MSc course in supply chain management.

Findings and analysis

The interview results disclosed that firms tried to prepare for and create resilience to deal with the water crisis. If threatened by flooding, machines were moved to higher floors. Various means were used to mitigate severity. Short-term action included temporarily shutting down production plants, distribution centres and offices, and delaying production plans and shipments. This disaster affected long-term strategic plans. Some firms decided to permanently relocate their plants to non-flooded areas while some permanently moved some production to their locations in other countries. Some firms had more than one production plant, distribution centre or branch in different locations. When it became urgent, they temporarily moved to non-flooded plants to continue operations. The firms studied dealt with the floods through their supply chain flexibility. They switched to other transport, standardized facilities and processes, and set up temporary offices and distribution centres.

1 One firm stated that during the flooding in 2011 they moved their HQ, warehouse and transport to another province, beyond Bangkok. Then, in 2012, their HQ and some indirect departments moved permanently to a Bangkok southern flood-free suburb.

2 Another firm temporarily moved all departments, and permanently relocated the production line of the main product to a non-flooded industrial estate.

3 In finding capacity elsewhere, one firm managed to survive by using capacity elsewhere in the Asia Pacific region (the firm has worldwide locations). It decided to move some product operations to a plant in China, and sent an engineering team to China to oversee this.

4 A big supermarket chain revealed that their first affected store was a supermarket. The biggest impact was the flooding of one of their food distribution centres (DCs). Its closure led to shortage of grocery products in many stores. A second, non-food, DC was disrupted by floodwater. Two other DCs, for fresh food products and express merchandise, were then also disrupted. As a result of the closure of the DCs 145 convenience stores had also to be closed. These were mini-stores, of small capacity. Then, some of their hypermarkets were threatened and had to close for two days because they expected to be flooded. They reopened after they were found to be safe and dry. The head office, in Bangkok, was closed for one month, and when seriously affected by flooding had to move temporarily to the National Exhibition Centre.

5 An electronics firm had to temporarily shut down. It suspended operations because of flooding in the surrounding areas of the industrial estate. The estate was without power, and government officials ordered an evacuation of the area. The company moved all equipment, raw materials and finished goods to the second floor before leaving.

6 A car-parts firm experienced a high flood level, interrupting their business and their whole supply chain. The firm was able to build barriers to protect the manufacturing area. But the area became flooded, so the HQ and manufacturing plant closed for three weeks. Employees were evacuated, and equipment and machines moved to a safe place for six weeks.

7 A jewellery firm realized that it should not risk putting all the firm's eggs in one basket. Eighty per cent of its sales worldwide are products made in Thailand. Before the floods, the company planned to set up a distribution centre in Thailand. After the floods, it decided to set it up in Singapore instead, even though the operating cost is higher. In addition, the company is building a new factory in Vietnam with a similar capacity to Thailand.

8 A large retail chain experienced stock shortage from local suppliers, so was able to switch to suppliers in Hong Kong, Malaysia and Taiwan, for essential basic items which customers desperately wanted. It took a week to deliver to Thailand, expensively, by plane. These new suppliers were well known for their quality and reliability because they only used quality manufacturers, and order quantities and delivery were guaranteed.

9 A Japanese car-assembly firm had ten factories inundated by floods, up to three-metres high. There was a review of overall sourcing strategy. Single sourcing for some parts would have to be changed to multiple sourcing, to reduce the risk of supply shortage from inbound disruptions.

10 In Thailand, trucks (vans, lorries) account for 88 per cent of transportation compared with 2 per cent for rail freight and 10 per cent for ship freight. A retailer revealed that the company had to use public transport such as trains and planes. They used train containers to deliver products to many provinces on three routes. The goods were prioritized and the most essential items allocated to these containers.

11 Many firms were able to continue production and operations by moving to non-flooded factories. As their plants and processes are identical, some employees were temporarily transferred, as in the case of a jeweller. After the Ayutthaya factory had to be closed, some workers were transferred to their smaller factory at an industrial estate where the company also provided living accommodation. Workers who could not manage the move, still received 100 per cent of their salaries. Totally unexpectedly, employees in Austria generously donated money to their Thai colleagues.

12 Some firms rented space for temporary offices or DCs. An electronics firm rented a temporary office in a Bangkok hotel, using it for joint recovery planning with its customers.

13 A retailer said that the biggest impact from flooding was the disabling of four DCs. The first thing was to set up temporary DCs. They first rented a place at the old northern Bangkok airport, but this area too became flooded, so it was moved to an exhibition centre in south Bangkok, which was also used as temporary HQ. Five stores were set up to be mother stores, hubs for upcountry distribution. They were provided for suppliers whose warehouse or factory was nearby. Due to limited space and time, these stores were mainly stocked with essential items, such as rice, water, and instant noodles. For non-urgent items they had to look for cooperation from their own suppliers to find ways to deliver goods to stores.

14 An auto firm said that some of its suppliers were flooded and could not continue. So, the firm halted production in three plants for five days. Japanese *keiretsu*, strong partnerships and a web of supply networks provided resilience. The firm then ordered parts from Indonesia and Japan instead. But it was not enough to fulfil an order from the Middle East. There were many backlogs. But the Thai domestic market turned out not to be a problem as many Thai customers requested a delay in selling them a car in troubled times. Ordering imported engines in big quantities from suppliers in Indonesia and Japan by plane lasted only for a short period. But when those new suppliers realized that their own local suppliers for small parts could not meet the increased demand, they also stopped delivering to Thailand. So, the production plan was reduced to one shift instead of two. Workers were asked to be on the production line for six hours, with two hours spent on safety activities. Supplier

disruptions lasted a month before all production resumed.

15 The experience of a retail chain was that direct delivery to stores was one way to fulfil customer needs, but that needed a lot of cooperation from suppliers who now had to deliver the stocks to stores by themselves. They had to use their own trucks or third-party logistics providers (3PL). However, if the product quantity of each supplier was small or suppliers could not manage such transportation, all orders from those suppliers were consolidated and divided into appropriate regions. Suppliers with better capability were assigned to be representatives to deliver orders or use 3PL. However, it took time to consolidate orders and distribute them to stores, because suppliers themselves were also in trouble and many orders were rejected by 3PL. The delivery flow was not as planned.

16 In addition to collaborative relationships with supply chain partners, some firms tried unusual survival resilience by working with a competitor. Such was the case of a leading hypermarket operator. In the floods some provinces were devastated, and the firm had difficulty in delivering to the flooded areas as highways were closed. So, they invented 'co-opetition', that is collaboration with the competition. The firm agreed to share 3PL, DC and truck loads. Collaboration between competitors is not new, but is rarely seen in Thailand's retail industry. As the firm's supply chain manager said: 'A time of crisis forces us to think and act differently. Things which normally would be impossible or unthinkable become possible. Part is a survival instinct and part is the Thai way of helping each other – we are all Thais. Our collaboration with a direct competitor may seem unthinkable – but this was a crisis.'

17 In an auto firm, due to its just-in-time lean manufacturing strategy, the disruptions of supply networks caused parts shortages, and the assembly line had to stop. Its suppliers could not operate and therefore could not supply parts. This meant that no parts were available to manufacture cars, so there were many backlogs for overseas and domestic orders. Three plants had to be shut down for a month to plan and solve the problems. Normal roads were cut off, so the firm could not receive parts on time, which affected production plans. The firm delayed the production plan and shut down the night shift for two months, and delayed shipments to customers.

18 For a retailer, the most serious issue is distribution centres. So, it is planning to build more DCs upcountry so that stores that were not flooded would not be affected by DCs that were. The firm has made a list of essential items necessary in a crisis, and is sourcing goods from more overseas suppliers.

19 An electronics firm identified two key external risks: natural disaster risks and political risks. The firm has developed a contingency disaster plan after its bad flood experience. The company now has a risk-management team to identify all risks and find alternative ways to handle them. It has transferred the disaster risk to insurers who cover flood losses and business interruption losses. For political risks, the interviewee believed that politics contributed to the drawn-out (four months) flooding. It seemed that the government did not have an adequate plan to manage the disaster and enhance recovery. Since then, the government has set up a flood-protection policy, for instance, early-warning systems, preparedness, an emergency response protocol during crises and flooding mitigation systems. The government has established two major plans to provide flood protection in both the short term and long term: a main flood-protection plan with a budget of US$100 billion, and a national catastrophe insurance fund with a budget of US$1.6 billion.

20 A car-parts firm disclosed that the firm now manages the risk through a pre-prepared action and protection plan, risk mitigation and training. It said that supply risk is its focus, which is identified and managed according to the location of each supplier (flooded/non-flooded area) and by applying portfolio analysis to different parts in terms of their value potential and risk. A jewellery firm decided that communication from the government to the public was not reliable. The company now spreads its risks through different geographical areas, Vietnam and Singapore, because concentrating 80 per cent of its production base in Thailand is now seen to be too risky.

21 A 3PL focuses on the natural disaster risk, and has moved its indirect department away from flood areas. Its direct departments (warehouse and transport) have produced a business continuity plan (BCP) and have explained it to employees and customers. An auto firm said that a flood team was set up during the flood period. Flood risk is now identified by this firm according to 'the water level above mean sea level' (MSL), with corresponding action, including wrapping parts in plastic, and intense monitoring.

References

Chongvilaivan, A (2012) Managing global supply chain disruptions: Experience from Thailand's 2011 flooding. Paper presented at the APEC Study Centers Consortium Conference on Establishing Reliable Supply Chains, Kazan, Russia, 26–27 May

Christopher, M and Peck, H (2004) Building the resilient supply chain, *The International Journal of Logistics Management*, 15(2), pp 1–14

Ho, CF, Chi, YP and Tai, YM (2005) A structural approach to measuring uncertainty in supply chains, *International Journal of Electronic Commerce*, 9(3), pp 91–114

Schlegel, GL and Trent, RJ (2012) Risk management: welcome to the new normal, *Supply Chain Management Review*, 14(16), pp 42–45

Sheffi, Y (2007) *Resilient Enterprise: Overcoming Vulnerability for Competitive Advantage*, MIT Press, Cambridge, MA

Srivantaneeyakul, Yongyuy (2011) The need for a business continuity plan, *Journal of Supply Chain Management: Research & Practice*, 5(1–3), pp 1–3

Tang, CS (2006) Perspectives in supply chain risk management, *International Journal of Production Economics*, 103(2), 451–488

Waters, D (2011) *Supply Chain Risk Management: Vulnerability and Resilience in Logistics*, 2nd edn, Kogan Page, London

World Bank (2012) Thai flood 2011: Rapid assessment for resilient recovery and reconstruction planning [online] http://www.gfdrr.org (retrieved 27 April 2012)

Questions

1 Categorize the interviewees' statements into the two forms of resilience: redundancy and flexibility, and list specific examples (eg find other suppliers).

2 Which of these resilience responses do you think would be those of your organization to a catastrophic flood, and would there be other responses?

3 Which of these resilience actions were probably planned before the floods, or have been planned since?

4 Produce a draft business continuity plan for your own organization, based on the model above but adding some specific details.

If possible, work this case study with colleagues, and compare decisions; or decide each answer as a discussion group, with all opinions having to be justified.

Answers

1 Categorize the interviewees' statements into the two forms of resilience: redundancy and flexibility, and list specific examples (eg find other suppliers).

Most are examples of reacting to the flood by being flexible. Redundancies have to be planned beforehand, and can be costly if nothing happens or be more costly than an actual disaster as redundancy measures have to be maintained, year in and year out; yet the pressure is always on profit this year.

Let us take each of the numbered items above, in turn.

- 1 to 6: These are examples of flexibility.
- 7: This is an example of redundancy – dispersing its activities and making sure not all eggs are in one basket. However as it happened after the flood, not before, it is flexibility after the event.
- 8: This could be redundancy if pre-planned but again is flexibility as the change was made after the event, not planned before.
- 9: This too is flexibility – after the event, caused by the event, not a pre-planned response.
- 10: Pure flexibility.
- 11: Redundancy in that plants and processes are identical, through this again seems by chance rather than pre-planned, and therefore flexibility. Also flexibility in staff transfers.
- 12: Flexibility, a response to the event, not pre-planned.
- 13: Pure flexibility.
- 14: Redundancy was built in, because this sort of supportive interlocked system is typical for Japanese big businesses. But it was not enough, so flexibility was tried, but also failed.
- 15, 16: Flexibility.
- 17: This company operates just-in-time and lean which hates expensive redundancy. Shutting down plants is not flexibility but despair.
- 18: This is another example of redundancy – but after the event, not pre-planned.
- 19: Neither redundancy nor flexibility, transferring risk to

insurers is certainly pre-planned action. Whether it is redundancy depends on the firm's financial position and whether this was in the longer term too expensive. Government plans remain to be tested for effectiveness, and are a form of redundancy as extra-expensive mitigators of future floods.

- 20: The car firm, after the event, has been galvanized into preparing for the next flood. We do not know details of what it did in this 2011 flood. The jewellery firm, after the event will spread its risks, which could be redundancy if that adds expense.

- 21: Mainly flexibility by both firms – after this event but good for the next.

To summarize, most of the responses are examples of flexibility. Or, they could be said to be reactive, and maybe a desperate attempt to do something. There is not much evidence of pre-disaster control plans, or continuity plans. Let's hope that more firms have now become proactive.

2 Which of these resilience responses do you think would be those of your organization to a catastrophic flood, and would there be other responses?

It is not possible for a definitive comment to be made as firms can be so different in their risks and needs. Be honest, however: has the firm got a proactive plan? Has it diversified suppliers, inventory, factories, even countries as a deliberate redundancy policy? Or is it relying on being flexible on the day of a disaster? If it has faced and survived a disaster, what did the company do? Did it also progress to making a continuity plan? Who in the company oversees this and is it clearly communicated to the organization?

3 Which of these resilience actions were probably planned before the floods, or have been planned since?

Only the last few comments by interviewees are about planning for the future. This fits with the answer to Question 1, and also human reluctance to anticipate bad events. Thailand is a heavily Buddhist country, with great belief in *karma* (you will get what you deserve, it's fate, so don't tempt fate). The enduring power of a person's culture is grossly underestimated. We are all born into an ethnic or national or regional culture, often influenced by religion, ways of thinking and behaving. It is part of our weaning, is hard-wired and is very resistant to change. Thais differ from the Chinese or the French differ from the English and this is further nuanced by the fact that we are also individuals. We are largely ignorant of our own cultural conditioning, and think that other cultures are wrong because they appear different.

4 Produce a draft business continuity plan for your own organization, based on the model above but adding some specific details.

Follow the 5 to 7 steps at the end of the literature review, and interviewee comments 19–22. Firms vary, in so many ways: one size does not fit all. The major influence on a continuity plan is the motivation by an influential person in the firm, who sees the danger and wants to foresee and control as much of it as possible. The constituent parts are not hard to understand, but it needs will and cooperative action to identify and evaluate the risks and choose how to install a plan and tangibles (people, equipment, alternatives) that people understand and allows them to recognize their own responsibilities.

Note	I am grateful to Dr Piyawan Puttibarncharoensri for permission to use some of her research materia

Supply chain management and return on total net assets

Understanding the impact of SCM decisions on financial performance

Simon Templar

AUTHOR BIOGRAPHY

DR SIMON TEMPLAR is Visiting Fellow at the Centre for Logistics and Supply Chain Management at Cranfield School of Management.

Introduction

This case illustrates the impact that typical supply chain decisions can have on the elements that make up the income statement and balance sheet, but also key financial ratios, which are used by stakeholders to appraise the financial performance of an organization and its management.

Supply chain decisions will have an impact on the organization's revenue and its operating expenses and therefore profitability (income statement). A typical supply chain comprises non-current assets (property, plant and equipment) and working capital (current assets minus current liabilities), which are elements that are included on the organization's balance sheet. Typical current assets include inventories, accounts receivables and cash, while current liabilities are short-term debts, such as accounts payable to suppliers, proposed dividends to shareholders and taxes owed to the government.

Let's pause for moment and move away from the financial detail and just consider how the following are delivered to us as consumers: a glass of water, a mobile-phone call and the electricity used to power our appliances. To fulfil customer needs there is a considerable amount of money invested in the total assets of each of these supply chains. Just think of the number of mobile-phone masts, electricity pylons and the miles of water pipes that make up the physical infrastructure of each of these networks, but also the monies spent on operating expenses to deliver these products and services to us as consumers.

A fictional company FMCG Co has been used in this case to illustrate the impact of supply chain decisions on the financial performance of a business. The assumptions and costs used in the scenarios are indicative and are only to be used for training purposes, as they just illustrate the cause and effect relationship between supply chain decisions and financial performance. The full figures can be found in the Appendix. The traditional DuPont model has been adapted to illustrate the impact of supply chain decisions on return on total net assets rather than return on equity.

Balance sheet, income statement and return on total net assets

Before we can explore the impact of our supply chain decisions on the financial performance of a business, it is essential that we examine the balance sheet and income statement in more depth and importantly their relationship with the financial ratios used to measure business performance.

The balance sheet tells us two things:

1 where the company has raised the money to fund its operations;

2 where the company has spent these funds.

In essence the balance sheet is an equation, which has two equal halves. One half illustrates the capital employed in the business (where the money has come from) and the other half illustrates the total net assets of the organization (where the money has been spent). If we now take a look at FMCG Co balance sheet (see Appendix) we can see that the company's capital employed is £1.2 billion and their total net assets (non-current assets plus current assets minus current liabilities) are also £1.2 billion, and therefore the balance sheet is in equilibrium.

We will now explore each half of the balance sheet in greater detail, as it is important for us as supply chain managers to identify which elements our decisions have a direct impact on.

Capital employed includes the shareholder funds such as share capital, reserves and retained profits plus any long-term liabilities such as bank loans. Total net assets are the organization's fixed assets, which includes tangible (property, plant and equipment) and intangible (goodwill) assets plus working capital, which is calculated by taking the organization's current assets (inventory, accounts receivables and cash) and deducting its current liabilities (accounts payables, proposed dividends and any tax outstanding) from them.

The decisions that supply chain managers take will generally be concerned with the components that make up the organization's total net assets rather than where the organization sources its capital.

The income statement (profit and loss account) in its simplest form is another equation, as it derives the organization's earnings (profit) by subtracting expenses from its sales revenue. If sales revenue is greater than expenses then the business is earning a profit; if not then the organization will be making a loss. FMCG Co's income statement (see Appendix) illustrates that the company has revenue of £2.4 billion, and when all expenses for the financial year are included the company has retained earnings of £177 million. Retained earnings for each year are added to the previous year's earnings and are included in the capital employed part of the balance sheet.

Supply chain managers can have a positive impact on revenue generation by designing distribution channels that enhance customer service and optimize transportation thus reducing operating costs.

Return on capital employed (ROCE) is a financial ratio used by analysts to measure the return (earnings) as a percentage of capital employed invested in the business.

ROCE is calculated by dividing earnings before interest and tax (EBIT) by capital employed and multiplied by 100 to give a percentage. An important point to recognize is that capital employed is equal to total net assets and they can be substituted for one another in the ROCE ratio. Therefore in this case study we refer to return on total net assets (ROTNA) rather than ROCE as the decisions taken by supply chain managers will impact on the variables that make up total net assets.

Supply chain managers can have a positive impact on ROTNA by making decisions that improve the numerator EBIT (revenue *minus* cost of goods sold *minus* operating expenses) or reduce total net assets (denominator); often a supply chain initiative such as improving inventory management can have an impact on both the numerator and denominator.

FMCG Co currently has a ROTNA of 25 per cent, calculated by dividing EBIT/TNA multiplying by 100 to give a percentage, which means that for every £1 invested in TNA the company is making a return of £0.25. The organization's stakeholder can use the output of this ratio as a benchmark to compare alternative investments or returns from companies operating in this industrial sector. Alternatively, ROTNA can be derived by multiplying together two other ratios EBIT percentage and TNA turnover multiplier. FMCG Co have an EBIT percentage of 12.5 per cent (EBIT divided by sales revenue expressed as a percentage); this means that for every £1 of sales, the company earns £0.125 earnings before interest and tax. The company has a TNA turnover multiplier of 2 (sales revenue divided by TNA), which means that for every £1 invested in TNA, it produces £2 in sales revenue. Therefore supply chain managers need to recognize the importance of the relationship between these two financial ratios when making supply chain decisions. This relationship between EBIT and TNA turnover and their input to ROTNA is illustrated in Figure 1. The figure also highlights the elements from the income statement and balance sheet (see Appendix) that influence ROTNA, EBIT and TNA and this diagram is typically referred to as the DuPont model.

Figure 1 FMCG Co's return on total net assets

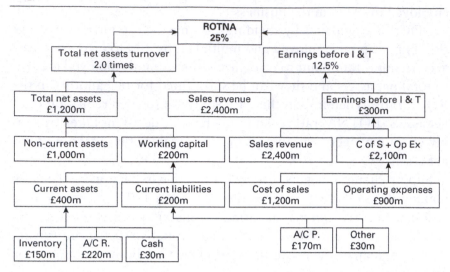

We shall now look at three typical supply chain management scenarios and explore the impact of each scenario separately on the FMCG Co's financial statements and ratios as depicted in the DuPont model. The three scenarios are:

- a reduction in inventories;
- an outsourcing opportunity;
- an extension of account payable days.

Inventory reduction

The financial impact of reducing inventory will reduce current assets, improve cash flow and reduce operating expenses and therefore have a positive impact on the organization's earning and also reduce total net assets on the balance sheet. Reducing inventory will have a direct effect on the organization's cash-to-cash cycle (C2C) as the number of days inventory held by the business is lower, which is a key component of the C2C calculation.

FMCG Co has decided to review its procurement strategy. As a result of improving their demand forecast accuracy, they are now able to reduce the quantities of raw materials purchased from its suppliers thus reducing inventory levels. The reduction in inventory levels will also reduce the cost of holding inventory, typically 25 per cent of the inventory's cost or net realizable value as assumed by FMCG Co. The reduction in inventory will not impact on customer service. The company anticipates that a 30 per cent reduction in inventory levels can be achieved, which equates to £45 million for the year. This additional cash will now be used to repay long-term debt. The company's cost of holding inventory is 25 per cent, therefore there will be a saving of £11.25 million in operating expenses and an increase in earnings.

Improving inventory management has increased the organization's EBIT percentage to 13 per cent and their TNA turnover multiplier to 2.08, resulting in an increase in ROTNA from 25 per cent to 27 per cent.

Figure 2 illustrates the impact of the inventory reduction using the DuPont model on ROTNA. It is now possible to see how the inventory reduction impacts on the components of both the balance sheet and income statement. A reduction in inventories reduces total net assets; if sales are unchanged then the TNA multiplier is improved. The costs of holding inventory have reduced therefore reducing operating expenses; if revenues do not change then the company's earnings will increase, improving the EBIT percentage.

Figure 2 Inventory reductions and ROTNA

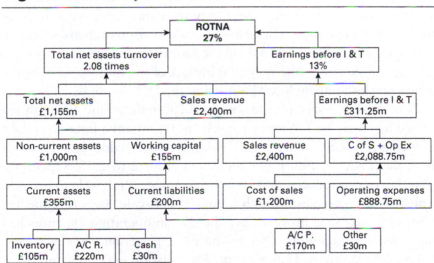

An improvement in the TNA multiplier and EBIT percentage cause the ROTNA percentage to increase, therefore illustrating the relationship between supply chain management decisions with an improvement in the financial performance of the business.

Outsourcing opportunity

FMCG Co is considering outsourcing its fleet of distribution vehicles to a third-party logistics company (3PL). The vehicle fleet will be sold to the 3PL resulting in a reduction of non-current assets on the balance sheet and an injection of cash (current asset). The cash from the disposal of the vehicles could be used to invest in other assets, reduce debt or return cash to their shareholders as dividends. FMCG Co has decided to repay some of their long-term debt.

With the sale of their vehicle fleet, FMCG Co no longer has standing and running costs. However, they will have the charge from the 3PL for delivering goods to their customers. As distribution is the core business of the 3PL, FMCG Co should also be able to benefit from lower distribution charges from the 3PL, as they can leverage cost savings due to economies of scale, increased vehicle utilization and standardization of vehicle type. FMCG Co now has the opportunity to utilize the 3PL network coverage enabling them to potentially reach more customers than they were able to do with their own fleet.

Additional cash-flow benefits include no longer having to buy new vehicles and the potential opportunity to reduce C2C cycle times as the 3PL payment terms will be longer than previous expenses such as driver salaries, which were paid in the month that they were incurred.

Figure 3 illustrates the potential impact of the outsourcing opportunity on the company's ROTNA using the DuPont model.

Non-current assets are reduced by £100 million and the cash received has been used to repay some of the company's long-term debt reducing it to £200 million. As TNA have been reduced to £1.1 billion, the TNA multiplier has improved from 2 to 2.18. Operating costs have been reduced by £50 million, as the 3PL is able to provide transportation savings through economies of scale. Sales revenue has remained the same; however, a reduction in operating expenses has increased earnings and therefore the EBIT percentage has increased from 12.5 per cent to 14.6 per cent. The outsourcing opportunity has

Figure 3 Outsourcing opportunity

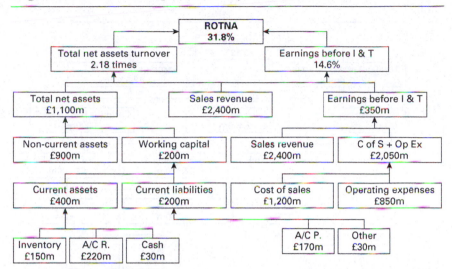

resulted in an improvement in both financial ratios and therefore ROTNA has increased from 25 per cent to 31.8 per cent.

Extending accounts payable

The treasury and procurement functions of FMCG Co are considering extending the time it takes to pay its suppliers and at the same time putting their suppliers on a supply chain finance (SCF) programme provided by the company's bank. It is assumed that the SCF programme will not incur any additional costs to FMCG Co. The impact of this decision will potentially increase FMCG's accounts payables at the end of financial year from £170 million to £340 million. The decision with have a negative impact on their liquidity ratios (current and acid test ratios); however, the company's cash conversion cycle will be improved as its C2C cycle time (inventory days plus accounts receivable days minus accounts payable days) will be reduced as a result of extending its suppliers payment period.

The impact of extending accounts payables on ROTNA has increased the ratio from 25 per cent to 29.12 per cent as illustrated in Figure 4.

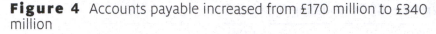

Figure 4 Accounts payable increased from £170 million to £340 million

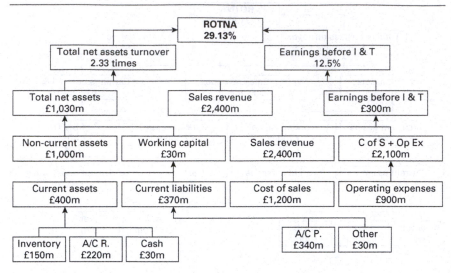

Increasing accounts payable by £170 million has also increased current liabilities to £370 million, which has reduced the company's working capital and also the value of the TNA, improving the company's total net asset turnover multiplier and the ROTNA percentage.

Conclusion

The aim of this case study was to confirm that supply chain management decisions would have a direct bearing on the financial performance of a business. Supply chain managers need to be aware of the important role that their decisions have on organizational financial performance and need to be able to recognize and articulate the impact their decisions have on the income statement, balance sheet and also in the financial ratios, which are used to measure performance such as the examples used in this case (ROTNA, EBIT and TNA turnover).

A fictional company and indicative financial figures were used to illustrate the impact of three typical supply chain scenarios: reducing inventory, outsourcing and extending accounts payables. The impact of each scenario was compared with the base case using the DuPont model and the impact on the financial ratios was discussed. A summary of the results from the different scenarios are illustrated in Table 1.

Table 1 Summary of results by scenario

Financial ratios	Base case	Inventory management	Outsourcing opportunity	Account payables
ROTNA %	25.00	27.00	31.80	29.13
EBIT %	12.50	13.00	14.60	12.50
TNA multiplier	2.00	2.08	2.18	2.33

Although the figures used in the case are indicative they illustrate the cause and effect relationship between supply chain decisions and financial performance. This is an important point as supply chain managers need to take a holistic perspective when considering the impact of their decisions on the financial performance of their organization.

Appendix: FMCG Co financial statements

FMCG Co balance sheet as at 31.03.XX	£m
Non-current assets	1,000
Current assets	400
Current liabilities	200
Total net assets	1,200
Equity	
Ordinary shares	600
Retained earnings	300
Total equity	900
Non-current liabilities	
Borrowings	300
Total equity and liabilities	1,200

Total Net Assets = Equity + Non-current liabilities

FMCG Co income statement for year ending 31.03.XX	£m
Revenue	2,400
Less cost of goods sold	1,200
Gross profit	1,200
Operating expenses	900
Interest paid	3
Earnings before tax	297
Corporation tax	60
Earnings after tax	237
Dividends	60
Retained earnings for the year	177

Questions

1 Which elements of the income statement and the balance sheet can be impacted by supply chain management decisions?

2 The following figures have been extracted from the financial statements of a company.

Non-current assets	£80 million
Current assets	£40 million
Current liabilities	£20 million
Sales	£200 million
Cost of goods sold	£75 million
Operating expenses	£45 million

Calculate the following financial ratios:

a) total net asset turnover ratio;

b) EBIT percentage;

c) ROCE percentage.

3 Procurement has decide to source a major component from a new supplier at significant discount; however, they are required to increase the size of the order quantity and the lead time will now increase from 20 to 60 days. What are the potential impacts of this decision on:

a) sales revenue;

b) costs;

c) non-current assets;

d) working capital.

4 The sales and marketing team of a FMCG company are planning to offer the customer additional choice and are prepared to increase the number of stock-keeping units from 50,000 to 75,000. What are the potential impacts of this decision on the supply chain and for the elements that make up the ROCE calculations?

5 The following figures have been extracted from the financial statements of a company. You are required to carry out a scenario analysis.

Non-current assets	£80 million
Current assets	£40 million
Current liabilities	£20 million
Sales	£200 million
Cost of goods sold	£75 million
Operating expenses	£45 million

Calculate the change in ROCE percentage based on all the following changes:

a) Sales have increased by 10 per cent due to a successful promotion.

b) An alternative supplier has been discovered that has decreased the cost of goods by 5 per cent.

c) Current assets have increased by 2 per cent due to the additional inventory held to meet the promotion.

d) Non-current assets have been reduced by 5 per cent as surplus assets have been disposed of and the cash used to reduce the company's long-term debt.

Answers

1 Which elements of the income statement and the balance sheet can be impacted by supply chain management decisions?

Supply chain management decisions will have an impact on numerous elements of the income statement and the balance sheet.

Income Statement	Sales	Demand fulfilment and availability of products
	Costs	Procurement, transport and warehousing
Balance Sheet	Non-current assets	Network optimization and utilization of assets
	Working capital	Inventory management, perfect order and outsourcing

2 Calculate the following financial ratios:

   a) total net asset turnover ratio;

   b) EBIT percentage;

   c) ROCE percentage.

Ratio	Formula	Workings	Calculation
TNA turnover	Sales/Total net assets	200/100	2.0
EBIT %	(EBIT/Sales)*100	(80/200)*100	40%
ROCE %	(EBIT/ROCE)*100	(80/100)*100	80%

3 Procurement has decide to source a major component from a new
  supplier at significant discount; however, they are required to increase
  the size of the order quantity and the lead time will now increase from
  20 to 60 days. What are the potential impacts of this decision on:

  a) sales revenue;

  b) costs;

  c) non-current assets;

  d) working capital.

Elements	Procurement decision
Sales revenue	The discount may enable sales and marketing to offer competitive prices to customers that generate additional sales revenue.
Costs	The discount will have a favourable impact on the cost of goods sold calculation, but as additional volume is required it may have an increase in the costs of holding inventory due to increased size of the order.
Non-current assets	Additional warehousing capacity may be required to store the extra inventory. If a new distribution centre is purchased them this will increase non-current assets.
Working Capital	The additional lead time and increased order size will impact on the level of inventory from 20 to 60 days held by the organization.

4 The sales and marketing team of a FMCG company are planning to offer the customer additional choice and are prepared to increase the number of stock-keeping units from 50,000 to 75,000. What are the potential impacts of this decision on the supply chain and for the elements that make up the ROCE calculations?

Elements	Potential impact
EBIT	The potential increasing the number of stock-keeping units from 50,000 to 75,000 will generate additional sales revenue. Additional inventory holding costs, sales and marketing and distribution costs will erode into the additional revenue generated by the additional stock-keeping units.
TNA	If additional warehousing capacity is required to hold extra inventory. If the company decides to own it themselves this will increase non-current assets on the balance sheet, current assets will increase as a result of the increase in stock-keeping units, accounts receivables may increase as the additional sales are purchased on credit, additional sales will generate additional cash. Accounts payables will increase as the additional stock-keeping units are purchased from suppliers on credit.

5 Calculate the change in ROCE percentage based on all the following changes:

a) Sales have increased by 10 per cent due to a successful promotion.

b) An alternative supplier has been discovered that has decreased the cost of goods by 5 per cent.

c) Current assets have increased by 2 per cent due to the additional inventory held to meet the promotion.

d) Non-current assets have been reduced by 5 per cent as surplus assets have been disposed of and the cash used to reduce the company's long-term debt.

The following figures have been extracted from the financial statements of a company.

	Original £m	Change	Revised £m
Non-current assets	80	0.95	76.00
Current assets	40	1.02	40.80
Current liabilities	20	1	20.00
Sales	200	1.1	220.00
Cost of goods sold	75	0.95	71.25
Operating expenses	45	1	45.00

Financial ratio	Original	Change	Revised
TNA turnover	2.0	13.64%	2.27
EBIT	40%	17.90%	47.16%
ROCE	80%	33.97%	107.18%

CASE STUDY 2.13

Managing workers' interests across global supply chain networks
Case studies of the garment manufacturing and offshore construction industries

Patsy Perry and Mohamed Abdel-Wahab

AUTHOR BIOGRAPHIES

DR PATSY PERRY is a Lecturer in Fashion Marketing in the School of Materials at the University of Manchester. Her research interests include corporate social responsibility in fashion supply chains and she has published a number of book chapters and academic journal papers in this area.

DR MOHAMED ABDEL-WAHAB is a Lecturer in Construction Technology at Heriot-Watt University. He is a member of the Royal Academy of Engineering Centre of Excellence in Sustainable Building Design and has published extensively on construction skills and training issues, including the link between skills/training and performance, skills policy, implication of new technologies for skills development and training, and the facilitation of learning from construction practice.

Introduction

Garment manufacturing and construction are key industries in the economy. Garment manufacturing is a key export industry for many developing countries while construction is a key contributor to gross domestic product (GDP) in both developing and developed countries. Both sectors have long and geographically complex supply chains, with materials sourced from different countries, as well as labour-intensive production processes that can rely significantly on migrant workers, particularly in developing countries. Ethical scandals involving exploitation of workers have made news headlines in both industries in recent years. In 2013, the garment industry's worst ever industrial disaster occurred in Dhaka, Bangladesh when the Rana Plaza garment factory collapsed and resulted in the deaths of over 1,100 people. Many Western fashion brands were implicated in the disaster as they had been outsourcing production to companies in the Rana Plaza building. Whilst ethical scandals are commonly associated with developing countries, they may also occur in developed countries. In 2015, a study by the Ethical Trading Initiative found evidence of sweatshop working conditions in garment factories in Leicester, England, including a lack of employment contracts, pay levels below the minimum wage and breaches in health and safety practices. Recently, the situation of migrant construction workers in Qatar has made news headlines with hundreds of reported deaths due to poor health and safety practices, and working conditions. Workers are unable to leave the country without the permission of their sponsors and are often forced to accept lower wages and unsanitary, cramped and dangerous living conditions.

Therefore, an important aspect of managing global supply chains is managing worker issues, especially in industries which are labour intensive, low skilled and under pressure for cost and lead time reduction (such as garment manufacturing and construction). Multinational corporations that control these complex supply chains are becoming increasingly conscious of the need to manage ethical issues relating to human-resource exploitation as part of their sustainability agenda.

It is interesting to note that the social aspect of sustainability encompasses labour relations issues, such as safe and healthy working conditions, forced and child labour, fair wages, working hours and holidays, equality, skills and training, and community relations.

Corporate social responsibility (CSR) is a way of responding to ethical issues, commonly managed by multinational corporations via a code of conduct to protect workers' interests. However, codes of conduct do not always protect companies from the risk of ethical scandals involving their workers. In this case, we explore the reasons for this and provide examples of how companies in garment manufacturing and construction industries may promote and protect worker interests in global supply chains. We focus, first, on garment manufacturing in Sri Lanka, which promotes itself as the world's number one ethical sourcing location for garments and, second, on construction in the north-east of England, which has historically suffered from labour and union issues. Both of these case studies clearly illustrate the issues that should be considered when managing people in global supply chain networks, both in developed and developing countries.

CASE STUDY
Garment manufacturing in Sri Lanka

Background

The mass outsourcing of garment manufacturing to lower labour cost countries in recent years allows global fashion retailers to make significant supply chain cost savings and thus offer consumers greater varieties of fashion garments at lower prices. However, global outsourcing may also result in the exploitation of workers in global garment supply chains, which includes issues of working conditions, wages and working hours, freedom of association, discrimination, child and forced labour. In developed countries, workers' issues are protected via institutional frameworks such as trade unions, but in developing countries freedom of association and collective bargaining may be illegal. In many developing countries, the minimum wage may be set below the living wage in order to attract foreign investment, while in other cases inflation may cause the living wage to rise above the minimum wage. In certain developing countries, the presence of child labour may be endemic due to poverty and the inability of parents to pay for their child's education. Industry sector factors such as retail buyers' unreasonable expectations of cost and lead time may put pressure on factory managers to cut corners and the consequent lack of regard for workers' rights may be evidenced by poor levels of pay, long working hours and forced overtime, bullying and harassment. In the fashion sector in particular, with its high levels of cost and lead time pressure as retailers demand cheaper and faster shipments of garments, it is challenging to manage cost efficiency as well as protecting workers' interests in the supply chain.

Sri Lanka is a key garment sourcing country that supplies casual-wear, sportswear and intimate apparel for a number of international fashion brands such as Marks & Spencer, Next, Gap, Nike and Victoria's Secret. Garments are now the country's main export category. Recent investments in backward integration and an industry association campaign to brand the country as a risk-free ethical sourcing destination for international fashion retailers has resulted in a sophisticated industry capable of servicing international fashion brands whilst also protecting workers' interests. What are the factors that enabled Sri Lanka to achieve this? We now explore the challenges faced by Sri Lankan garment manufacturers in the global apparel supply chain and their responses to these challenges, which enabled them to remain competitive whilst protecting workers' interests.

The issues

A lack of long-term written contracts from retail buyers

One reason for the ability of Sri Lankan garment suppliers to balance protection of worker interests alongside commercial pressures for low cost is the nature of suppliers' trading relationships with international retail buyers. Despite little evidence of formal commitments for future orders, there was an unwritten assumption of continuity based on the duration of the relationship and satisfactory past performance. Garment manufacturers developed strong relationships with large US and European retailers over long time periods, with trading relationships of 10–20 years commonplace within the sector.

Pressure on cost and lead time

Cost and lead time pressure in global garment supply chains can result in factory managers cutting corners and sacrificing worker welfare for the sake of expediting orders in the short term. However, in the long term, harmonious labour relations between workers and management in factories lead to increased productivity levels, which in turn reduce unnecessary overtime. Happy workers are more reliable, productive and loyal. Addressing worker welfare enables factory managers to maximize workers' output and encourage higher levels of motivation and retention. In larger factories, the payment of an attendance incentive, production bonus and overtime payments discouraged absenteeism and encouraged workers to perform to the best of their ability in order to increase their wages. Training and development opportunities were provided to enable employees to become multi-skilled operators and earn higher wages.

Increased collaboration and coordination between retail buyers and garment suppliers helps to reduce cost as well as lead time by improving responsiveness rather than sacrificing worker welfare. Some garment suppliers built state-of-the-art product development centres where buyers could come and work alongside the production team to speed up the product development process and reduce lead time, without having a detrimental impact on worker welfare. Others worked closely with their retail buyers to make cost savings in the production process. Provision of technical training seminars and collaboration between suppliers and retail buyers on cost-reduction measures reduced the likelihood of suppliers cutting corners on worker welfare in order to cut costs.

Inability to compete on cost against other garment-producing developing countries

With increasing global scrutiny of ethical standards in global fashion supply chains, low-cost sourcing of garments is no longer the sole supply chain priority for international fashion brands and retailers. Sourcing from low-risk locations helps to avoid ethical misconduct and the risk of negative media publicity, which could harm brand image and reputation. A combination of factors has uniquely placed Sri Lanka to be able to offer reasonable cost alongside low ethical risk for brands and retailers concerned about protecting their reputation.

Most importantly, strict labour laws have been in place for a long time, well before the advent of retailer codes of conduct. Sri Lanka's national labour laws limit working hours and overtime, especially for female workers. The country also has a long history of corporate philanthropy. Buddhism is the main religion and its tenets of moral discipline and ethical behaviour, such as not discriminating against others or exploiting those beneath, provide a strong foundation for the protection of worker interests in business. Sri Lanka's nationwide system of free education prevents the need for poor families to send their children to work, as books and uniforms are provided by the government for all children. Cultural traditions such as family meal-times and the protection of females' moral character further provide a foundation for the protection of worker interests in business, for example by establishing limits on overtime working and an outright ban on harassment and bullying. These factors supported the development of the 'Garments Without Guilt' scheme in 2006, which assures retail buyers that garments produced in Sri Lanka were made under ethical conditions. The five guiding principles of the scheme are:

- ethical working conditions;
- free of child labour;
- free of forced labour;
- free of discrimination on any grounds;
- free of sweatshop practices, in terms of working hours and overtime, pay and benefits, freedom of association, health and safety.

Factories are independently certified and monitored to confirm they are operating in accordance with these principles. Sri Lanka's lack of child labour and high health and safety standards enabled the industry to command a strong position relative to other garment manufacturing countries in the developing world. For international fashion retailers, sourcing from such accredited locations helps to protect the reputation of the retail brand from the risk of ethical scandals.

Conclusion

Sri Lanka has succeeded in carving out a unique position in the highly competitive global garment industry through industrial upgrading and building a reputation for low-risk ethical garment manufacturing that protects workers' interests. Garment manufacturers are aware of the long-term benefits of protecting worker interests, in terms of staff retention and productivity improvements. However, protecting worker interests must always be balanced against the garment industry imperatives of cost and lead time pressure. Therefore, it remains to be seen whether Sri Lanka will retain its world-class reputation as other developing countries upgrade their garment manufacturing capabilities and further increase global competition.

CASE STUDY
Offshore oil and gas rig construction in the North-East of England

Background

The construction materials industry is facing growing stakeholder expectations about the accountability, transparency and legitimacy of its operations. Responsible sourcing can be defined as the management of sustainability objectives throughout the construction products supply chain. It covers environmental, social and economic issues, including ethical concerns relating to workers within the entire supply chain, from extraction activities through to end-use.

An oil and gas company based in Aberdeen, with worldwide operations, was commissioning the construction of a part of its offshore platform to companies based in the north-east of England. Before commissioning the work, the company's aim was to understand labour-relations issues in the region which could then provide a basis for informing its decisions when selecting subcontractors for the project. Most importantly, the company aimed to establish the extent to which labour lockouts (work stoppage) posed a risk to its project.

Whilst work stoppage is an extreme form of industrial action, other forms of industrial action (that would not necessarily result in work stoppage) could potentially impinge on the progress of construction projects, such as work-to-rules and go-slows. Work-to-rule refers to workers doing no more than the minimum required by their contract and precisely following rules in order to cause a slowdown, whilst go-slows refer to workers performing their duties but not necessarily working to their full productivity potential. Such actions emanate from workers' demotivation and lack of job satisfaction. Therefore, the client should identify labour-relations issues early on in the project and put provisions in place from the outset of the project to minimize the risk of any form of industrial action. This is particularly important if a project is working towards a very tight timescale.

The issues

- *The existence of a pay agreement* is paramount given that work stoppages are primarily caused by pay disputes. Decreasing the likelihood of pay disputes could be achieved by:
  - A *collective agreement* could be negotiated to agree a level of pay from the outset of a project. Such agreement could form a part of the contractual arrangements which should be underpinned by the philosophy that systems and procedures should bring the objectives of all parties in line with the project objectives.
  - A *pay and productivity bonus scheme* could be introduced. In other major construction projects, such as London Heathrow Airport's Terminal 5, bonus schemes have proved successful and resulted in productivity gains, improved industrial relations and collaborative team-working. If workers are well incentivized, they are more likely to do their best for the benefit of the project.
- *Good working conditions* are an important factor to consider because it could be a potential source of motivating workers and thereby enhancing performance. Poor working conditions could be detrimental to workers' morale and create a divisive culture in the organization of 'us' (workers) and 'them' (management). This could also create negative publicity, which could be detrimental to the company's image and may affect its future operations and ability to win contracts.
- *Health and safety* (H&S) is crucial in the north-east of England construction industry. Recently, the Health and Safety Executive (HSE) encouraged workers to report any health and safety violations in the workplace. Having a third party to enforce H&S standards is not an optimal solution. Not only may this expose the company's poor H&S practices, which could affect its reputation, but it may also trigger potential conflict between the company and its workers. As such, it is

important that adequate H&S practices are implemented and maintained throughout the project. After all, if workers feel safer, they will have a better chance of performing to their full potential.

- *Duration and patterns of working hours* should not be at the expense of the well-being of workers. Working hours in the UK are generally higher than in Europe. However, longer and unsociable working hours do not necessarily lead to better productivity performance. In fact, research suggests that extended working hours results in lower productivity levels on construction projects. Furthermore, extended working hours could be at the expense of workers' well-being and family life, and it is therefore not surprising that the construction industry has one of the highest divorce rates compared with other sectors.

- *Staffing and work allocation* should be reflected in the duration and patterns of working hours. So, if the project is understaffed (whether because of skills shortages or with the intention of saving money), then it is more likely that workers will work for extended hours. This approach is too risky for a project that is working towards a tight deadline. Thus, it is important to ensure that adequate levels of staffing have been planned in advance and work allocation decided accordingly, which could be achieved through a formal human resource planning (HRP) exercise.

- *Fringe benefits and team bonding* are essential so that workers can establish a sense of belonging to the project. For example, a social event could be organized in order to produce some cohesiveness within the workforce and a sense of identity with the project. This becomes particularly important when considering the temporary setting of the project.

The Aberdeen-based oil and gas company incorporated the afore-mentioned labour-relations issues in their tender documents to establish to what extent shortlisted subcontractors had provisions in place for addressing those issues. This informed the company's selection process for a subcontractor. The company was proactive in its attempts to address workers' issues, for example by taking the unusual step of directly approaching trade-union representatives for guidance. In this way, the company hoped to avoid any problems such as industrial action that could result in delays to its project. However, such an informal approach is not legally binding, unless the aforementioned issues are incorporated as a part of the contractual agreement. This raises the question of what other approaches could be adopted to effectively deal with trade unions in order to address labour-relations issues. There are four approaches for managing labour or employee relations:

1 *Adversarial:* The organization decides what it wants to do, and employees are expected to comply. Employees only exercise power by refusing to cooperate;

2 *Traditional:* A good day-to-day working relationship exists but management proposes and the workforce reacts through its elected representatives;

3 *Partnership:* The organization involves employees in the drawing-up and execution of organizational policies, but retains the right to manage;

4 *Power sharing:* Employees are involved in both day-to-day and strategic decision-making.

The case of the Aberdeen-based oil and gas company fits within the category of an informal partnership agreement. However, such a partnership agreement could be formalized under the National Agreement for Engineering Construction Industry (NAECI). The NAECI is a comprehensive framework for managing labour relationships to ensure completions to time and budget. It is administered by the National Joint Council for the Engineering Construction Industry (NJC) and is a legally binding agreement that has proved successful on a number of projects. In order to implement the NAECI, a company should become a member of the Engineering Construction Industry Association (ECIA) who could then act on behalf of the company brokering an agreement with trade unions (Unite and GMB). However, this may involve an additional cost (on top of ECIA membership fee), for example an independent auditor and levy fee. The Aberdeen-based oil and gas company did not opt for the NAECI as it only had a one-off project in the north-east of England. The benefit of a formalized approach is that it can provide a framework for guidance. This becomes particularly important given the uncertainty as to the best approach to adopt for dealing with unions, when considering the multiple numbers of trade-union bodies available and the complexity of the issues involved. At the same time, using an intermediary as opposed to dealing directly with the union might signal that there is mistrust when dealing directly with the union.

Conclusion

Whilst the risk of labour lockouts in the north-east of England construction industry appears less likely when compared with other industries, the risk of poor labour relations should be managed effectively, especially given the time constraint of the project commissioned by the Aberdeen-based company. In summary, experience suggests that workers have four key needs that should be met (but these needs should be confirmed with workers prior to the project):

1 Fair payment: not less than similar crafts on other sites or other crafts on the same site.

2 Some control over how much time they spend at work and when they spend it.

3 Proven and visible respect for craft pride and competence.

4 Opportunities for friendship with other workers.

Poor labour relations can potentially put a project in peril. Labour-relations issues should therefore be addressed from the outset of a project. If workers are happy, well motivated and feel safe in their workplace they will be more productive which will be for the benefit of a project and the company. Finally, a company must choose the most appropriate approach to adopt for effective management of labour relations. Regardless of the situation, a company should always opt for a more engaging approach towards trade unions, namely partnership or power sharing, as opposed to adversarial or traditional approaches. After all, aren't people the most important asset for an organization?

Questions

1 How can a region's history and culture influence labour relations? Explain your answer providing examples from different countries.

2 How do industry-sector characteristics impact upon workers' issues in global supply chains?

3 What are the risks of ignoring workers' issues across the supply chain?

4 What are the benefits of addressing workers' issues across the supply chain?

5 Discuss the approaches for effective management of workers' issues across the supply chain.

6 How could organizations address workers' needs?

7 Compare and contrast the management of workers' issues in a developed and a developing country.

Answers

1 How can a region's history and culture influence labour relations? Explain your answer providing examples from different countries.

It can provide a foundation for the management of labour relations. The Sri Lankan culture and national labour law provided a strong foundation for protecting workers' interests and promoting harmonious labour relations. The historical strength of the trade unions in the north-east of England also provided a strong foundation for better labour relations.

2 How do industry-sector characteristics impact upon workers' issues in global supply chains?

Industry-sector factors such as retail buyers' unreasonable expectations of cost and lead time may put pressure on factory managers to cut corners and the consequent lack of regard for workers' rights may be evidenced by poor levels of pay, long working hours and forced overtime, bullying and harassment.

3 What are the risks of ignoring workers' issues across the supply chain?

The garment manufacturing case identified risks of ignoring workers' issues such as the potential of ethical scandals and negative media publicity, as well as lower productivity, higher absenteeism and higher labour turnover levels.

The construction case shows how industrial action can result if workers are unhappy with their working conditions. For example, work stoppage (an extreme form of industrial action), as well other forms of industrial action (that would not necessarily result in work stoppage) could potentially impinge on the progress of construction projects, such as work-to-rules and go-slows. Such actions emanate from workers' demotivation and lack of job satisfaction. Industrial action can result in delays to the project, which could have significant consequences, especially if a project is working towards a very tight timescale.

4 What are the benefits of addressing workers' issues across the supply chain?

Happy workers are more reliable, productive and loyal. Addressing worker welfare enables factory managers to maximize workers' output and encourage higher levels of motivation and staff retention. Harmonious labour relations between workers and management in factories lead to increased productivity levels, which in turn reduce unnecessary overtime.

5 Discuss the approaches for effective management of workers' issues across the supply chain.

The garment manufacturing case showed how the development of strong relationships between manufacturers and retailers over long time periods enabled them to collaborate and thus overcome some of the challenges of cost and lead time pressure, which might otherwise have an adverse effect on workers. Payment of an attendance incentive, production bonus and overtime payments discouraged absenteeism and encouraged workers to perform to the best of their ability in order to increase their wages. The provision of training and development opportunities enabled employees to become multi-skilled operators and earn higher wages.

The construction case explained four approaches for managing labour or employee relations:

- *Adversarial:* The organization decides what it wants to do, and employees are expected to comply – employees only exercise power by refusing to cooperate;
- *Traditional:* A good day-to-day working relationship exists but management proposes and the workforce reacts through its elected representatives;
- *Partnership:* The organization involves employees in the drawing-up and execution of organizational policies, but retains the right to manage;
- *Power sharing:* Employees are involved in both day-to-day and strategic decision-making – an informal power-sharing agreement can empower the employees and help in creating loyalty to the project.

6 How could organizations address workers' needs?

The garment-manufacturing case shows how companies may follow the principles of the 'Garments Without Guilt' scheme or adhere to a retailer's ethical code of conduct to ensure workers' needs were met. Specific examples include:

- Providing training and development opportunities.
- Establishing limits on overtime working.
- Banning harassment and bullying.

In the construction case, specific ways of addressing workers' needs include:

- Provision of fair payment: not less than similar crafts on other sites or other crafts on the same site.
- Allowing workers some control over how much time they spend at work and when they spend it.
- Ensuring proven and visible respect for craft pride and competence.
- Providing opportunities for friendship with other workers.

7 Compare and contrast the management of workers' issues in a developed and a developing country.

In developed countries, workers issues are protected via institutional frameworks such as trade unions, but in developing countries freedom of association and collective bargaining may be illegal. The garment manufacturing case showed how workers' issues were managed via a voluntary industry-led scheme 'Garments Without Guilt'. Factories were independently audited to ensure they adhered to the principles of the scheme. The construction case introduced the legally binding agreement NAECI (National Agreement for Engineering Construction Industry), which is a comprehensive framework for managing labour relationships to ensure project completions to time and budget. It is administered by the National Joint Council for the Engineering Construction Industry (NJC). In order to implement the NAECI, a company should become a member of the Engineering Construction Industry Association (ECIA) who could then act on behalf of the company brokering an agreement with trade unions (Unite and GMB). However, this may involve an additional cost (on top of ECIA membership fee), for example an independent auditor and levy fee.

Strategic cost management
Lean production at a global vehicle manufacturer

Gerard Chick

AUTHOR BIOGRAPHY

GERARD CHICK is Chief Knowledge Officer at Optimum Procurement Group. He has considerable experience working with some of the keenest minds at the most senior level in supply management today. He is regularly invited to make keynote presentations and deliver workshops on strategic procurement issues to senior executive teams across the world.

Introduction

This case study covers the strategic, organizational and operational decisions involved in an automobile manufacturer's efforts to balance its goals of productivity and high quality with the more elusive goal of supplier-development integration.

The case material is based on the real-life experiences of supplier development, integration, socialization and trust, which are core and integral components of a global vehicle manufacturer's overall direction.

Background

The global vehicle manufacturer was built upon a cost-management culture from the time the company began. The company founder sought to move into the automotive industry from a motorcycle base, despite government blockades, and found that the automotive supply base in Japan was unwilling to support his business. As such, he developed his motorcycle-component suppliers into automotive-component suppliers through supplier development, financial support and, most importantly, relationships and trust.

This loyalty to suppliers, under any circumstances, still exists today. The global vehicle manufacturer will not 'fire' a supplier unless the supplier requests them to do so. They will support and invest in suppliers who are going through difficult periods, but expect the same leeway when economic times become difficult in the automotive industry. This long-term view towards co-destiny has paid off. Moreover, like a strict but loving parent, the manufacturer demands a lot from its suppliers, including multiple visits to their site to drive improvement with a refusal to take 'no' for an answer. This concept of supplier development, integration and ongoing socialization and trust is a core and integral component of the manufacturer's business model.

The business model

The global vehicle manufacturer's business model has always been focused around:

- A six-year plan, which is highly dependent on a small group of committed suppliers who are involved upfront for the entire six years.
- 100 per cent understanding of all factors of product cost, with a high level of precision.

- Lean supplier development engineering, with a large population of field engineers working closely with key suppliers on every aspect of their production process.

- Flawless new product launch – the manufacturer is a firm believer in extreme attention to detail in every aspect of component, subsystem and system development.

- A 'same part, same place, same process' mind-set with an emphasis on multiple visits and meetings with suppliers during prototype development and ramp-up, to ensure that products coming off the supplier's line are of 'first product' quality and ready to go to market when production conditions occur.

- *Communication*: the quality, frequency, and content of every communication that takes place between the manufacturer and its dealers, suppliers, and stakeholders is reviewed, and is systematically controlled for in every aspect of their business model – communications are seen as the foundation for inter-organizational relationships.

The global vehicle manufacturer's 'deep smarts'

Measurement systems support all cost-management decisions. Initial metrics in the design include the price that the final product could be introduced at in the market. The price/value relationship for the manufacturer's customer is a focal point for debate and discussion. What price level at the retail level can provide the required profit at the manufacturing level? A production cost is established at a high level as a target, and then R&D, manufacturing and supply chain work on how to achieve it, separating manufacturing and supply cost to make that unit.

They breaks costs down component by component in building up to the target price. Certain types of quality characteristics are set in stone (five-star crash ratings, eight airbags, and so forth).

There is then an ongoing effort by suppliers and supply management to share ideas and innovation with R&D teams early on to discover how to reduce expense, along with adding more value and features. Price is the first differentiator, followed by quality. Target cost elements are based on activity based costing procedures, derived from historical analysis conducted by key R&D groups who are capable of estimating realistic manufacturing and supplier expenses.

These are broken down into budgets developed by category teams. Trade-offs are always a point of discussion at category team meetings. This is a stressful and rigorous process, as multiple teams each work on their own target costs, all seeking to meet the market price.

Cost engineers (procurement) at the manufacturers are aligned by the specific types of suppliers they work with, and are dedicated to this role with the objective of becoming global experts. For example, a cost engineer can visit any given supplier of stampings, and produce a lengthy report documenting the level of capability associated with that supplier, based on one visit. There is a high level of capability and knowledge regarding what to look for, which is designed into the culture.

All of the procurement groups meet regularly (once a quarter) to discuss integrated global supply management strategy. At this meeting, the discussion focuses on opportunities for commonality and standardization, coordination with marketing's export strategy, new product planning, cost management and technology transfer issues within the supply base.

An important part of this strategy meeting also focuses on development of a truly 'global' supply base. All divisions and business units come together on a regular basis to discuss and share global platform development, common supply strategies and ongoing cost management objectives. Opportunities for learning and identification of lessons learned are a major part of this effort.

The manufacturer continues to measure cost against attributes such as customer value, ensuring that its new vehicle costs do not rise even though global material costs are rising, and also to add features that ensure customers have a safe, innovative and fulfilling driving experience.

The corporate influence included the firm's highly effective version of lean manufacturing, which it and other Japanese manufacturers pioneered. Lean practices had, of course, been largely adopted in the manufacturer's US operations. A corporate policy of localization, however, permitted some lean practices and other manufacturing practices to be modified and adapted to local conditions in the Ohio plants.

Conclusion

Overall, the global vehicle manufacturer case illustrates the difficulty of balancing competing internal factors (such as a lean manufacturing strategy) and context considerations (such as environmental regulatory pressures) in strategic decision-making and organizational design considerations. A central idea to take away from the case is the complexity of managerial decision-making when carrying out these balancing acts. Such challenges often resist simple quantification and involve high levels of uncertainty.

Questions

1 What are the benefits of lean?

2 Lean production emphasizes waste reduction. Generally, what are the implications of 'lean' for the environment?

3 Is the manufacturer's goal enough to meet all social or corporate environmental goals?

4 Organizational design: the manufacturer vs Toyota: What are the benefits and drawbacks of the manufacturer's approach to organization with respect to other issues such as environment regulations?

Answers

1 What are the benefits of lean?

The implementation of lean manufacturing in a business enables value to flow through the company's manufacturing process. This is known as just-in-time (JIT) manufacturing and is 'pulled' by customer demand. JIT prevents or rather eliminates waste in the manufacturing process.

Here waste is categorized into seven distinct activities:

1 transport;

2 inventory;

3 motion;

4 waiting;

5 over-processing;

6 overproduction;

7 defects.

All of these activities directly impact on costs. This is because they add no value to the manufacturing process. Since they add no tangible value customers would not be happy to pay for what is essentially wasteful expenditure in your process or service.

The accepted view in manufacturing is that businesses only add value for around 5 per cent of the time within their operation. It follows then that the remaining 95 per cent of that time is regarded as waste. The goal in a lean manufacturing process is to find ways of reducing as much of the 95 per cent wasted time and effort, and as a consequence improving:

- performance, fewer defects and rework (in house and at customer);
- reducing process interruptions;
- reducing levels of inventory;
- improving stock turnover;
- reducing storage space requirements;
- improving efficiencies, more output per hour;
- improving delivery performance;
- improving manufacturing developments;
- greater customer satisfaction;
- improved employee morale and involvement;
- improved supplier relations;
- increased profits;
- increased business demand.

2 Lean production emphasizes waste reduction. Generally, what are the implications of 'lean' for the environment?

Areas in which lean production may complement the environment are outlined in the case. This concept points to the win–win scenarios for business and the environment. Additional complementarities and many trade-offs between the two can be envisioned. They can be organized in three areas:

1 waste reduction;

2 procurement practices;

3 measurement and continuous improvement.

The waste reduction mentality, which permeates the manufacturer's operations globally, can have obvious benefits for the environment, such as reducing the use of toxic chemicals that involve expensive waste disposal and recycling more materials that would have become waste. However, the lean waste reduction ethic may hinder some environmental goals. While encouraging efficiency, waste reduction on its own does not provide a sufficient mechanism to meet all social or company environmental goals. Waste reduction can increase environmental performance but only up to a point.

The environmental goal of reducing industrial toxic chemical use is not served well by lean production strategies. Lean production seeks to reduce the costs of waste, an activity that does not minimize toxicity correspondingly because environmental regulations and markets do not see theses toxic materials in the same way.

Cross-boundary working can lead to more creative and pragmatic solutions to environmental issues because workers who know the details of plant operations can have an input into environmental decision-making. Cost reduction is one example. Employees may have ideas about how to reduce scrap waste, which benefits everyone; however, they may be less able to contribute to a discussion regarding how to make sophisticated equipment at the plant more efficient.

The use of information systems that focus on measurement and continuous improvement allows documentation and tracking of environmental issues within the plant by showing the progress that can be made.

They can also help link environmental benefits to cost reduction and other manufacturing advantages. However, an emphasis on measurement and continuous improvement could be problematic when applied to the environment.

Striving for continuous improvement in manufacturing may interfere with environmental performance. The just-in-time element of lean production, in which parts are continually shipped to the manufacturer in batches just large enough to meet the current demands of the consumer, can have significant implications not only for traffic congestion (owing to increased trucking deliveries) but also for air emissions and energy consumption.

3 Is the manufacturer's goal enough to meet all social or corporate environmental goals?

The student needs to determine the real problem presented. There are two possible (broad) responses:

- First, the problem is to articulate how the manufacturer might optimize the trade-off between lean manufacturing and the environment, because both are important, and different approaches have different implications for manufacturing success. With regard to the environment this would involve the student discussing the manufacturer's approach to the organization of their plant to reflect both the integration of lean manufacturing and giving full consideration to the environment impact of that decision.

- Second, to examine how to optimize a trade-off because in pure business terms no trade-off should be made. The core business is making the best cars at least cost. The environment needs to be served, but it should be addressed through an organizational structure and activities that do not interfere with the lean manufacturing practices.

4 Organizational design: the manufacturer vs Toyota: What are the benefits and drawbacks of the manufacturer's approach to organization with respect to other issues such as environment regulations?

Discussing the positive and negative interactions between lean production and the environment helps address the question of: how to design the organization to maximize complementarities and minimize trade-offs. As is so often the case there is no right answer to this question. It is analogous to other issues in which core business activities have to be balanced with pressures to behave in a socially responsible manner and the general business context has to be incorporated into strategic thinking about the organization's design and activities.

This question has several aspects, two of which are considered here. One gives consideration to the overall level of control afforded to local manufacturing plants. The broad options for corporate versus local control are suggested by looking at the manufacturer and Toyota:

- A top-down and centralized management ensures uniform quality and control over procurement policies. This option can easily capitalize on an optimized system of production put into place globally, often leading to economies of scale and lower costs. However, inflexible systems can suffer when facing local constraints and contextual variation.

- Management that is flexible and able to respond to local environmental regulations, input prices and stakeholder demands is the other option. However, flexibility may lead to greater variation in local production costs, and average costs may be higher across all plants because core activities are allowed to be disrupted to adapt to local conditions.

Another aspect of organizational design is the extent to which environmental activities are integrated into manufacturing activities. Integration can be achieved through goal-setting policies (such as waste reduction), human-resource practices (such as training and quality circles) and the use of information system methods (such as developing metrics for comparing environmental and other performance in areas of manufacturing). Broad options here include:

- An integrated approach, in which environmental activities and staff are blended or dispersed across departments in the organization. For example, responsibility for environmental regulations might be assigned as a part-time duty of a team member within procurement or at a lower level.

- A buffered approach, in which environmental activities and staff are centralized. For example, a team of regulatory compliance specialists housed in a headquarters building or plant management building would rarely interact with other staff. Changes to improve environmental performance might more likely originate from this department and become part of the working practices of other staff.

Optimizing shipment options
An application of the transportation problem

Andrea Genovese and Mike Simpson

AUTHOR BIOGRAPHIES

DR ANDREA GENOVESE AND DR MIKE SIMPSON
ANDREA GENOVESE is a Lecturer in Logistics and Supply Chain
Management at The University of Sheffield Management School.

Introduction and useful definitions

- *Many-to-many distribution:* A logistic distribution mode where
  items are shipped from multiple sources to multiple
  destinations.
- *Integer decision variable:* A problem unknown that can just
  assume integer (and not fractional) values.

The transportation problem is a simple freight traffic assignment
problem in a many-to-many distribution context. The objective of the
problem is to find a minimum-cost routing plan for goods from their
origins (eg their manufacturing plants) to their destinations (eg retail
points). The problem is characterized by the following notation:

I a set of origins, whose generic element can be indicated as i

J a set of destinations, whose generic element can be indicated as j

s_i the available supply at origin i

d_j the requested demand at destination j

c_{ij} the cost of shipping one unit of demand from origin i to destination j

x_{ij} an integer decision variable indicating the amount of demand at j served by i

The problem can be described by using the following mathematical model (characterized by a linear structure):

$$\sum_{i \in I} \sum_{j \in J} c_{ij} x_{ij} \quad min! \tag{1}$$

Subject to:

$$\sum_{i \in I} x_{ij} = d_j \qquad \forall j \in J \tag{2}$$

$$\sum_{j \in J} x_{ij} \leq s_i \qquad \forall i \in I \tag{3}$$

$$x_{ij} \geq 0 \qquad \forall i \in I, \forall j \in J \tag{4}$$

The objective function (1) represents the minimization of the total transportation cost. The set of constraints (2) states that each destination has to receive an amount of goods exactly equal to the amount of requested goods. The set of constraints (3) states that each origin i cannot supply more goods than a given availability threshold s_i. The last set of constraints simply expresses that the amount of goods cannot be negative.

Problems related to this mathematical model can be easily solved by using MS Excel Solver. However, pen-and-paper procedures based on heuristic algorithms are also possible. Indeed, several methods are available to obtain a feasible solution to the transportation problem; some of these (such as the least-cost method and the north-west corner method) will be illustrated in the following short case.

Transportation planning

A third-party transportation firm has to transfer empty containers from six warehouses (located in Birmingham, Leeds, Manchester, Newcastle, Sheffield and York), to five destinations (Cardiff, Edinburgh, Felixstowe, Glasgow, Southampton) where they are needed. The following tables report the containers' availability at each warehouse location and the containers' demand at each port. Containers are transported among these locations by truck. The transportation cost of each container is proportional to the distance covered by the truck that is transporting it; distances between origins and destinations are reported below in Table 3; the average transportation cost per container is equal to 1.9 £/km.

TABLE 1 Available containers at warehouse locations

Warehouse	Available containers
Birmingham	38
Leeds	10
Manchester	22
Newcastle	24
Sheffield	16
York	10

TABLE 2 Required containers at destinations

Port	Required containers
Cardiff	20
Edinburgh	15
Felixstowe	25
Glasgow	33
Southampton	21

TABLE 3 Distances (in kilometres) between origins and destinations

	Cardiff	Edinburgh	Felixstowe	Glasgow	Southampton
Birmingham	115	291	165	290	143
Leeds	235	218	215	220	242
Manchester	203	219	255	218	234
Newcastle	321	121	295	152	328
Sheffield	206	255	197	256	213
York	248	209	223	212	255

Questions

1 Work out the transportation plan that minimizes the total costs by fulfilling all the requirements and respecting all the constraints.

2 What happens if the company has to consider a further constraint regarding a maximum number of ten containers that can be shipped from any origin to any destination?
How would the transportation plan change?

Answers

1 Work out the transportation plan that minimizes the total costs by fulfilling all the requirements and respecting all the constraints.

The *least-cost* method can be utilized for this purpose. Very simply, this method first of all identifies the lowest-cost route, allocates as much to that as is possible, then moves on to the next lowest-cost route, and so on until everything has been allocated.

In this case, the lowest-cost route is Birmingham–Cardiff (115 miles). Twenty containers are required in Cardiff, and 38 containers are available in Birmingham. Therefore, 20 containers are allocated to this particular route. As all the 20 containers required from Cardiff have been allocated, this destination can be removed from further considerations, while 18 containers are still available in Birmingham.

The next lowest-cost route is that between Newcastle and Edinburgh (121 miles). Twenty-four containers are available in Newcastle; 15 are required in Edinburgh. Therefore, the entire demand expressed in Edinburgh can be fulfilled and no more considerations about Edinburgh need to be done; 9 containers will be still available in Newcastle.

The next lowest-cost route is that between Birmingham and Southampton (143 miles). Twenty-one containers are required in Southampton; however, just 18 of them are available in Birmingham. Therefore, all of them will be allocated to Southampton; however, 3 containers will still need to be supplied to Southampton (from another origin). Birmingham can be excluded from further considerations, as there are no more containers available to be shipped.

Reiterating the procedure, the following allocations can be performed:

- 9 containers, from Newcastle to Glasgow (and no more containers are available in Newcastle);
- 16 containers, from Sheffield to Felixstowe (and no more containers are available in Sheffield);
- 10 containers, from York to Glasgow (and no more containers are available in York);
- 14 containers, from Manchester to Glasgow (and no more containers are required in Glasgow);
- 9 containers, from Leeds to Felixstowe (and no more containers are required in Felixstowe);
- 3 containers from Manchester to Southampton (and no more containers are required in Southampton).

Therefore, the solution reported in Table 4 below is obtained.

TABLE 4   Solution obtained through the least-cost method

	Cardiff	Edinburgh	Felixstowe	Glasgow	Southampton	Available containers
Birmingham	20				18	0
Leeds			9			1
Manchester				14	3	5
Newcastle		15		9		0
Sheffield			16			0
York				10		0
Required containers	0	0	0	0	0	

The total cost associated with this solution can be obtained by multiplying the number of containers times the respective distances in miles times 1.9 £/km (transportation costs) as follows:

$$\text{Total Cost} = 1.9*(20*115 + 15*121 + 9*215 + 16*197 + 14*218 +$$
$$9*152 + 10*212 + 18*143 + 3*234)$$
$$= £36,134.2$$

Improving the solution

This solution can be further improved by performing some empirical considerations. For example, it would be much more convenient shipping all the containers direct to Southampton from Birmingham, as the distance is just 143 miles. Currently, 3 containers out of 21 are shipped from Manchester. Re-allocating these three containers to Southampton would imply that Birmingham would not be able to supply Cardiff with 20 containers, as just 17 containers would then be available. Therefore, the three containers from Manchester that were previously allocated to Southampton could be directed to Cardiff. This would result in the new solution shown below in Table 5.

TABLE 5   Improved solution

	Cardiff	Edinburgh	Felixstowe	Glasgow	Southampton	Available containers
Birmingham	17				21	0
Leeds			9			1
Manchester	3			14		5
Newcastle		15		9		0
Sheffield			16			0
York				10		0
Required containers	0	0	0	0	0	

To check if these changes to the solution produce an improvement, the difference in the total cost should be calculated. This can be done by performing the following evaluation, which compares the new routes (203 miles from Manchester to Cardiff plus 143 miles from Birmingham to Southampton) to the previous ones (234 miles from Manchester to Southampton plus 115 miles from Birmingham to Cardiff):

$$\text{Cost Difference} = 1.9*3*[(203 + 143) - (115 + 234)] = -£17.1$$

The negative cost difference implies that this new solution allows achieving a saving; therefore, it can be implemented. Similarly, further improvements can be produced.

2 What happens if the company has to consider a further constraint regarding a maximum number of ten containers that can be shipped from any origin to any destination? How would the transportation plan change?

Additional constraint

If a further constraint regarding a maximum number of ten containers that can be shipped from any origin to any destination has to be considered, the *least-cost* method needs to be modified. Indeed, the allocation to the remaining lowest-cost route can be still performed; however, no more than ten containers can be allocated to each route. A solution is shown below in Table 6.

It is easy to verify that the presence of the additional constraint produces a solution whose cost value is higher than the previous one.

TABLE 6   Constrained solution

	Cardiff	Edinburgh	Felixstowe	Glasgow	Southampton	Available containers
Birmingham	10		10	3	10	5
Leeds			5	5		0
Manchester	10			10	2	0
Newcastle		10		10	3	1
Sheffield			10		6	0
York		5		5		0
Required containers	0	0	0	0	0	

The north-west corner method

The north-west corner method is the most straightforward way of solving the transportation problem and allocating product to routes. It simply involves starting at the top left-hand cell (the north-west corner of the matrix) and allocating goods to this cell in such a way that all the requirements are satisfied for the destination or all the capacity is used from the source.

An example of application of this method is shown below (Table 7).

Starting from the top left-hand cell of the matrix, it can be seen that it is possible, respecting the constraints, allocating 20 containers currently stored in Birmingham to Cardiff. This would saturate the entire demand required in Cardiff, still leaving 18 containers in Birmingham. Fifteen of these can be allocated to Edinburgh, by satisfying the whole demand. Moving to the right in the matrix, the residual three containers stored in Birmingham can then be allocated to Felixstowe.

Still, 22 containers will be required in Felixstowe. Moving to the next row, all of the 10 containers stored in Leeds can be directed there; this would allocate the entire number of containers available in Leeds. Therefore, to saturate the demand requirements for Felixstowe (still 12 containers are required), the next row in the matrix (Manchester) should be considered. Twelve containers can be shipped from Manchester to Felixstowe, leaving 10 containers available; these, moving towards the right in the matrix, can be shipped to Glasgow, where still 23 containers will be required. To saturate this requirement, the next row in the matrix needs to be considered; of the 24 containers available in Newcastle, 23 can be sent to Glasgow (completely satisfying the residual demand), while the remaining one can be sent to Southampton (where 21 containers are required). Moving to the next row, all the 16 containers from Sheffield can be sent to Southampton, leaving a further demand of 4 units, that can be satisfied (looking at the next row) by using some of the available containers in York, where an unused surplus of 6 containers will result at the end of the allocation process.

It can be easily noticed that the quality of the solution produced by this method is significantly worse, as it just tries to get a solution that satisfies the constraints.

TABLE 7   Solution obtained through the north-west corner method

	Cardiff	Edinburgh	Felixstowe	Glasgow	Southampton	Available containers
Birmingham	20	15	3			0
Leeds			10			0
Manchester			12	10		0
Newcastle				23	1	0
Sheffield					16	0
York					4	6
Required containers	0	0	0	0	0	

Total Cost =
   1.9*(20*115 + 15*291 + 3*165 + 10*215 + 12*255 + 10*218 +
   23*152 + 1*328 + 16*213 + 4*255)
   = £43,323.8

Indeed, it can be easily computed that the total cost is equal to
£43,323.8, higher than the solution obtained with the *least-cost*
method. This method can just be utilized to get a feasible starting
solution to the problem, which can then be improved by employing
the heuristic method shown above.

Alternative approaches

Students may like to implement the proposed problem in MS Excel
and find the optimal solution to it through the Solver application,
comparing it with the ones derived through the heuristic pen-and-
paper methods.

INDEX

9780749 475956

CPSIA information can be obtained
at www.ICGtesting.com
Printed in the USA
LVOW13*2007070518

576284LV00021B/322/P

WITHDRAWN
Wake Tech Community College Libraries
RTP Campus
10908 Chapel Hill Road
Morrisville, NC 27560

DATE DUE

GAYLORD PRINTED IN U.S.A.